THE AXE AND THE TREE

How bloody persecution sowed the seeds
of new life in Zimbabwe

Stephen Griffiths

MONARCH
BOOKS

Oxford, UK, and Grand Rapids, Michigan, USA

To Tim and Rachel

Published by Monarch Books
an imprint of
Lion Hudson IP Ltd
Wilkinson House, Jordan Hill Road,
Oxford OX2 8DR, England
Email: monarch@lionhudson.com
www.lionhudson.com/monarch

ISBN 978 0 85721 789 9
e-ISBN 978 0 85721 790 5

First edition 2017

Acknowledgments
Scripture quotations taken from Scripture quotations marked RSV are from The Revised Standard Version of the Bible copyright © 1946, 1952 and 1971 by the Division of Christian Education of the National Council of Churches in the USA. Used by permission. All Rights Reserved.
Scripture quotations marked NIV taken from the Holy Bible, New International Version Anglicised. Copyright © 1979, 1984, 2011 Biblica, formerly International Bible Society. Used by permission of Hodder & Stoughton Ltd, an Hachette UK company. All rights reserved. "NIV" is a registered trademark of Biblica. UK trademark number 1448790.
Extracts from marked KJV taken from The Authorized (King James) Version. Rights in the Authorized Version are vested in the Crown. Reproduced by permission of the Crown's patentee, Cambridge University Press.

Cover image: Lion Hudson

A catalogue record for this book is available from the British Library

Printed and bound in Great Britain by Marston Book Services Ltd, Oxfordshire

"I couldn't stop reading until I'd finished. Tragedy, triumph, tenacity; grace and faith; suffering beyond words, with love for the Lord, his gospel and his people: this book has them all. Read – and pray for Zimbabwe, as Peter Griffiths would have wished."
Rose Dowsett, missionary leader

"I could not put the book down nor could I read it without tears in my eyes. The strength of the story that Steve tells is that he is also part of it, he knew the people he writes about and he brings each character to life as if they were alive today. I am indebted to his diligence in unearthing history and telling it accurately. This book will never be old."
Paul Hudson, Elim International Missions Director

"This story of a Christian community, vividly brought to life through the memories of a missionary family, offers a compelling example of forgiveness and redemption in the face of one of the darkest moments of Zimbabwe's recent past. Through it we come to understand the deep roots of the Zimbabwean Church."
Dr David Maxwell, Dixie Professor of Ecclesiastical History at Emmanuel College, Cambridge

"Your book moved us to tears. It is so well written, so well researched, and does not flinch from the hard political and theological questions raised by the massacre. A significant contribution to the history of Christian mission."
David and Rosemary Harley, OMF

"This book is a moving account of triumphant faith in endeavour and suffering for the cause of Christ and his kingdom. It is thoroughly researched and impressively written by a first hand observer of events which drew the attention of the world to the work of Christian missions."
Professor Don Evans, University of Otago, New Zealand

"Steve pours heart and mind into the most moving of quests: the mystery of God's ways in the face of palpable evil and suffering and faith."
Revd Fiona Barnard Smith, Chaplain, St Andrew's University

"I wept tears of sadness at the terrible suffering this book describes; tears of joy at the power of forgiveness it conveys."
Revd Rupert Standring, vicar of St Peter's Church, Fulham

CONTENTS

"*Therefore every scribe (γραμματεύς – grammateus – writer) who has been trained for the kingdom of heaven is like a master of a house who brings out of his treasure what is new and what is old.*"

Jesus of Nazareth, Matthew 13:52

THE DREAM

Chinokanganwa idemo, chitsiga hachikanganwe.[1]
(What forgets is the axe, the wood does not forget.)

Startled awake, I stare into the cone of mosquito netting over my head. I am disorientated. My heart thumps in my ears. The bright square of the curtained window helps me to regain my bearings in the darkness. I creep to the end of my bed and cautiously raise one corner of the curtain, absurdly careful not to move it too much and draw unwanted attention.

The huge African moon pours silver light over the familiar scene, so bright that one can read by it and even discern colours. Shadows are drawn razor sharp and jet black. Anything, anyone standing quietly in the shadows would be invisible. I stare out and then scoot back down under my sheet – all I need in the heat of the lowveld of north-eastern Rhodesia.

I have a secret nightmare. I confess it to no one, afraid that it might come true. One night I shall look out into the still moonlight and they will be there. Holding their weapons at half port, they march in a ragged skirmish line. My heart closes in fear and I cannot shout.

Suddenly we are out of the house, running desperately into the night. Bushes whip my face as I run. Roots and thorns tug at my legs, leaving bloody beaded stripes. I trip and fall, scraping my knees and making my hands raw. My father is alongside me, scooping me up and hissing at me to run again. We rush on, our fear growing as we hear the shouts of angry men behind us. The thudding of booted feet and the sound of bodies crashing through the brush come closer.

We turn a corner round an enormous rock and throw ourselves desperately up its side. We climb higher and higher and fling ourselves down on its flat top, spent. My father locks eyes with each of us in turn, warning us to silence with a fierce glance. I creep closer to the edge, almost paralysed with terror yet fascinated by the source of my fear.

The rock is pointed and I stare down as if from the bow of a ship riding the moon-silvered waves of elephant grass. Capped heads force their way through the grass and then, as they meet the rock, slide down each side of it and are lost in the dark ocean of the night behind us.

I awake, shivering in the sunlight streaming through the windows.

STREAM OF THE LION SPIRIT

It was a dry, clear day, the sun ablaze in a vault of blue. An ancient one-tonne Ford truck rattled a dusty trail down an escarpment road winding through the Ruwangwe mountain range in eastern Rhodesia. As the driver and his wife peered through the windscreen they saw below them a broad plain spreading across towards Portuguese East Africa, dotted with kopjes,[1] hilly rocky outcrops. At the foot of the mountain range, the road petered out. Undeterred, husband and wife picked up heavy-bladed knives and began to cut their way through brush so thick that Native Commissioners patrolling the area a generation before had to dismount their horses and proceed on foot. Local Hwesa people appeared and helped them cut open a path through the undergrowth. They threaded their way among trees, inching their vehicle along until they came to a stop by a perennial stream flowing down from the mountains behind them: the Manjanja, or the "Stream of the Lion Spirit". It was August 1951.

Cecil Brien, a tall, angular, austere man worked alongside Mary, his vivacious wife, to pitch a tent just a few metres from the river. It was to be their home for the following eighteen months.

Together they built a mud hut to serve as their kitchen and dining room. Long-drop toilets were dug a little way from the camp. They cooked on an open fire and went to bed with the sunset.

These elemental conditions didn't hold them back from their medical work. The truck bed was turned into a medical storeroom, extended with a framework of poles covered with a tarpaulin: a rudimentary dispensary. An ironing board was set up for their microscope: their laboratory. Cecil and Mary cleared a space under a spreading flat-topped mupfuti tree. Beneath the feathered red spring leaves they shared their skills and the Word of God with those who came seeking medical help.

Their first operation was a hernia repair performed in the mud hut on their kitchen table. Mary Brien, a specialist anaesthetist, dropped ether onto a Schimmelbusch inhaler and held it to her patient's face. Surgeon Cecil Brien performed the operation while an assistant held a hurricane lamp and knocked away the insects attracted by the light. That first patient lived to tell the tale.

The rains came, sweeping across the dry, parched land, and the Manjanja turned from a stream to a raging torrent. No common rainy season, these were the heaviest downpours in living memory. Foodstuffs had been kept in a "food safe" submerged in the river, the only way to keep them a little fresh. But as the river rose, so their supplies were all swept away. Hurrying off to the Eastern Highlands town of Umtali to replenish their stock, the Briens returned to find "white ants" – termites – laying heavy red tunnels of clay over their stored clothes and surgical linen, busily eating their way into and destroying them.

It wasn't only the climate or the insects that made those early days difficult. Speculating over possible motives for the newcomers to live as they did, many local people were deeply suspicious of the Briens. Many believed that they were carrying out reconnaissance in the area before engaging in a major cattle-rustling operation. As cattle were the main measure of wealth among the Hwesa, there was great concern, especially given the history of contact with the outside world.

* * *

The north-eastern area in which the Briens arrived was remote and inaccessible, lowlands lying beyond the edge of the central Southern Rhodesian high plateau. The two principal African powers of the mid-1800s, the Ndebele to the south and Gaza to the east, had left the area largely untouched.

The Portuguese artillery officer Joaquim Carlos Paiva de Andrada had attempted to expand Portuguese control west into the Ruwangwe Valley. He had been welcomed into the valley by the *mambo* or lord of the area, Chief Katerere, on 13 September 1885.[2] In their first meeting, Paiva de Andrada declared his government's desire to befriend the chief. Without apparent irony, Paiva de Andrada followed up his initial comments with a demonstration of the accuracy and speed of fire of his Winchester Express rifle, leaving Chief Katerere "very impressed" by the holes blown in several trees. Later that day, the chief visited Paiva de Andrada's encampment to invite him to travel to a gold-panning area, fortuitously right on the edge of the chief's sphere of influence. The young artillery officer unsuspectingly took the bait.

Nine days later, Paiva de Andrada was surprised to encounter a delegation of local elders accompanied by 100 armed men and a lion spirit medium.[3] Paiva de Andrada described the lion cult as mere superstition but regretfully recognized that "the chief did nothing without consulting the medium". The oracle had declared that Paiva de Andrada's mission was to cheat the people and ultimately to war against them. The elders ordered him to retrace his steps and never enter the area again, and reinforced their message with a night full of dancing and drumming. Before dawn the following day, a sleepless Paiva de Andrada was hastily on his way, and his official recommendation to the Lisbon government was that the border of Portuguese East Africa be drawn to the east of the Ruwangwe Valley.

Nearly ten years later the Ruwangwe Valley was brought under the nominal political control of the British South Africa Company (BSAC). The BSAC came into being through colonial adventurer Cecil Rhodes' efforts to exploit the mineral wealth of Rhodesia. A Royal Charter was granted to the BSAC in 1889, similar to that of the British East India Company. Company representatives attempted to impose a hut tax of ten shillings from every household in the Valley each year, despite the absence of any services being provided. Other parts of Rhodesia saw the introduction of some infrastructure and services as part of the trappings of a colonial state. In contrast, the colonial government left the Ruwangwe area largely marginalized.

The hut tax forced a people who held their wealth in livestock to send their sons far away to enter the Company cash economy. If they could not pay, the Hwesa faced the confiscation of their precious cattle. This stirred deep emotions. Having successfully repelled one would-be exploiter, the Hwesa under Chief Katerere attempted to mobilize in revolt. This time, a force of thirty-two BSAC police marched into the area. A brief public demonstration of firepower with a Maxim gun left Chief Katerere[4] with nothing to say, except that he was quite willing to pay the government tax.[5]

That the arrival of the Briens was greeted with suspicion was unsurprising. Any protestation of friendship, any expressed motivation of love, any apparent disinterested concern for the welfare of the people was unlikely to gain a sympathetic hearing. But despite the seemingly isolated nature of the area, significant groundwork had been carried out before the Briens' arrival. There were not enough missionaries to account for the remarkable growth and expansion of Christianity in Africa.

Often, far more was going on than appeared in the popular and missionary-centred stories that were published in the countries that had sent them.

Cecil and Mary Brien had arrived in an area under the control of the Katerere chieftainship, which had been in place for around 200 years by that time.[6] Despite the fact that there was little penetration of the area by the apparatus of the state, many local people had ventured out into the wider world. The colonial government's hated hut tax had forced many young men into the cash economy to meet the obligations placed on their families. The tax had to be paid in Rhodesian currency, which had restricted the easier eastward trade into Portuguese East Africa, forcing the Hwesa west and south to find ways to earn money.

Harry Tsengerai and Mateu Marongedza were two young men from the area who had gone to work in the mines at Gatooma in central Rhodesia. Some of their fellow miners were Pentecostal Christians, members of the Apostolic Faith Mission, by that time a largely black African independent church movement spreading north from its roots in South Africa. The Apostolic Faith Mission kept evangelism at the centre of its priorities, strongly encouraging African enterprise and leadership while discouraging engagement with health and education, which Apostolic Faith Mission leaders saw as a diversion from the main task of soul winning.

Harry and Mateu had come to faith in Jesus Christ and left the mines to return home to Katerere in 1946, wanting to establish a church there. They saw ancestor veneration and spirit possession as entirely negative, at odds with the Holy Spirit of the God they had met while working underground in the mines. Critically, they did not seek to deny the existence of the spirit world but rather saw it in a new light. They wanted to see Pentecostal mission work begin in their home area, and they wanted to work alongside missionaries in transforming both the religious world view and the quality of life of their people, incidentally subverting some Apostolic Faith Mission teaching. In the face of suspicion and fear of the Briens, these two young men argued that they should stay. As relatively wealthy, independent younger men, their status enabled them to challenge the old order of society and religion and to overcome. Harry and Mateu returned home to Katerere at just the right time to cut open the way for the Briens culturally and relationally, just as they had cut the brush back physically.

* * *

Cecil Brien was born in 1905 in Enniskillen, County Fermanagh in Ireland and trained as a pharmacist[7] before entering Queens University Medical School in Belfast. He was an intense, fiery man with a deep evangelical Christian faith. While a medical student in Belfast he spent time on the streets distributing tracts along with his best friend, a bus conductor. Qualifying as a doctor in 1934, he would earn himself a dressing-down from his senior colleagues in the Rhondda, in Wales, for his regular habit of preaching in the open air and so bringing disrepute on the medical profession.

While at Queens, Cecil Brien met Mary Campbell Chambers, a doctor's daughter from Dannhauser, Natal, in South Africa. Beautiful, intelligent, and strong-willed, Mary followed in her father's medical footsteps, and she became the only female junior doctor at Belfast's Royal Victoria Hospital. She was more than a match for the quick, intense, hard-driving Cecil. They married in 1936 and decided to study at the Bible College of Wales, where they were influenced by Rees Howells, the principal.

Howells had come to faith during the Welsh revival of 1904–05. He was a man with a reputation for prayer and a gift for healing and had worked for many years at the South Africa General Mission's Rusitu Mission in Southern Rhodesia. Rusitu

Mission was the epicentre of rapid church growth between 1915 and 1920. This growth was partly driven by a remarkable episode during the post-First World War Spanish influenza pandemic. The death rate soared across the country, often bringing even basic services to a halt. Entire households lay sick or dying. Southern Rhodesia's medical director feared that entire peoples might be wiped out, and wrote, "People were numbed and staggered with the immensity of the disaster."[8] When Howells declared the Mission a place of safety, saying that no one on the Mission station would die, hundreds of people fled there for refuge, and none died.[9] Howells' reliance on prayer and his preference for seeking divine healing had a powerful influence on the young, medically trained Briens.

During his studies, Cecil was exercised as to what he should do: stay in Britain and serve as a doctor or go abroad as a medical missionary. He spent a weekend on retreat, during which he asked Howells what he should do. The strange advice he received was, "Go back and do what your senior partner tells you to do!"[10]

On the following Monday, his senior partner called him in to admonish him yet again, rather flippantly rebuking him, "Dr Brien, this business of your preaching in the streets of the town is most unbecoming to a man in the medical profession. You ought to be a missionary in Africa!"[11] Cecil was thunderstruck at the words of what he saw as divine guidance coming so promptly after the advice he had been given by the principal – and he determined to take that advice. He had developed a keen interest in surgery, which led him back to the Albert and Edward Royal Infirmary in Wigan for surgical training. He wanted to prepare as thoroughly as possible for life abroad as a medical missionary.

World events took a dramatic turn, however, threatening Cecil's sense of destiny and purpose. Call-up papers arrived at the outbreak of the Second World War, but he refused to enlist. A socially and professionally disastrous decision in the atmosphere of the time, he was brought before a Conscientious Objection Tribunal chaired by a judge. Cecil objected to being labelled as a "conchie". His refusal to enlist was not because he objected to warfare as a means of settling international disputes. Rather, he told the tribunal, "I have placed myself fully at the disposal of God. How then could I obey the orders of a commanding officer to go where God has not sent me?"[12]

The tribunal discharged him, giving him full exemption from military service. Reported in the local press, the judge chairman of the tribunal summed up, "I have never been so convinced of the sincerity of any man as I have of Cecil Brien. Dr Brien is free to go to serve his God."

Years later, Dr Brien commented wryly, "From that moment God trapped me. Many better, braver, Christian men than I went abroad to serve and die. I could do no less for God than they had done for their country."[13]

As it turned out, the Briens remained in the United Kingdom for the duration of the war, while Cecil continued to gain valuable experience as Residential Surgical Officer in the Albert and Edward Royal Infirmary. It was only in 1948 that the couple set sail on the converted hospital ship *Llandovery Castle*, taking seven weeks at sea and travelling through a romantic roll-call of Mediterranean and African ports: Gibraltar, Genoa, Suez, Port Sudan, Aden, Mombasa, Zanzibar, and Dar es Salaam. Finally they disembarked in Beira, a coastal town in Portuguese East Africa. Swung out of the hold of the ship were hospital beds, an operating table, and hundreds of surgical instruments that the Briens had collected.

The Briens began work in Southern Rhodesia's Zambezi Valley with the Evangelical Alliance Mission (EAM). They spent their first two years at a small hospital in the Mvuradona area, a rugged area of mountains and miombo woodland on the Zambezi escarpment.

Then an opportunity to pioneer a medical work in a new area came up, and the Briens seized it eagerly – for more than one reason. They were frustrated because of EAM rejection of Pentecostal practice, seeing this as the agency's refusal to take seriously both the power of God and the supernatural world view of the people they were trying to reach. The Briens had also been invited by Harry Tsengerai and Mateu Marongedza, who were determined to mediate with both the chief and Cecil and Mary Brien to ensure that the missionary work was born out of behaviour which was acceptable to the traditional authorities of the area. Through the hard, careful groundwork of these two young local Christians and the willingness of the Briens to listen to advice from nationals, the local people of influence in the Ruwangwe Valley felt that the Briens came into the area in a way that was respectful of local custom.

* * *

Inching forward month by month, the Briens slowly expanded from a tent and a mud hut to a two-roomed cottage and a two-ward hospital. Their early years were poverty stricken, as their missionary society was unable to pay them either salary or grants for buildings and equipment. The lack of finance would have frustrated many, but during their years at Bible College they had learned to do without what many would call essential. They had also learned to live from day to day, trusting God to answer their prayers.

Despite his fiery intensity, Cecil Brien was a shy, self-effacing man. He had been deeply impressed by a passage from the prophet Jeremiah: "Should you then seek great things for yourself? Do not seek them!"[14] He consequently felt constrained to shun any publicity but rather sought to glorify only God. In practice this meant that very few photographs were taken of Cecil and Mary or their early work. In spite of no income from an established agency and of their deliberate principled refusal to appeal for funds or seek any kind of publicity,[15] they were able to survive and grow their work through unsolicited gifts from around the world. Both were entrepreneurial, ingenious, and willing to listen, qualities which, combined with their deep faith, served them well.

Cecil learned to mould and burn bricks, lay foundations, and put roofs on buildings, and taught others to do so too. Throughout the dry season while building was possible, he would rise at 5.00 a.m. in order to get the building work going before his first ward round, and then would work late into the night. He became a well-known figure among demolition teams and second-hand dealers in Salisbury (now Harare). The Umtali Municipality Building was demolished in 1962. Cecil and a colleague hovered at the site like a pair of vultures, waiting to seize hold of the discarded double entrance doors and load them onto the Mission truck. The doors were built into the church right next to the hospital and remain there still, solid and imposing, more than half a century after being discarded by the municipality. Walking around the hospital with Cecil, visitors would often be told where every piece of asbestos sheeting, door, and window frame was salvaged from!

The hospital grew into a seventy-bed institution by the mid-1950s. The annual reports made impressive reading: 250 major operations performed, more than 600 babies delivered, around 4,000 sick people admitted, and 15,000 treated as outpatients. But that was not the only aspect of their work. Cecil opened thirteen primary schools throughout the area, becoming school manager of them all in addition to his medical work.

Although the Briens were careful to listen to local believers and acted in respectful ways towards the people of the area, that respect did not extend to traditional religious practices. Ancestor veneration, the practice of spirit possession, the use of charms or fetishes,[16] the brewing of beer which was part of spirit worship ceremonies and consequent public drunkenness were all seen as being part of the entrapment and enslavery of Satan, to be confronted not compromised with.

Encounters with the spiritual powers seen to be at work in the area came through fervent preaching, the casting out of evil spirits through exorcism, periodic all-night prayer meetings, the public confession of sin, and the burning of objects related to spirit possession. A key factor in the Briens' approach was that they did not deny or downplay the spirit world of the Hwesa, as other more conservative missionaries had done.[17] They saw the Hwesa spirit world as real and the spirits as powerful, but knew they could be overcome by the greater power of the Holy Spirit. As Pentecostal Christians, the Briens and their colleagues were able to engage effectively with this world view, not to dismiss the world of the supernatural but to help transform it, not to replace it with Western rationalism but rather to embrace an authentic folk Christianity which took both the spirit world of rural Zimbabwe and the Holy Spirit seriously. The kind of Christianity I saw expressed in the rural areas of Rhodesia was a far cry from the serious, quiet, conservative Protestantism of urban European life.

The Briens, as highly trained health professionals, integrated their medical skills and their Pentecostal beliefs into a potent approach to healing and well-being. Each day, patients and relatives gathered together with the hospital staff to dance, sing, pray, and hear the Word expounded in the local language. The Briens thought nothing of combining medical techniques with fervent appeals to God. They wrote enthusiastically of such cases as a patient with severe peritonitis and kidney failure who was beyond their medical ability to heal, yet who made a full recovery when the only option was the laying-on of hands and prayer. Frequently, as patients recovered, they and their families would become Christians.

A less dramatic but very welcome service was the drawing of painful teeth. Decades later, as a young medical student, I travelled from village to village, working at clinics in the Katerere area. Many of the older folk, on realizing who I was, would command my attention and then jerk back a lip to show an empty gap in a row of teeth and describe the relief that Cecil Brien had brought them! Many with hearing problems, lameness, or long-standing eye disease also found help. Echoes were seen in the singing and telling of the stories of Jesus each morning with what was happening in the wards of the hospital and the clinics across the area.

A dishevelled and fatigued man appeared at the hospital one day asking to see the doctor who was "like Jesus". The link between the stories and the healing was diffusing widely into the local community. The exhausted man had walked for four hours through the bush to seek an encounter with Cecil. He was a *n'anga*, a traditional healer. His wife had arrived at the hospital because of prolonged childbirth and had been close to death. Even though the child had died, the *n'anga* had been deeply moved by the care and expertise of the newcomers in saving his wife's life. He listened to what the Briens had to say about Jesus Christ. As a result, he turned away from his old practices and embraced this new way of life, walking those twenty-four kilometres to church every Sunday.

Unknown to the Briens, the site they chose for the Mission was close to a useful source of water, where local people would leave clay pots of beer in homage to a *mhondoro*, a royal ancestral or lion spirit. The spirit was known as Chikumbirike, and the spirit's medium lived just outside the Mission. But through the preaching and work of the Briens, the Tsengerai and Marongedza families, and other new believers in the area, first the medium's wife converted and refused to participate in the necessary ceremonies enabling her husband's possession. Then his two daughters became followers of the new way. The stream where once the lion spirit was honoured became the place where vigorous baptismal services were held; the drumming, clapping, singing, ululating, and dancing in worship were now directed to the God of Israel. The medium still fell into trances, but the words that spilled from him were curses for those who had brought such change.[18]

* * *

Caring for both spirit and body of those they were serving, Cecil and Mary Brien also focused intentionally on the mind. Thomas Morgan Thomas, a Welshman and former miner turned missionary sent by the London Missionary Society, is credited with starting the very first school in Rhodesia in 1857 among the Ndebele people one hundred years earlier.[19] Radically for his day, Thomas Morgan Thomas wrote:

> *That [the Ndebele] will carry with him into the great Church of Christ some of the traits of his present character is very likely, and that those traits will have their place, use and glory, in the great family of regenerated men, seems also clear... Much has been said and written in order to prove the inferiority of the African as compared with the Asiatic and European, and to show the impossibility, as it were, of his ever distinguishing himself in anything that is truly great, sublime or original. This to me appears invalid and incorrect.[20]*

However, this missionary commitment to education was viewed with ambivalence or downright hostility. The colonial government of Southern Rhodesia invested little in education for black citizens. While education for white children was made free and compulsory in 1935, education for the black population remained a privilege. The government spent twenty-one times as much on each white student as on each black student. Missionaries had been involved in education even before the colonial era, becoming responsible for more than 90 per cent of black education. But opportunities for black students remained limited. Even in the 1970s, just over 40 per cent of black school-aged children were in school.[21] Government concerns about "over-education" of the black population by missions led to the creation of the Department of Native Education to inspect mission schools and consequently to open a handful of government schools for black pupils.

A hundred years after the pioneering work of Thomas Morgan Thomas, the 1950s were a time of rapid educational development, and the Doctors Brien were not to be left behind. As good northern Irish Protestants, they were deeply concerned by the steps being taken by nearby Irish Catholic missions to expand their work into the area, with their rosaries and scapulars,[22] Latin liturgy and hymns, shrines, and statues. The roots of the differences between the work of neighbouring missions were partly theological but also reflected the political and socio-economic struggles and prejudices of Northern Ireland. Cecil Brien, on seeing a building that needed repainting or a thatched roof that was unkempt, would comment, "That looks very Catholic. We need to take steps to get that looking more Protestant!"

Although some aspects of the competition between Catholic and Protestant missionaries seem both comical and sub-Christian, this was during the time before the Second Vatican Council[23] which addressed relations between the Catholic Church and the modern world. Pope John XXIII would call on the council to "open the windows of the Catholic Church to let in fresh air".[24] The council was to revise liturgy, allow translation of the liturgy into local languages, look to make the teaching of the

Catholic Church clear to a modern world, and prioritize efforts to improve Christian unity, seeking common ground on some issues with Protestant churches.

However, for the Briens and their Catholic neighbours, Vatican II still lay in the future. The sometimes unyielding struggle between the Elim Mission led by Cecil Brien and the neighbouring Catholic missions turned into a kind of educational "arms race". Both sought government permission to expand the area of their control, presenting themselves to the Native Commissioner in the best possible light and taking opportunities to do down their neighbours. Sadly, the Native Commissioner observed that "the prevailing spirit of relationships is quite unChristian".[25] This spirit was to change as more missionaries who were not from Ireland, and therefore less partisan, arrived on the scene.

One result of the spiritual and physical needs of the area combined with the less savoury inter-church competition was an urgent desire to grow the Elim missionary team. The Briens issued an "SOS for Prayer" for new workers, especially teachers for their newly established schools. This call was taken up in the UK and published in the *Elim Evangel*, the magazine of the Elim Pentecostal Church movement.[26] Not satisfied, the Briens went back to the UK to look for new workers themselves, their only visit home in the first seventeen years of pioneer missionary work, such was their dedication. But it would prove to be life-changing for two young people.

PECULIAR PEOPLE
AND PUBLICANS

Walking out to Gande village in the starlight, Brenda pushed her way through the maize plants which towered three metres into the air. An eerie whispering followed the little group of travellers as the spiral leaves of the maize twisted and turned in the light night air. As they tramped along the narrow track on the far side of the field, the tall elephant grass tickled their necks and faces. Reaching the Musarudzi, Brenda balanced on a tree which had been felled to straddle the river as a crude bridge. Holding her breath, she danced across the trunk and jumped to safety, climbed the sandy bank, and wended her way through fields of groundnuts and rice. She picked her way carefully along the path, eroded here and there by recent heavy rain or interrupted by columns of marching ants. She and her companions arrived in the village to find a fire burning and a low table ready for the hissing pressure lamp. A welcoming crowd had gathered, ready to sing along with the piano accordion and hear what Brenda had to say.

A few weeks later at Sangoma village it was a different story. From the darkness at the other end of the village, considerable noise emanated from a beer party. The small group of women and children was joined by four drunken men who had heard the singing. Brenda was frightened when she saw them lurch out of the darkness, and wondered how many more would appear. Feeling very alone, she opened her Bible and read, "God is with us," and decided to continue. When she began to preach, to her guilty relief two of the drunks struggled to their feet and ambled off into the gloom. Another gazed at her with a disconcerting, fixed glare before slowly toppling forward to lie flat out and begin snoring. Stubbornly, Brenda pressed on, despite the remaining drunk adding ripe comment to everything she said. The wretched state of the drunks replaced her fear with pity.

Later, back in her home which nestled under the looming bulk of the Ruwangwe escarpment, Brenda recounted her experiences to her colleague, and discovered she had escaped lightly. That same night her colleague Catherine Picken, while visiting a different village, had been repeatedly interrupted by the headman who had chosen to do a drunken, shouting, shuffling dance in the middle of the group. He had then pulled his belt out of his trousers and slashed wildly at all around him, causing the crowd to scatter and regroup, while he laughed and jeered. It all seemed a very long way from Essex!

* * *

Essex girl Brenda Hurrell was born in 1932, and grew up in a loving but unusual home. Her father, Bernard, was a warm, gentle man. Fastidious and precise, he worked as an articled clerk. During the Second World War he served with the Royal Air Force Volunteer Reserve on the ground staff in North Africa and had been mentioned in dispatches.[1] Bernard and Gladys had three children: an older brother, Brenda, and a younger sister. Bernard loved his children deeply in a quiet but affectionate way.

Brenda's mother, Gladys, was very different. Gladys had been born to a couple who belonged to the "Peculiar People", members of a Pentecostal sect that originated in East Essex. They took their name from a letter of the apostle Peter: "But ye are a chosen generation, a royal priesthood, an holy nation, a *peculiar people*; that ye should shew forth the praises of him who hath called you out of darkness into his marvellous light."[2]

While adhering to aspects of orthodox Christianity, the Peculiar People had a sometimes deserved reputation for eccentric beliefs and dangerous actions. Brenda's grandfather, Herbert Henry Carter, an elder of the Peculiars, once advised a young couple with a child who was desperately ill with diphtheria to seek divine healing. They took his advice and avoided seeking the God-given wisdom of a doctor. The child died. Justice Ridley, sitting at Chelmsford, sentenced the boy's father to serve a month in jail, and Herbert Henry Carter to two months in jail for the tragic results of his advice. Sadly, Brenda's grandfather Carter considered his sentence as persecution by the authorities, and on his release he was greeted with singing by his congregation.

Although she considered herself to be deeply committed to God, some of Gladys' beliefs were unhelpfully shaped by her family background. When she developed a small spot on the side of her face, she attempted to ignore it. As it slowly enlarged she reluctantly agreed to see a doctor. He diagnosed a "rodent ulcer", a basal cell carcinoma, which would have been easily cured with a relatively minor surgical procedure. But owing to her deep-seated aversion to medical care, and encouraged by the example of her father, she refused treatment.

Over the years, Gladys came to the fixed belief that God would heal her miraculously, as "a sign to the nations", although this might have been a subconscious attempt to rationalize her decision not to seek medical treatment. No one could shake her from her position even though the carcinoma continued to grow slowly and eat into the structures of the left side of her face.

Resolutely refusing help and risking her life, it seemed she was trying to compel God into vindicating her obstinacy.

Embarrassed by the unsightly tumour, Gladys hid the lesion under a bulky dressing with a scarf, even indoors. Eventually she had to stop attending church as the smell emanating from beneath her bandages was keeping others away. Finally, maggots were to be seen writhing in the depths of the enormous, stinking lesion on the side of Gladys' head. Not long after that she became mute and stopped eating.

Bernard outlined what happened next in a few stark sentences in a letter to Brenda who by then was already working in Rhodesia. He found his wife collapsed in her room, convulsing uncontrollably. The doctor came, examined her, and called an ambulance. Pathetically, Bernard attempted to reassure Brenda and wrote, "She will now have the best treatment possible," but he couldn't resist adding that it was "a great pity she didn't have treatment early when they wanted to deal with it."

Within days of Gladys' admission to hospital, the tumour eroded into a blood vessel and she died of a torrential haemorrhage. Instead of a humble faith, awareness of human frailty and the possibility of mistake, yet a confidence in the greatness and goodness of God, she had placed her confidence in her own beliefs, seeing her stubbornness as a virtue. Her "faith", rather than demonstrating the greatness of God, had only served to belittle Him and make Him less.

Throughout her illness, Brenda had been grieved by her mother's hardness of heart, but she was able to recognize that her mother had confused wilful obstinacy with faithful obedience. Brenda might have inherited her mother's sense of commitment and willingness to stand for what she believed in, but this was tempered with her father's gentle reserve and reflective nature.

* * *

A few weeks before Easter 1956, tall, slim twenty-three-year-old Brenda, with her wavy hair stylishly cut, was leafing idly through her church magazine. Arrested by the bold word "Teachers" on one page, she scanned the urgent plea from the Briens in the *Elim Evangel* and then hastily turned the page. Brenda Hurrell might have been a trained secretary and primary school teacher, but she was working towards her dream of living and teaching in Canada. She definitely did not want to bury herself in some remote part of Africa so early in life! But the article lingered in her mind.

Brenda was a member of the first Elim Church established in England, in Leigh-on-Sea, Essex.[3] George Jeffreys had founded the Elim Movement in Northern Ireland, a British Pentecostal Church which had its roots in a remarkable wave of revivalist activity that took place between 1900 and 1910 in diverse locations around the world, among them Azusa Street in California,[4] Wonsan in Korea,[5] South Africa, and the Welsh valleys. Each Easter, the Elim Movement gathered in the Royal Albert Hall in London. Brenda heard that Cecil Brien was to speak at the evening service. Curious, she wondered what her reaction would be on hearing him call for teachers.

There were thousands at the event. During one of the breaks as she wandered in the teeming crowds, Brenda felt her arm gripped by a member of her church who excitedly drew her along to introduce her to a stranger. Brenda was alarmed to hear, "This is Dr Cecil Brien." Cecil had just asked if there were any teachers in the Leigh church as Brenda walked by. Sensing Brenda's reluctance to discuss service abroad, with uncharacteristic gentleness Cecil said, "I'm not going to ask you to come to Rhodesia. God will have to ask you because the work is hard."

She found his words disturbing. A man's words she could reject. But what if it was God who was speaking? Hearing Brien's passionate public call for help a few moments later, she found it deeply provocative, but once again tried to shunt it to one side in her thinking. That night, as was her custom, she opened her Bible to read a chapter before going to bed. It was Acts 7, Stephen on trial for his life, reminding his religious leaders what God had said to Abraham centuries earlier. Brenda read, "Go out from your land and from your kindred and go into the land that I will show you."

Struck by the words and in turmoil of mind, she wrote to mature Christian friends who replied in the words of Jesus: "If any man's will is to do his will, he shall know,"[6] and reassured her of their prayers for her.

Seven weeks later, at the Whitsun Convention, Brenda was alarmed to see Cecil Brien ascend the platform to speak again of the role of teachers within the context of the spiritual needs of Rhodesia. In her diary Brenda recorded, "A deep sense of conviction such as I have not felt before came over me. I was facing a challenge that went deep in my soul." Wildly, she looked around for an exit so she could run out, afraid of the appeal for workers that she knew would be made at the end of the meeting. But she was trapped in the middle of a very long row, and she heard the speaker invite to stand those who felt that God was challenging them to missionary service, quietly adding the words of Jesus, "If you cling to your life, you will lose it; but if you give up your life for me, you will find it."[7] Reluctantly, unwillingly, amid great conflict of spirit, Brenda stood to ask God to have His way in her life.

Caught up in the melee at the end of the service as people streamed out into the darkness, Brenda found herself invited by a friend to supper. She accepted, only to find the Briens were at the supper too! As she asked questions and heard more about Rhodesia, Brenda felt peace stealing over her troubled mind.

After consulting with her minister, Brenda completed application forms and dropped them into the post box. It was

June 1956. As she stood, one hand resting on the post box, she felt a surge of relief. She had done what she could. The rest was out of her hands. A response came within a few days. Tearing it open, she read a most unexpected letter. It was not women that were wanted in Rhodesia but men. Her application had been rejected on the grounds of her gender. She thought, "I've done all I could. I have been obedient. I don't have to go." She turned, with a sense of reprieve, back to everyday life. At the back of her mind, though, there remained a niggling sense that somehow her life and Rhodesia would remain intertwined.

Fully engaged with her pupils, enjoying her music and art, and thinking through her plans for Canada, the months fled by. Then in October, out of the blue, a large envelope landed on the mat. Apologetically, the Missionary Secretary had written again. There had been a mistake. Her application was welcome after all. The need remained urgent. Would Miss Hurrell be willing to attend an interview? Ruefully, Brenda smiled, recognizing the guidance of God in the twist of events.

Trim, attractive, artistic in temperament with a passion for music, Brenda was not the usual picture of a missionary in 1950s churchgoers' minds. Indeed, she seemed to become something of a "poster girl" for the Elim Pentecostal Missionary Society. Just three months later, on 16 January 1957, at the age of twenty-four, Brenda sailed from England on the *Braemar Castle* to begin her service with the Elim Missionary Society. She travelled up from Cape Town by train: three slow, hot days through South Africa, across the Kalahari Desert to her final destination – the tiny hamlet of Penhalonga in Eastern Rhodesia.

Elim Mission had two centres in the country. The first in the remote, arid north-eastern lowlands of Katerere, largely beyond the reach of the colonial government, was where the Briens were based. The second was in Penhalonga, close to the border of Portuguese East Africa among the lush, rolling forests of the

Eastern Highlands, just a few kilometres from the urban centre of Umtali.

Upon her arrival on 10 February, Brenda sent her parents a telegram: "=Arrived Penhalonga Staying= Brenda"! Here Brenda began her teaching duties and started to learn the Shona language. She also learned to drive. Finding enough traffic to interact with for her driving test was a challenge. There were no traffic lights and only a single crossroads in the entire village!

Two years later, Brenda moved to join the Briens further north in Katerere.

* * *

Three years after Brenda had left her home, Peter Griffiths, a startlingly fresh-faced youth, left his parents in South Wales and sailed for Africa. Stanley Griffiths, Peter's father, grew up in a working-class Welsh-speaking family in South Wales. An intelligent and athletic boy, he passed the exam to go to Dynevor Grammar School,[8] However, his family were unable to afford further education and he was obliged to work instead. He joined the British Army and served in India with the Irish Guards. He was a fine soldier and played on the championship-winning regimental football team. On leaving the army, he laboured at the tin works.

Hannah Robbins, a "pretty slip of a thing", fell in love with Stanley at a works dance. They married on 3 March 1931. In due course, their first son Ken was born.

Life seemed carefree then, as Hannah recalled: a little two-roomed house, a tin bath hung outside for weekly use, her husband working hard but regular hours, and a young son to love. One clear day, Ken climbed up on a high wall, across the road from the house. While prancing along the top, as he had seen the older boys do, he slipped and fell heavily to the ground. Dragging himself to his feet, he weaved across the road, calling for his father, and then never spoke again. He was rushed to hospital, where X-rays showed fractures of the skull. He died the following day, 8 April 1936, at the age of four.

Stanley and Hannah were broken by their loss. They couldn't even bear to go back to the house where they had been so happy. For a while they separated, each returning to live with their parents, buried in their grief and unable to comfort one another. Stanley developed a stomach ulcer, and the subsequent complications were to trouble him for the rest of his life. He never managed a day at the tin works again. Hannah displayed an amazing strength of character. During Stanley's long illness she worked for the Provident Company which loaned money to the poor. She tramped all over Plasmarl and Morriston to collect repayments and then pay in the collected cash at the headquarters in Swansea.

Eventually, Stanley and Hannah were able to set up as publicans in the Imperial Hotel, working for themselves. Life began to change for the better. The work was interminable: cleaning the pub, doing the accounts, ordering in food and drink, and then night after night serving behind the bar. Stanley took it all very seriously. Hannah recovered her high spirits and was always ready for a bit of fun and a dance. On one memorable occasion she was out at a dance, "tripping the light fantastic" on a table top. Stanley burst in, shouting, "Quick, Hannah, give us a hand. The Imperial's on fire."

"Let it burn," cried Hannah, as the dance continued. The fire was eventually brought under control without Hannah's help!

Those nights of laughter, swirl, and colour were all too few as the threat of war grew.

Peter, Stanley and Hannah's second son, was born on 15 September 1937, shortly before the onset of the Second World War. Before long Swansea burned around him, the docks pounded by German bombers. Like many of his generation, it seemed like an adventure, "war games" on a grand scale. Collecting shrapnel, aircraft recognition, and playing on bomb sites were part of everyday life. With his gang of grubby, skiving street urchins he swam in the yellow, polluted waters of the local canal, scrapped with kids from other streets, played football on rough ground, pinched tyres from a tyre yard to burn, and played endless tricks on the long-suffering residents of the area.

One day, Peter complained of a sore throat and began to run a fever. The days lost their structure, blurred, and melted into one long delirium. Several times he approached death, and his parents were distraught at the prospect of losing a second child. Eventually he was given penicillin, a precious drug in very short supply. His urine was collected and the penicillin extracted from it to be used again.

Weeks later Peter awoke to find himself in a hospital bed. As he convalesced he counted the cracks in the ceiling, imagining them into a map, into a picture, into anything that would relieve the endless tedium. He had survived rheumatic fever but remained in hospital for nearly a year because his heart had been badly damaged. Eventually he was discharged, pale-skinned, feeble, and skeletal. He had to repeat a whole year at school but did well in the eleven-plus exams, gaining a place at Bishop Gore Grammar School. The group of boys he befriended as a result of his delayed schooling was to change the direction of his life.

On leaving school, Peter worked as a chemist at the Steel Company of Wales. Analysing samples taken from the blast furnaces, he would tell the furnace-men what adjustments to make to produce the right quality of steel. Irrepressible and full of fun like his mother, he and the other chemists didn't take their jobs very seriously. They would play football in the laboratory round the workbenches, using large rubber bungs as balls. Often the analysis results were merely plucked from thin air and jotted on the official forms. Head Office, unsure of how their technical staff seemed to have so much free time, kept increasing the workload.

Then Peter developed an inexplicable hunger for spiritual things. He plunged into attending a local Methodist church, which he described as "lifeless and as dry as dust". Accepting invitations to preach short sermons in the church, he simply repeated dogma about a Christ he didn't yet know personally.

At seventeen years old, Peter was engaged in a public debate with a group of older Christadelphians. Among the crowd that gathered to listen was Bill Sheehan, a young Irish house painter. Bill listened with amusement to Peter, who wasn't allowing a lack of knowledge to get in the way of his enthusiastic arguments! As the verbal clash ended, Bill introduced himself to Peter. Together they walked the couple of kilometres to Peter's home, talking all the way. A warm friendship sprang up, and over the next few months Bill took Peter, step by step, into a new understanding of the Christian faith. Peter eventually met with Jesus through Bill's friendship and explanation of the Bible (and Bill's secret, fervent prayer).

Peter's new-found faith immediately impacted his work at the Steel Company of Wales. Instead of making up the results, he began to do all the analyses carefully. He found that he didn't have the time to carry out properly all the work assigned to him, so he would stay late to complete it. Although the blast furnaces may have functioned better, his new desire to do a proper job led to criticism from his work colleagues, who were concerned that his approach would get them into trouble. In the very earliest days of his faith, Peter learned something about the total impact of the gospel on every area of life. He realized that following Jesus Christ might often mean conflict rather than comfort, opposition rather than affirmation.

His new friend Bill Sheehan was well acquainted with conflict. Orphaned before the age of two, Bill with his three sisters had been brought up by his uncle and aunt in Swansea's Irish Catholic community. Working as a house painter, Bill was hired by Leslie Green, pastor of a Pentecostal church in Swansea. Leslie was a warm, godly man who struck up a friendship with Bill. He talked to him about Jesus, about sin and forgiveness and grace. Instead of an arid, nominal system of rules, Leslie appeared to have a faith that was liberating and meaningful. Bill was both alarmed and intrigued. Leslie invited him to go along to church.

One Sunday, trembling with fear, Bill slipped into the back of a Protestant church for the first time in his life. These were pre-Vatican II days when it was still a sin for a Catholic to attend any Protestant church. Bill listened to what Leslie had to say, asked questions, took away and read a Bible, and finally prayed, declaring his need for salvation and his desire to give Jesus his allegiance. His conversion brought him a sense of purpose and joy. Delighted with his new understanding and spiritual insight, he tried to share what he had found with his uncle and aunt, only to have a storm break around his head. They did not speak to him for six months.

Such hostility towards his new-found faith was not confined to his family. Some of his Catholic friends surrounded him in the street, jostling and spitting on him. Suddenly, one of them headbutted Bill, knocking him to the ground and breaking his nose. With blood streaming from his face, Bill's first stunned thought was his new gabardine coat. The pastor he sought help from said, "Isn't it wonderful to suffer for Christ?" and Bill thought, "Well, hopefully it will be your turn next…"

Finally, Bill's uncle came to his room and told him to get out. For all the cold silences and the physical abuse, Bill later said that the most difficult moment was when his sister came to him with tears in her eyes, put her arms around his neck, and urged him to give up his new ideas and return to the family faith. Bill stood firm in his trust in Christ, despite the pain that he endured. In the face of such opposition, Bill's faith had matured quickly.

Thus began an extraordinary phase in the lives of both Peter and Bill. A group of young men who had been in Peter's class at school gathered round Bill in the local Elim Pentecostal church. Bill led them into a living faith, he prayed for them and with them, and he taught them to read and study the Bible for themselves. While enjoying energetic horseplay and merriment, with Bill's help they also put down deep roots into thoughtful biblical faith. In Peter's Bible, nearly every verse was highlighted in a different coloured pencil depending on theme or subject. It was worn, pored over, marked and annotated. Unafraid as Bill was to think and work through the implications of his faith, he taught these young men to do so too.

From this one man's example and words to a small Christian group in a small town in depressed South Wales came unexpected results. David Griffiths trained as an Anglican clergyman, going first to Japan and then to the Philippines as a missionary, working for decades with the Overseas Missionary Fellowship. Alan Mutter became an educationalist. Alan Crispin became a mathematician. Don Evans trained in philosophy and went on to become a professor of biomedical ethics, founding departments of bioethics at universities in Europe and New Zealand. Then there was Peter. What was to become of this young man who had recently come to faith and been discipled by Bill?

Peter met the Doctors Brien in 1956 while they were on that brief visit to Britain, their first furlough in seventeen years of pioneer missionary work. They were both passionate and persuasive about their work in north-eastern Rhodesia, and spoke of the need for more missionary teachers in their network of twenty-five very basic schools spread along the eastern border of Rhodesia. Peter corresponded with the Briens, and eventually left the Steel Company of Wales to train as a teacher in response to the Briens' guidance on preparation for cross-cultural service. He found himself the lone man within a cohort of female trainee teachers – a situation he clearly enjoyed!

Peter earned his teaching certificate with distinction, but his practice with C-stream pupils in a 1959 boys' secondary modern school in inner-city Birmingham was a rude awakening. Once, in December 1959, when he punished a boy for lying, he found the boy waiting for him after school, so filled with rage that tears were running freely down his face. The furious student threatened to lash Peter with his studded belt, stab, and then strangle him. Internally terrified, Peter told him that the really tough thing to do was to accept responsibility for doing wrong and take his deserved punishment like a man! A week later, much to Peter's surprise, the boy approached him, admitted he had lost his temper, and apologized. Despite this encouragement, Peter found the double pressure of his first year of teaching combined with the struggle for class control so stressful that he broke out in a rash. A few days later he wrote to Bill Sheehan that he was struggling to sleep and felt on the edge of "cracking up". But he understood his weakness as an opportunity to rely on God, telling Bill that because of his struggle with health, "so I had liberty in the pulpit".

Towards the end of 1959, Peter had an inner conviction that he should apply to work in Rhodesia. But he was very concerned for his mother, who had already lost one son. How would she cope with the loss of a second son to prolonged service abroad? Bill's history came to mind, confronted as he had been with the choice of either remaining faithful to God or falling in line with the wishes of his family. He wrote to Bill, not for advice but simply to request prayer, aware that Bill would know just how painful such a dilemma could be. Peter didn't know if he was taking the right step in seeking missionary work but added, "I am determined to follow Him withersoever He leadeth." Taking the words of Jesus at face value, "I am the light of the world. Whoever follows me will not walk in darkness,"[9] he told Bill he would take the plunge of applying, trusting that God would make clear the way forward, whatever that might be.

He completed his application to the Elim Mission Society on 6 January 1960. Specifically asked if he had been baptized in the Holy Spirit, the key "second experience" of Pentecostalism, he answered with admirable candour that he had not. He went on to tell the Mission Society that he was applying not because of a supernatural experience of being called by God but rather because he had "a desire to do God's perfect will, see the tremendous need, have the academic qualifications necessary, am young and healthy, and I believe I have a God-given vision of a lost world that needs the gospel of Jesus Christ. I have committed my way to the Lord and I believe that if it is not His will that I should go He will bar the way."

Peter then discovered that Margaret, a young woman from his home town of Swansea, had also offered herself for short-term service in Rhodesia. Peter was greatly concerned that Margaret would be out there before him, as if she was "waiting for him". His alarm was reinforced when an article appeared on 23 March in a local newspaper, the *Swansea Voice*. "Didn't like the bit that said I was going out to meet Margaret," he wrote to Bill, asking for his help to kill any rumours of romantic entanglement.

Just a month before leaving for Rhodesia, on 8 March 1960, he took a trip into London, exclaiming, "I actually took part in an Anglican Communion service at Oak Hill – it was according to the prayer book but quite good. I went to All Souls and heard John Stott preach on Amos – he was very good. It was strange to hear a man dressed in a red cassock and surplice preach evangelical truths." He also enjoyed hearing Martin Lloyd-Jones preach at Westminster in the evening. Alongside some lofty reflections on Lloyd-Jones' sermon, Peter added that he "gave the slipper" to nine boys he caught smoking in the toilets.

Peter expected that it would be about a year before he might leave. Wrestling with doubt and wondering if he had made a mistake and was about to permanently shipwreck his life, he was comforted by reading through Genesis, being reminded that even when Abram made mistakes, God acted in sovereign power to bring Abram back to the "straight and narrow". He had vigorously underlined the word "sovereign" in his Bible!

Despite his responses, the Mission Society responded with alacrity. Within eight weeks, Peter had been interviewed and medically screened, his references had been taken up, an opening on the Rhodesia field had been confirmed, he had been vaccinated against smallpox, and his passage out to Cape Town by ship had been booked for April 1960, one month later. All this despite the fact that he didn't even own a passport!

* * *

January 1960 had seen British Conservative Prime Minister, Harold Macmillan, visit the West African nation of Ghana. Black nationalists there were among the first to campaign for independence from Britain even before the Second World War. Led by Kwame Nkrumah, the British colony of the Gold Coast became the independent nation of Ghana, the first to achieve independence, in 1957. There was an air of excitement and optimism which Macmillan reflected in his famous speech that he delivered first in Accra:

> *The wind of change is blowing through this continent.*
> *Whether we like it or not, this growth of national*
> *consciousness is a political fact. We must all accept it as*
> *a fact, and our national policies must take account of it.*

This subtle declaration of a British determination to provide independence for its African colonies went unremarked upon until Macmillan repeated his speech in Cape Town on 3 February 1960 before Hendrik Verwoerd, President of the Republic of South Africa. He added that the South African policy of apartheid under development at the time made "it impossible for us [to support South Africa] without being false to our own deep convictions about the political destinies of free men to which in our own territories we are trying to give effect".

Visibly shocked during Macmillan's speech, Verwoerd rapidly collected his thoughts and responded vigorously that he would protect and seek justice for white people in Africa, many of whom had no other home. Critically, Verwoerd stated that South Africa was grounded in what he saw as Christian values and so would take a strong stance against Communism, thus unhappily conflating black aspirations for independence with Cold War politics.[10] The following month, on 21 March, South African police killed sixty-nine unarmed citizens in Sharpeville who were protesting draconian pass laws which restricted and controlled the movements of black South Africans in their own country. The news of what became known as the "Sharpeville Massacre" flashed around the world.

While preparing to travel out to Rhodesia as soon as he could, Peter reflected on the headline stories featuring African issues. He wrote to Bill Sheehan on 30 March, just two weeks before sailing: "There seems to be big trouble starting up in Africa. Perhaps if I don't get in now all the doors will close in the near future." Rather than the negative news daunting Peter, it seemed to spur him on.

A reporter and a photographer from *The Herald of Wales* arrived at the Griffiths' door. Twenty-two-year-old Peter was photographed standing on Mumbles Rocks in Swansea and looking dramatically out to sea. "A young missionary off to Africa" was the front-page headline. Although Hannah and Stanley had worked hard and "kept a clean pub", there is a hint in a yellowed newspaper clipping of the opprobrium and social pressure that the publican felt in chapel-going South Wales all those years ago. Stanley was reported as saying, "This just goes to show that, despite what people say, publicans can raise their children just as well as anyone else." Privately, Stanley had warned Peter that his new-found enthusiasm for the Christian faith was just a phase, that he mustn't allow it to get the better of him or he would develop "religious mania". Stanley had mistaken passion for insanity. Peter was not mad, but rather passionate for the Lord of Life and the Word of God, and that passion was to carry him and sustain him through extraordinary times. It was not Peter who changed but, many years later, Stanley.

Peter Griffiths was commissioned for cross-cultural service in the packed Elim Church, Swansea, on 10 April 1960. Despite his extreme youth, as he spoke in the service it was reported that people sensed an authority and wisdom beyond his years. Four days later, on 14 April 1960, the *Edinburgh Castle* sailed from Southampton with Peter on board. Hannah wasn't there. She could not bear to see Peter off. Having buried Ken and then seen Peter almost die, his marvellous recovery from a life-threatening illness was a gift she didn't want to lose. After his departure she mourned as if she had lost a second son. As far as Hannah was concerned, Rhodesia was beyond the end of the world, and the six-year first term of service Peter had signed up for was an eternity.

THE RIVER CUTS
NEW CHANNELS

Much to Hannah Griffiths' surprise and relief, light blue aerogrammes bearing exotic stamps, postmarked with names of places she had never heard of, began to drop through the letter box. Peter had made the long sea voyage safely and was enjoying a much-needed rest after the hectic months leading to his departure. The 2,500 kilometre train journey from Cape Town through the parched expanse of the Karoo then into Botswana across the Kalahari Desert before finally entering Rhodesia was uneventful. Peter arrived on May Day 1960: "It was a real thrill to round the last bend and to see Umtali nestling among the majestic mountains of Rhodesia's Eastern Highlands. As I gazed at the place to which God has called me I was overwhelmed with joy."

Peter had enclosed a photo of himself, taken in his humble thatched cottage in Penhalonga. Clearly visible on the table in front of him was a bottle of tomato sauce, an essential addition to almost every meal he had eaten in Wales. Hannah was glad to think of her boy having at least one of the comforts of home even in far-off Rhodesia.

Hannah had lost her first son to death. The loss of her second son not to death but to long-term service overseas seemed to be a key moment in Hannah's own spiritual journey. Peter wrote to the mission board just two months after his arrival in Rhodesia, "Since I have come here, my mother Hannah has given her life to the Lord… The Lord is certainly no man's debtor. We have given each other up for a time but He has seen that we will be together for eternity."

Peter plunged wholeheartedly into his new life as a schoolteacher in the Elim Mission station just outside the village of Penhalonga. Many of the "children" he was teaching were older than he was. In contrast to his battles with British pupils in inner-city Birmingham, he was deeply impressed with the passionate, almost fanatical approach to learning that the young black people of Rhodesia displayed. Education was seen as a key to unlock a prosperous future as well as a passport out of the drudgery and boredom of subsistence farming, just as it had been a way out of the Welsh coalmines a generation before.

On top of his teaching commitments, Peter gave himself to the demanding discipline of language learning that every cross-cultural worker knows well. He found it humiliating and frustrating to be reduced linguistically to being a child again. Not to be discouraged for long, however, he persuaded one of the local teachers, Agnes Mdhluli, to translate for him, so that at least he could begin to preach while his Shona skills were being honed. To his relief, he discovered that Margaret (the young woman from Swansea who appeared to have set her sights on him) was working up in Katerere while he was much further south on the mission station in Penhalonga.

Most of the students at Elim Primary School came from a very poor background. To earn money for his fees, one of the students, Dannie, agreed to help Peter with his housework. Like many young black students in Rhodesia at the time, Dannie had experienced many interruptions in his education, so even though he was at primary school there was little difference in age between the two young men, and they became fast friends. Dannie delighted in correcting Peter's stumbling attempts at speaking Shona, and provided answers to his innumerable questions.

Peter was a lover of practical jokes, but he could go too far, especially before he understood enough about the new culture that surrounded him. Dannie told Peter about *mitupo*, or totems, which linked a Shona clan together through creatures that they were then forbidden even to touch, and certainly never to kill or eat. Dannie told Peter that his totem animal was the freshwater crab. Peter received a tiny tin of freshwater crabmeat from home, and he held the tin in his hand, concealing the label, and skewered a chunk of the meat. He offered it to Dannie, who took it cautiously into his mouth and then chewed it with increasing enthusiasm. The two young men enjoyed the tin of meat together. Only when it was finished did Peter turn the tin around to reveal a picture of a crab on the label. Dannie's eyes widened with shock and horror. He pleaded with Peter to keep their shared meal a secret.

Despite Peter's crass cultural insensitivity, Dannie grew close to him. Just how close became clear when, having previously told Dannie of his heart damage, Peter suddenly grasped at his chest and feigned a collapse while he and Dannie were talking. With a yell, Dannie sprinted out of the house, which was situated at the top of a long hill, and raced down the slope. Pleased with the reaction he had provoked, Peter sauntered out onto his veranda, calling Dannie's name and waving cheerfully. Dannie stopped and turned around. To his immediate shame, Peter saw tears running freely down Dannie's cheeks, who shouted reproachfully, "Don't do that again! Don't ever do that again!"

Gregarious and outgoing, Peter enjoyed the warm relationships he was developing. Life was full and very demanding. But returning to his cottage in which he camped in bachelor style was sometimes very lonely.

* * *

A year after his arrival in Rhodesia, on 1 July 1961, Peter was asked to help with a transport challenge. Nurse Olive Garbutt was to collect her car from Umtali and needed a lift there from Katerere. Brenda was to take Olive from Katerere to a halfway point at Juliasdale, a tiny hamlet in the Eastern Highlands, and then turn back. As the only driver on the team in Penhalonga, Peter was to meet the two women in Juliasdale and drive Olive on to Umtali. Brenda rose at 3.30 a.m. to start the long drive with Olive, only to find that Margaret was waiting by the Land Rover too, anxious to join in the adventure.

Outside the agreed meeting point, the modest emporium of Juliasdale Store, Margaret captured the moment of their rendezvous with her camera. Under the clear, blue winter sky, pine trees and blooming yellow wattle lining the road's edge, Peter stood with one foot up on the bumper of his Ford truck, confident, smiling, and with his bush hat pushed far back on his head. Behind him, demure and pretty in a striking striped swing dress, fashionable flats on her feet, Brenda leaned casually against the front of her Land Rover, arms by her sides. Grinning widely while balancing on the back bumper of the truck was Boniface,[1] one of Brenda's students who had agreed to keep her company on the long, dusty drive back to Katerere.

Unknowingly, Margaret also captured the moment that ended any chance she might have had of winning Peter's heart. It was a twist of irony that it was Margaret's camera that snapped the scene. Her hope of seeing Peter and delight that she was to be in his company, even if only for a few snatched moments, was soon clouded by the chemistry that sparked and crackled between the two drivers as they stood by the dusty road, untroubled by the occasional vehicle that raced by, stirring clouds of acrid, choking dust.

Peter and Brenda chatted with growing enthusiasm. Although Brenda had three years more experience than Peter, they had much in common: they were both far from home, living on the remote eastern border of Rhodesia, among a people and in a culture not their own, coping with a monotonous diet, and facing similar struggles of language learning and loneliness. But the rugged beauty of the landscapes, a satisfaction in testing their ability to thrive in simple, even spartan conditions, an enjoyment in forging new friendships across cultural divides and, above all, a sense of fulfilling a divine purpose, brought more than adequate compensation for their hardships.

Summarizing her feelings about the life she had chosen to lead at the end of that conversation, Brenda quoted a line to Peter from John Buchan's 1941 novel *Sick Heart River*, in which the dying central character confronts the questions of the meaning of life in the Canadian wilderness. Finding it a situation that resonated with her own, she quoted, "It's a great life, if you don't weaken!" She was finding her life of obedient faith demanding, but rewarding.

Hidden away in an old sea trunk, wrapped in fragile, crumbling tissue paper and tied with a dusty length of pink ribbon, Brenda kept the letters that Peter wrote to her during their secret courtship, sparked by that short meeting under the yellow wattle trees at the side of a mountain track in the Eastern Highlands. As two young, single missionaries working in different locations separated by hours of driving on dirt roads with very little free time and few excuses to see each other, letters became a channel through which their feelings, fears, hopes, and dreams were poured.

Feeling somewhat in awe of Brenda's command of English that she had demonstrated at their meeting, Peter warned her not to expect too much of his writing, claiming he always needed a dictionary beside him and was the "world's worst speller". But, encouraged by a rapid response from Brenda, just a few days later, on 24 May, he daringly scribbled, "Please don't feel obliged to answer my letters as I don't want to take up too much of your time. Just write every day!"

As members of close-knit teams where little could be concealed, neither Peter nor Brenda wanted to endure the inevitable pressure that would potentially crush even the slightest evidence of budding feelings for one another. Both wanted space to allow the relationship to take its course. Right from the start, they were both desperately concerned that their highly respected but austere and demanding senior missionaries, Cecil and Mary Brien, would hear of their nascent friendship and either forbid it or want it formalized. With the high view of authority that they both shared, neither Peter nor Brenda would want to disobey those they saw as their divinely appointed leaders. Yet neither wanted to stop writing. So by mutual consent they went to great lengths to mask the frequency of their correspondence.

Envelopes were alternately handwritten and typed, as Mary Brien sorted all the mail that arrived at Elim Mission in Katerere and would be quick to recognize handwriting and spot any patterns in a flow of correspondence. Missives were posted from off the mission when opportunities arose, to add variety to the postmarks. To avoid any familiarity with a particular style of stationery, different colours, types, and sizes of envelopes were used. When possible, letters were hand delivered by colleagues travelling between the mission stations. By offering to provide minor services to all their colleagues they justified writing and receiving letters purporting to watch repairs, developing photos and the like. For a period they successfully managed an "exam paper exchange", where they claimed to be swapping experiences and expertise on developing sets of examinations for their pupils.

In Peter's letters, I met a younger, emerging version of the mature man I knew so well. His writing was touchingly earnest, breathlessly energetic, a passionate screed on a multitude of subjects. A concern for the glory of God was frequently his focus. Scripture quotations were liberally sprinkled throughout his letters. He mentioned often his prayerful longing for a movement similar to the 1904 Welsh revival to sweep across Southern Africa.

Peter tried out his sermon outlines on his long-suffering sweetheart, acknowledging that some of the better ones he had "borrowed" from Bill Sheehan. His approach to preaching changed from quoting single verses plucked apparently at random. To illustrate a point, he began to think through long passages or entire books, reflecting on themes and contexts and developing a more profound view both of the work of the Holy Spirit and of the nature of the Trinity.

Disconcertingly honest, Peter frequently confessed his weaknesses, failings, and sins to Brenda in his letters. On 18 February 1962 he outlined sources of friction with a colleague and asked Brenda for prayer. He told her a month later, on 11 March, that he was still working hard not to be critical. "I'm a wonderful theorist you know, oh to be a doer of the word! A dear friend once told me that my piety outstripped my character," he wrote a few months later, on 21 July.

Frequently travelling off to preach and visit, wandering through the area on foot, by bus, or with borrowed transport, Peter often sought the company of an experienced, older, black pastor, Mufundisi Chiwara. Peter crammed his missives with a bewildering record of preaching locations: in the local villages scattered throughout the mountains along the border with Mozambique; among illiterate, undernourished plantation workers at Palmers and Imbeza; to the educated elite at Umtali Teacher Training College; following the temporary Road Department camps filled with gangs of itinerant workers; to "native constables" and their families at the Police Camp; among the sinewy, tough miners gathered in Liverpool compound at Rezende Gold Mine. At Premier Estate, the first farm established by Cecil Rhodes the previous century, Elim Mission had opened a school and a church, and Peter would preach there too. The mixed-race Baptist church in the poorer area of Umtali invited him regularly, and he could preach there in English. Since all these regular preaching engagements were extra-curricular, all the preparation, travel, and preaching had to be done in his spare time after his teaching day was done.

Peter's and Brenda's correspondence was also filled with practical details. Committed to learning the language, Peter sought out those who were willing to correct and teach him. In his letters he recorded the insights and wisdom of black colleagues who analysed, critiqued, and corrected his sermons, talks, and papers. Although food and hobbies were never mentioned, they were both enjoying learning Shona, and this became the language of affection between them. Peter began his letters with *Mudikani* ("my lover") and signed off with loving Shona phrases. Although he frequently included Shona tags or phrases in his letters, Peter said little about nuances of language or culture, scenery, flora, or fauna in his letters. He made an exception for fauna that was dangerous in some way. Snakes figured often. This was part of the heroic and pioneering picture presented by many missionaries at the time and so, literally, was something "worth writing home about".

Brenda's diary noted details and wonderings about Shona customs, proverbs, and beliefs. She painstakingly typed up folk tales that had been passed on by her students. She described the indigenous trees, so new and different. If two people met, who was to offer greetings first? What was the correct way for children to serve their elders with food? How did a chief qualify to become a *mhondoro* or lion spirit? There were disturbing elements of the culture that she recorded too; for example, if twins were born, they would be placed in a large pot and hot coals would be poured in.

White Rhodesian society was frequently patronizing and discriminatory towards black people. But even when writing to Brenda informally, Peter would use the proper names of his black contacts, colleagues, and friends, along with their honorifics. Thus Mufundisi Chiwara, Mistress Agnes Mdhluli, Mrs Mabambe, Teacher Nzou, and many others featured in his letters. Brenda's photograph albums featured pictures of her students, both individuals and in groups, carefully labelled with their full names.

Peter was cheerfully egalitarian, driven partly by his theology that all peoples were created equal by God, all had equally fallen into sin, all needed to stand before the cross of Christ, and all could find forgiveness there. Perhaps his tough Welsh working-class background also helped him. He felt little concern for position or title, had no airs and graces, and shared a sense of oppression by the ruling class! He engaged daily with some of the most intelligent and hard-working young people in the country.

Working close to Umtali and frequently running errands into town, he encountered and was angered by the petty racist approaches of the day. While they had not yet hardened into the ruthless divisions of apartheid, they were humiliating and dehumanizing. He ranted to Brenda about the separate queues for black and white customers in the post office. His boss, school principal Mr Sithole, was taken suddenly ill. Driving him into Umtali General Hospital, Peter sat in the queue with him as he waited to be seen by the doctor. Despite the fact that a young Peter was supporting an obviously much older man who was fully capable of speaking for himself, the white nurse gestured towards Mr Sithole and asked Peter, "Is this your boy?"

Angry, Peter retorted, "He is my headmaster!" much to the surprise of the nurse.

Apparently, minor social divisions reflected greater injustices related to ownership of land and the right to vote. The Southern Rhodesia African National Congress (SRANC) was formed in 1957 and was the first black mass movement committed to the reform of increasingly discriminatory laws controlling voting rights, distribution of land, and access to education for the black majority. Despite the SRANC's principles of civil disobedience and non-violence in pursuit of their political aims, inspired by Martin Luther King's civil rights campaign in the United States, the SRANC was banned by the colonial government.

Undaunted, its leaders formed a new National Democratic Party (NDP) in January 1960. Inspired by political change led by Kwame Nkrumah in Ghana and Jomo Kenyatta in Kenya, NDP leaders cast a larger vision, not just seeking justice from the government but seeking also to become the government.

A referendum was held in Rhodesia on 26 July 1961 on a new constitution proposed by the Rhodesian government. The NDP rejected this, and tensions rose as they tried to force security to the top of the agenda in an effort to persuade the distant Westminster government to take a more active role in the management of their colony, hoping they would force the local white government to back down on their drive towards discrimination.

The rapid realization of this vision was threatened by polarizing events. To the north of the relatively peaceful British Crown Colony of Rhodesia, a crisis in the Central African colony of the Belgian Congo exploded in 1960. On 30 June, the Belgian government granted independence to its grossly underdeveloped territory, with a minimum of preparation. A very rapid descent into anarchy followed, with rival factions emerging within the new black government who violently opposed one another.

This so-called Congo Crisis took a disturbing new direction when assistance was requested from the Soviet Union by one of the Congolese factions. More than a thousand Soviet military advisors were dispatched, alarming the American Central Intelligence Agency who warned the American government that the Congo might follow Cuba, becoming a Communist state in the heart of Africa. A separate Maoist-inspired Simba rebellion in the east of the Congo was indeed supported by Cuba, which sent a military team led by Che Guevara to advise the Simbas on tactics and doctrine.

Already trying to stop the spread of Communism in South-East Asia and anxious not to lose access to Congolese uranium, which it needed for its nuclear weapons programme, the United States was willing to prop up a Congolese government sympathetic to the West despite its corruption, inefficiency, and use of public violence. White mercenaries, of whom more than half were drawn from South Africa and Rhodesia, became a proxy militia for the pro-Western government, and were covertly supported by the US. But one of the mercenary leaders described his own men as "appalling thugs".

Various Congolese armed groups vented their frustration and anger towards Western intervention by capturing, humiliating, torturing, and killing Belgians and other white civilians who had chosen to stay after independence. Both Protestant and Catholic missionaries were also caught up in the terror, typified by young American missionary doctor, Paul Carlson, who was held for weeks, tortured, and finally gunned down by a young Simba rebel on a Stanleyville street. The picture of his body, eyes still open and staring lifelessly at the camera, transfixed and horrified all who saw it.

Belgian paratroopers with American air support eventually intervened to rescue European hostages. Their action was sharply criticized by independent African governments, who saw it as undue neo-colonial interference in a newly sovereign state. In the chaos, what industrial infrastructure had been developed in the Belgian colony was destroyed or fell quickly into disuse and disrepair. Both economic collapse and widespread violence brought a flood of white and black Congolese refugees into the Federation of Northern and Southern Rhodesia and Nyasaland.

Peaceful transitions to independence elsewhere on the African continent were forgotten in the very visible anarchy that had overwhelmed their giant neighbour. The Congo Crisis had a powerful negative impact on the white settler community of Southern Rhodesia. If these were the results of a few short years under black rule for the Congo, then the settlers swore that such a thing would never be allowed to happen in Rhodesia.

In the overheated atmosphere engendered by the rhetoric of both sides in the Cold War, it was believed by white governments in Rhodesia and South Africa that Moscow intended to create a series of satellite states in Africa. Although both the Chinese and Soviet governments were largely opportunistic, reacting to events in Africa rather than controlling them, white settler regimes played on fears of Communist expansionism to Western governments, seeing it as justification for their actions against nationalist movements.

For the small missionary team in eastern Rhodesia, the Congo Crisis had a positive outcome for team growth. Following the Léopoldville Riot on 4 January 1959 where an estimated 35,000 Congolese rampaged through the streets of what is now Kinshasa, unrest had spread across the country. Caught up in the violence, teacher Catherine Picken and nurse Olive Garbutt had been evacuated to Rhodesia.

Bespectacled Catherine was quiet and unassuming in manner, prosaic in her speech. Behind her diffident manner, she was capable, reliable, and a competent sportswoman, having played representative hockey in her youth. Reading Nigerian writer Chinua Achebe's 1958 novel *Things Fall Apart*, Achebe's reflections on African identity, nationalism, and decolonization enabled Cath to recognize the rapid changes that were taking place in her adopted continent and to empathize with those she served. In correspondence home, she observed that the kind of cultural and social change that took place in England over the course of 300 years had taken Africa just seventy. Like Peter, she too was struck by the deep hunger for education among young black people in Rhodesia. Cath also saw a far deeper need for that education to be anchored in a Christian world view. Perceptively, she grasped the role that mission schools could play in meeting both of these needs in Rhodesia. Despite her challenging experiences in the Congo, Cath decided to stay on in Rhodesia and give herself to teaching young black people there.

* * *

On 8 July 1961, Brenda wrote to Peter of her awareness of the growing tension in the country and locally. Political strains temporarily impacted the missionary team. Cecil Brien felt unable to be away from the Ruwangwe Valley overnight as this would have meant leaving the otherwise all-female team of missionaries. Peter impishly offered to drive up and be their protector. Writing of strikes, of armoured cars on the roads, of the call-up of police reservists, Peter described seeing truckloads of troops racing past and even spotter planes overhead, aerial surveillance teams looking for "unlawful gatherings". From his point of view, the main impact of nationalist activity and heavy-handed government response was that he was temporarily banned from travelling with Mufundisi Chiwara to the various outstations, which he found deeply frustrating.

Although the two young lovers noted the political developments that were taking place around them, Peter's earlier letters showed a naive disdain for the issues. Arriving at a road camp to preach, Peter had been unceremoniously bundled out by the white supervisor. Peter protested, but to no avail. Crossly, he grumbled, "I think that 'missionaries' who are dabbling in politics are closing doors to the gospel."

Ten months after his arrival, on 12 March 1961, he wrote to the Missionary Secretary back in the UK, "There is a very strong nationalistic spirit rising in this area. Leaders of the National Democratic Party held a big meeting in Penhalonga two weeks ago… I tended to argue a bit with them but the Lord clearly showed me that it is not my department. Jesus was living in an occupied country and He was surrounded by nationalists who would have loved Him to take their part, but He would have nothing to do with it. His Kingdom is not of this world, and our citizenship is in heaven. Jesus preached freedom from sin and not freedom from other nations, and that must clearly be our pattern."

But Peter's initial attempt to remain ignorant of the politics of nationalism while claiming the spiritual high ground became more difficult to maintain as engagement with the issues was forced upon him. Rumours spread about a government polio vaccination campaign, that the injections would cause sterility and were part of a conspiracy to limit the size of the black population. In October, health teams visited the Elim school in Penhalonga, provoking mass panic. Amid yelling chaos, Peter saw more than 200 pupils from other classes jumping from windows, pouring through doors, and bolting across the fields and into the nearby hills. Only Peter was able to keep his entire class in place while the vaccines were given.

But a distressing backlash took place when Peter went to preach the following day at Palmer's plantation. Angry parents barracked him, shouting that he was working with the white government to sterilize their children. Disturbing and painful though Peter found it, Elim got off lightly in comparison with other schools as the campaign became a flashpoint for unrest. There was rioting in every school in Sakubva Township, just outside Umtali. Student strikes were widespread, and many schools closed temporarily. And it was not only government schools that were caught up in the unrest; there had been petrol bombings and acts of arson, and a Salvation Army church and a Methodist school burned down in the area. In September the Rhodesian authorities had responded to the unrest by mobilizing the Territorial Army, raiding houses belonging to leaders of the National Democratic Party to make arrests and carrying out pro-government leaflet drops by plane.

Concerned about the possibility of an arson attack, Peter laughingly outlined his own foolhardiness in deciding to remove the highly flammable thatched roof from his house and replacing it with a corrugated iron roof while he was still living in the house! Not realizing what a dirty, dusty, prolonged job it would be, eventually he was forced to take refuge in a tent in one room, and found his camping spot to be "a furnace by day and a fridge by night"!

His concerns were not unreasonable. On 8 October 1962, the simple thatched classroom of Elim's Forest Primary School was burned down in a night-time arson attack. No one claimed responsibility, but the missionary team decided to invest their scanty financial resources in converting thatch to tin roofs. As Peter reflected on this unwelcome development he wrote, "God may intend allowing persecution to purify and shake the church out of its sleep… I don't think I have felt so burdened and tired for many a long day. I hope there is no self-pity but rather a longing for God to rend the heavens and come down with Holy Spirit revival."[2]

The Rhodesian Front had been formed in March 1962 by whites opposed to any immediate change to black majority rule and seeking to reverse even the modest rights granted to the country's black majority. The Rhodesian Front unexpectedly won power in the general election of December 1962, and this provoked widespread unrest among the black population. On 25 January 1963, back from her furlough, Brenda outlined the seriousness of the situation in restive Katerere under marginal state control. As Brenda knelt beside Mai Enesia, one of the first converts to Christianity in the Ruwangwe Valley, during a prayer meeting, Brenda was moved and alarmed to hear Mai Enesia tearfully pray "that the missionaries wouldn't have to die in Africa". Peter's response was dismissive, but Mai Enesia had prayed prophetically, possibly as someone who perceived the depth of public feeling with more clarity than the missionaries.

Peter grasped that "Europeans are afraid we will stir up the people against them", as he wrote on 1 September 1962. He began to see that the teaching of biblical values such as the equality and worth of all human beings regardless of their skin colour could be seen as a political act. Vigorously preaching the idea that everyone sinned implied that even the current leaders of the country might be doing wrong. As such values and ideas were inculcated by the missionary team, in addition to educating students to think for themselves, they were laying much of the groundwork for political change to become possible, even though this was often unwitting.

Not only politically naive, in February 1963 Peter wrote enthusiastically to Brenda, who was thinking of stopping teaching. "You'd be a missionary then and not a missionary teacher, which could mean that your spiritual ministry may double. We have been claiming that souls are to have the priority over schools. This may be a step towards it." At that point, he saw his missionary calling in dualistic terms: the physical versus the spiritual, the temporal versus the eternal. And yet he was repeatedly drawn into the practical aspects of everyday life. As someone who could drive, he transported mission mailbags to and from Umtali Post Office and ran dozens of other errands. He frequently took pregnant women to deliver in the labour ward at Umtali General Hospital, rushed sick people into the same hospital, and, inevitably, helped to transport dead bodies from time to time.

Despite his youth, he learned to conduct funerals. In October 1961 he described the sickening experience of transporting a body in a closed van; the person had been dead for some time and had been placed in a cheap coffin that didn't close properly. Cuttingly, he added that when he arrived at the church, "most mourners drank – it was an Anglican affair", referring to the fact that some liberal Anglican missionaries allowed mourners to hold beer ceremonies as a key part of traditional African religious funeral rites.

During his holidays, Peter ran Bible Schools, which included taking his students on visitation trips and encouraging them to conduct meetings in open-air markets and villages.

Asked to oversee the production of 25,000 bricks for two new classrooms and a teacher's house, Peter worked with three of his students. They started with the trampling of clay in pits, the filling of wooden moulds, and slow air-drying. This was followed by piling the sun-dried bricks into vast hollow stacks which were then filled with firewood and set alight. The kilns burned for days as the bricks were vitrified and then cooled.

The saga unfolded over weeks. At one point, in July 1962, overwhelmed by the physically hard labour and difficulties that he encountered in a complex task that demanded skills he felt he didn't have, Peter broke down and wept over the letter he was writing, which he began, "Man is of few days and full of trouble – rain is on the horizon and 9,000 unburnt bricks are on the ground." He knew that if the rain pelted down it would dissolve the sun-dried clay, and the hard labour of days would be lost. But he was learning to pray through and persevere in practical issues. His small team completed the kilns despite unseasonal driving rain. Finally, construction could begin!

A sense of expectancy came through repeatedly in Peter's and Brenda's correspondence, that God would do things, would convict people of their need for repentance, that He would speak through His Word, that their prayers would be answered, that people could be changed. Preaching at the Liverpool compound provoked loud jeering and dissent from the crowd that stopped to listen, but Peter recorded thirteen "decisions" in a single meeting.

Walking into a new area of the mountains with Mufundisi Chiwara in July 1961, they approached an unfamiliar village. Peter could see a large group gathered for a beer party in the middle of the day. Given the propensity for uninhibited heckling and the possibility for violence where alcohol was involved, Chiwara stopped in his tracks, to Peter's secret relief. Then he turned to Peter, "and said, 'Paul went and preached at a beer party,' and so continued forward. I would have liked the chapter and verse but at any rate I'm sure Paul would have preached at a beer party and so I nodded in agreement. We had a good listening as we seem to have caught the festivities in their early stages."

But how were these one-off encounters going to be built on? His preaching at the Liverpool compound continued, but he wrote candidly that despite all the "decisions" he recorded on the streets, he didn't believe a single person was really "going on with the Lord". He realized that a desire to please rather than a true conviction lay behind many of these "decisions".

Denominational differences he encountered stretched him too. He confessed that reading the delightfully named Anglican divine Octavius Winslow on *The Work of the Holy Spirit* convinced him that all professing Christians were indwelt by the Holy Spirit, not just Pentecostals. He took on John Calvin's seminal work of Protestant systematic theology, *The Institutes of the Christian Religion*. Peter also read biography and church history. Swiss historian Jean-Henri Merle d'Aubigné's *History of the Reformation* impacted him powerfully.

His honest conversations with national colleagues, warm relationships with missionary colleagues across denominational divides, and increasingly perceptive observations on cultural and political issues confronted Peter with pastoral and theological challenges he couldn't ignore. He wrestled with these challenges, his Bible heavily thumbed, annotated, and underlined.

His thinking was changing. He began to understand the work of seeing people come to faith and then nurtured and supported as they learned to live out the implications of that faith as a process more akin to farming than a "smash and grab" raid in enemy territory. Rather than seeing his wandering the hills of eastern Rhodesia as the "pure" missionary work and teaching as a necessary evil, he began to ponder how they could best fit together. Slowly, he began to see his role as a teacher in a new light, as an opportunity to share his life over a number of years with his charges.

In glowing terms, Brenda had written about one of her students, Ephraim Satuku. He had worked hard at school and his qualifications had opened the door to further study. Coming to faith through the witness of his teachers, Ephraim had chosen the uncertain path of Bible College rather than going into a more lucrative line of work – no easy choice in a culture where the influence of the extended family was so strong and where those able to earn were expected to provide for others. Ephraim had travelled from Katerere to Penhalonga for a visit. Peter wrote back to Brenda in June 1964, "Your Ephraim… took our services yesterday. I was very impressed with Ephraim, he seems outstanding. A few more like him and the mission would be expanding rapidly."

As Peter recognized leadership potential among black students as key to the future of the national church, it was but a short step from there to future leaders of the country. In contrast to the political hard line being taken by the white minority, Peter told

Brenda how important he believed it was that more leadership skills should be developed among young black Rhodesians. How would it be if the missionary team were to play their part under God in educating young people, seeking to see them soundly converted, nurturing them in faith, participating in creating a generation able to lead in either church or society? It was an exciting, radical thought.

* * *

It wasn't just the future of the country that stirred Peter's emotions. What of his own future? Would it involve Brenda? Less than twenty-four hours after Brenda had returned to the UK on furlough on 15 December 1961, Peter sat and scribbled daringly, "You mentioned that you didn't have the deportment (I think that is the right word) to be an air hostess – as you walked towards the plane I thought to myself, that girl has elegance *kupfuura* [transcending] all the air hostesses I've ever seen. The hat looked cute and you looked so sophisticated and tall and slim and upright."

A couple of weeks later, on 28 December, as he audaciously penned his thoughts on their possible future together, Peter talked of the fears he had of stepping out of the will of God. But he recognized that he wanted more than divine guidance. He wanted the strength and courage to accept where that guidance might take him and to follow faithfully. He recounted a trip into nearby Mozambique, at the time still a Portuguese colony: "On Christmas Day we visited the customs house on the border, to be greeted by Portuguese soldiers, probably waiting for Indians trying to flee into Rhodesia.[3] They allowed us to travel one and a half miles over the border to see a beautiful waterfall. We could gaze from the top of a mountain over a vast area, well populated but ignorant of the gospel. Once again I thought of you and of the vague possibility of us one day taking the gospel to those who sit in darkness. Probably a wild and immature dream. It is certain that God has a lot of moulding to do with my life before he would entrust me with such a task."

As a massive lightning strike smashed into the ground just outside his window, dark-bruised clouds discharged volleys of driving tropical rain to hammer down on the roof. Amid the cacophony Peter mused further in his letter of 11 January 1962, "I've just read a first-class book by Elizabeth Elliot, *The Savage My Kinsman*, about her work with the Auca Indians. The story contains some very practical and down-to-earth truths – Southern Rhodesia, Portuguese East Africa, Brazil, Formosa – it doesn't matter where. All that matters in the Christian's service is the little word 'obey'. Faraway places are certainly green, but if they are outside of God's plan the green is only surface deep covering a bog or quicksand."

Peter's strong sense of the need for obedience and a desire to remain within the will of God stayed with him all through his life. Pensively, on 4 February, he closed another letter, "The meetings are over for another Lord's day, another step closer to eternity. I wonder what has really been accomplished in the hearts of those who came to hear the Word of God today."

* * *

Peter had written in January to their senior missionaries to finally declare his interest in Brenda and that their relationship had been developing over time. The Briens' long-awaited response arrived. Peter confessed that he was shaking as he tore open Cecil Brien's response. But there was only the Briens' concern that such a romance existed undeclared to them! It was not for another five months that the Briens wrote again, at which point they expressed their anger at what they saw as Peter's and Brenda's deceit, describing them as conniving together in a conspiracy. Angry and hurt, Peter declaimed to Brenda that there was a difference between being discreet and being deceptive.

Nine months later, in September, the Briens were finally willing to talk about Peter's and Brenda's relationship and to give their blessing. Delighted, Peter commented to Brenda in a letter written in early October, "Not that there *is* a way through every difficulty but that God will *make* a way." Trying to see things from the Briens' point of view, he admitted to feeling somewhat guilty about being so secretive and advised Brenda that she could address her letters openly to him at last.

Displaying a fine disregard for superstition, Peter and Brenda were married on Friday 13 December 1963, the first day of the school holidays and thus the first day they were free. The rain thundered down on the tin roof of a rural church in Penhalonga, almost drowning the voices raised in song. Beneath a great sign, "*Isu Tiisu Kristo Wakomborerwa*", or "We preach Christ crucified", the young couple stood to be married by the delightfully named marriage officer, Reverend Sermon, a Baptist minister in Umtali. His hair barbered and Brylcreemed, Peter looked painfully young, but both he and Brenda exuded sheer delight! The young newlyweds set off on an adventurous road trip through Rhodesia and into Zambia in a borrowed car. True to form, Peter found fifteen opportunities to preach during their month-long honeymoon.

On their return to Rhodesia in January 1964 they were assigned back to their separate mission stations. Cecil Brien was concerned that any transfer would mean a loss of the government subsidy paid to Elim for each teacher by their location. Only a fraction of the subsidy was paid to the teacher, each choosing to live frugally so the remainder could be used for new buildings, medicines, and the like. Knowing what a sacrificial life the Briens themselves lived, Peter and Brenda decided to embrace this decision! Their correspondence continued as they obediently separated again.

School holidays meant they could spend some time together.

Peter wrote on Sunday 12 April with great anticipation about the two newlyweds meeting as the school term drew to a close: "Two people having the same famous and royal Welsh name of Griffiths will be united again. It will be a time for the daffodils to dance, the leeks to shed their richest aroma, and for the Welsh dragon to fire his hot arrows of love!" But even then, duty still called, as teaching was considered only part of their overall missionary work and each had congregations to serve and ministries to fulfil. Silently they endured, seeing their separation as being for the sake of Christ's kingdom, although Peter warned Brenda in his letter of 26 May not to go overboard and let the "nun" in her have too much sway! Trying to encourage her in her sorrow, he added, "Keep rejoicing – it makes the devil angry. Keep loving – for love is of God."

Outwardly cheerful, they gave vent to their feelings only in their letters. Seven months into their marriage, the strain of separation was becoming unbearable. Plans had been made several times but dashed. Peter wrote, "I was shattered when I received the news just after noon that you wouldn't be coming down. I had hardly slept through the night thinking of your visit. The Lord must have a purpose in it all although it is hard to understand how a Land Rover couldn't travel during the dry season and yet a message could get through by bus to make known the fact! 'Hope deferred makes the heart sick.'"

Catherine Picken, on furlough in the United Kingdom, heard about their separation and took drastic action. Typically loving and loyal, she cut short her much-needed rest and returned to Rhodesia early, arranging her posting so no subsidy was lost and that Peter and Brenda could be reunited.

Finally, in August 1964 the newlyweds could begin living together. Two and a half years of courtship and nine months of marriage had been conducted almost entirely by mail. In his own romantic style, Peter signed off his last letter, on 17 August 1964,

"I love you more than ever. England score at close of play 381 for 4. Peter."

* * *

In 1964 the Elim missionary team from both Mission stations met in conference in the halfway town of Inyanga. Elim had invested heavily in medical work in the Katerere area. Churches were scattered in villages around Penhalonga and Katerere. The education team had developed a network of primary schools. Together they were to discuss the opening of a secondary school with boarding facilities, drawing in students from beyond the Ruwangwe Valley. This would be a significant commitment of both staff and finance, a huge investment in institutional work.

Brenda recorded in her diary early in April that a weekend was given over to prayer, discussion, and decision. Peter was positive about the idea, seeing how it could contribute to a truly indigenous church, how such a work might be part of the fullness of "the whole Gospel for the whole man", to use the catchphrase of the day. One of the nursing team was also enthusiastic.

Two hours of intense discussion with the whole team ensued. Brenda recorded, somewhat generously, that the decision had been made through consensus. Despite the weight that the Briens' opinion inevitably carried, given their status as senior missionaries and the pioneers of the work to boot, they showed little sensitivity to allowing a balanced discussion! Cecil Brien was the strongest anyone had yet heard him about any missionary project, as he stated that opening a secondary school would be a distraction to the spiritual work and that "blessing wouldn't come through it".

Mary Brien said little, but when asked by Peter what advantages the school would bring, she retorted sharply, "None!"

The Briens' disapproval of the idea carried all before them. Peter responded that given their strong feelings it should not be built. The nurse said that the other missionaries didn't want to do anything the Briens felt they shouldn't. Brenda jotted in her diary, "All seemed happy and settled. Sang brightly and good fellowship."

Despite the clear opposition of the Briens and the agreement by all against the school, Brenda's sense that "all seemed happy and settled" soon evaporated. She scribbled a sentence from her Bible reading that evening and added her own thoughts: "'Not by might, nor by power but by my Spirit.'[4] Not power educationally – but His Spirit. If we had Sec. School we would hold that power in this Reserve." In contrast to some of her colleagues, Brenda recognized that the building of a secondary school could be a route to spiritual fruitfulness not a distraction from it. Troubled, she fell into uneasy sleep.

A wistful letter from Peter arrived.[5] "An open field to build, start, and lead a secondary school was very tempting – it really appealed to the schoolteacher in me and was a challenge… to be grasped." Accepting of the decision as he was, he, too, sensed the door was not yet closed: "If we should go in for a secondary school I am confident that HE will see that we will do so."

Alongside his prodigious appetite for work, Cecil Brien was someone who spent great periods of time in prayer. Each morning between 3.00 a.m. and 4.00 a.m., at noon and in the evening Cecil Brien was to be found on his knees. It was part of a lifestyle of intercession he had learned from his mentor, Rees Howells. In the quietness of his home in Katerere a few days after the conference, Cecil was on his knees when he heard God say, "You are to open a school and you will call it 'Emmanuel', for I will be with you." In his prayer Cecil had protested his lack of ability, as a doctor, to build and run such a place. It was fear of his own shortcomings to meet the demands of such a task that had driven his opposition to the secondary school. But he believed God who said that he would "not lack any willing, skilful worker".

Therefore, a few days after the momentous decision, Cecil walked from his home into the little office where Brenda was preparing lessons. In great humility, he told her that God had shown him that his opposition to the school had been wrong. The decision had to be reversed!

Never one to waste time, within days Cecil had written to the Rhodesian Department of Native Education asking if Elim Mission would be able to open Emmanuel Secondary School.

Permission for the school was granted, and Brenda privately recorded her relief. Quoting Amy Carmichael of Dohnavur, she scribbled, "It may be that decisions which seem to change the character of the work will have to be made. But if the root principles which have governed us from the beginning are held fast, there will be no real change. The river may flow in a new channel, but it will be the same river."

AMONG WORLDS

As you grow older, you'll see white men cheat black men every day of your life, but let me tell you something and don't you forget it – whenever a white man does that to a black man, no matter who he is, how rich he is, or how fine a family he comes from, that white man is trash.

Harper Lee[1]

I crouched, a small, blond-headed boy, eyes wide with wonder, one hand reaching out tentatively to touch the golden and black beauty lying on the ground. It was a leopard, powerful, sleek, and compact. The early morning sunlight streamed across the scene, lighting up to perfection the markings on the predator. There was a little blood on its head but otherwise it looked simply to be asleep, sprawled in lazy feline comfort. A teenage schoolboy stood in the background, one foot placed cockily on the rump of a beast normally treated with far more respect. Behind us the ground rose sharply into the mountain range behind our houses, the territory from which this magnificent animal came.

In the middle of the night, a veteran missionary had awoken in response to an uproar in a livestock pen not far from his small cottage. Walking into the night, in the wavering beam of his torch he caught a glimpse of a leopard that was killing the goats and chickens being raised to feed boarders at the school. He ran back to his house, snatched up an ancient Lee-Enfield bolt-action rifle, went back out into the dark, shot the leopard, and then returned to bed. After breakfast the next morning, my mother Brenda took my younger brother Paul and me the few steps from our back door to see the leopard, capturing the moment on camera.[2]

As small boys, our life in the African bush seems now both exotic and free but, knowing nothing else, we took it for granted. Peter and Brenda worked hard at the Mission school and entrusted their children, Paul and me, into the hands of local girls for part of the day. We usually escaped their care and roamed not only the sprawling Mission compound but also the surrounding bush.

Mangondoza's bus, a seventy-six seater monster, always crammed with people, its roof rack piled high with BSA bicycles, steel-springed bedframes, shiny brown cardboard suitcases, bags of maize, and makeshift cages full of chickens, plied the route between our remote enclave tucked up against the Mozambican border and the small town of Inyanga ninety kilometres and several hours south. Fearless in my ignorance, I wandered unattended along the gravel road that led to Inyanga. Mangondoza's driver rounded the corner, saw a three-year-old casually strolling in the middle of the road, and managed to bring his massive multi-tonne top-heavy behemoth to an emergency stop just inches from me – no mean feat on the shifting gravel surface.

Every night Simbisai Muwamba came up from the school to chop wood and light our boiler, a way of earning some cash to put towards his school fees. The boiler was outside our back door, a brick structure containing a forty-four-gallon drum lying on its side. The drum rested on short lengths of steel bar cemented into the structure. Below the drum was a space open at one end where a fire could be built. A chimney at the other end carried the smoke away, and an arrangement of pipes conveyed hot water from the base of the heated drum straight through the wall into our bathroom. It was crude but effective.

Paul and I were fascinated by what Simbisai could do. He could vigorously wield a heavy-bladed, wicked-looking axe, a tool we couldn't even lift momentarily off the ground. He would produce large, forbidding-looking, multicoloured spiny caterpillars, as long and thick as two of his fingers, which he found in the mopane trees that grew densely in the area. Simbisai showed us how to roast these caterpillars of the *Gonimbrasia belina* moth in the hot ash of the fire, break off the thick charred skin, and scoop the hot contents into our mouths. These caterpillars were high in protein, and when they were in season beef sales would drop.

We both wanted knives but were too young to be entrusted with the real thing, so Simbisai carved us wooden replicas. Even on his days off from school he would sometimes show up at the house, and together we would wander up the cool, shady banks of the Manjanja River. The river bubbled and roiled a winding boulder-strewn route down the mountain range behind the Mission compound. There we would "fish" for tadpoles and barbel. There was a cost to swimming though: I contracted bilharzia, a painless parasitic infestation in my bladder through water contaminated with tiny flukes released from infested freshwater snails. For days I was passing blood in my urine before my father found out. Sitting on the cool steel examining table down in the outpatient clinic, swinging my legs, I was delighted to overhear Dr Brien tell my mother that treatment didn't involve needles but a course of tablets.

Paul and I walked everywhere barefoot, the soles of our feet callused and cracked like old leather. Our blond crew cuts and white skins meant our fluency in Shona took people by surprise.

Down in the sweaty, roasting sauna of the boarding school kitchens, chest-high pots stood on legs anchored to the floor. Each pot had its own fire glowing beneath its great blackened bottom. In these the cooks prepared the thick maize meal porridge – *sadza* – the staple food in the students' diet. Once the rush was over, the cooks would feed us with crusty, toasted peelings from the inside of their giant cauldrons.

We wandered, half-dreaming in the breathless heat, through the thirsty mopane woodland for several kilometres to the store. This was a dark, cool cavern of delights that smelt of floor polish, Lifebuoy soap, and dried *kapenta* – tiny, silvery, dried fish. Right next door was a grinding mill, thudding away, driven by a rickety old engine. The exhaust pipe snaked out through a hole in the wall and reared up to above our heads. Its perforated bulbous ending puffed out black clouds, like a giant, smoking python. Both of us were more than a little afraid of the mill, and we would circle through the bush to avoid having to pass it. My mother would sometimes give us a *tickey* – two and a half cents – to spend on sweets. Sometimes we would go with no money at all, just for the joy of the walk and to look at all we couldn't afford.

Just outside the door of our kitchen was the outhouse, colloquially known as the long-drop. There was something satisfying about the pause between "bombs away" and the squelchy thud of impact, metres below. But I hated using the outside latrine at night, especially when it was raining. Childish imagination ran riot as I stood with one hand on the outhouse door knob, a feeble ring of torchlight just managing to push back the darkness around my feet as I hopped from one foot to the other, desperate to go but having to steel myself to face the terrors of the unknown darkness that lay behind that door. Who knew what might have crawled up from the abyss and be lying in wait below the seat?

At the dying of each day the twilight thickened until it was almost impossible to see the page of the book we were hunched over, or the tracks of the roads we graded through the dust for our Matchbox cars. Then came the duuuuh-duuuuh-duuh-duh-duh-du-du-du of the generator starting down at the hospital. Seconds later, the lights across the compound flickered and then begrudgingly yielded a sullen yellow glow, often to the faint sound of cheering from the boarding school. Every night we were tucked not just into bed but into netting tents to protect us from malaria-carrying mosquitos. We also had our weekly dose of Deltaprim, a drug to suppress the multiplication of any tiny malarial parasites in our blood.

Despite nets and drugs, I contracted malaria, and experienced the hallucinatory oddness of a very high temperature, the sense as I walked that my feet were unconnected to the rest of my body, and feeling desperately cold while pouring with sweat. Dreadfully afraid of injections, I tried to persuade my parents that all was well even as my teeth chattered and I shook the bed with a rigour. Dr Brien appeared at our house with a covered silver kidney dish in his hand, and I knew what was coming. Despite all my father's exhortations to be brave, I shamed myself by screaming, howling, and fighting viciously against firm restraining hands even as the needle went in.[3]

Once a week my mother crammed our feet into shoes, pursing her lips as we complained loudly and appealed to our father for relief. We stood silently before my father as he attempted to wrestle our hair into respectability, often with the assistance of Brylcreem hair pomade. "Goodness me, boys," he would say, "where did you get this hair from? It's like straw." In the few surviving childhood photographs, my hair looks astonishing – great ragged hunks of hair right next to bristling white stubble chopped back to the scalp, my fringe wavering and uneven. My father was neither skilled nor patient when it came to haircutting.

Thankfully, he discovered electrical clippers and it was goodbye to the bloody nicks in our ears, and the eye-watering yanking and pulling with ordinary scissors.

The reason for the shoes and combed hair was Sunday. Although my parents worked long hours at the school during the week, they also had their church work at weekends. Early Sunday morning, Paul and I were loaded, clean, shod, and slicked down, into the cab of a Land Rover pickup, clutching a favourite toy or a book. Often we were joined by boarding students, full of laughter and boisterous enthusiasm, delighted by the prospect of a morning's adventure away from the boarding school. They would clamber into the open back of the Land Rover, the cue for us to plead to ride in the back with them, to enjoy the rush of wind (and dust), the teasing and banter in Shona. My mother longed to keep us clean and presentable for at least part of the morning so our pleadings fell on deaf ears, and the four of us were crammed into the cab. As compensation, my father would allow us to change gear as he drove.

A narrow dirt track led north, a grassy strip marking the centre. Our ears were filled with a steady susurration, so evocative of African travel – the sound of thick grass brushing steadily against the underside of the vehicle. The bush pressed in on us from each side, pushed back by the mirrors angled sharply out from the boxy Land Rover mudguards, and then whipping back in an irregular rattle against the windscreen. The escarpment stretched away into the blue distance to our left. We would track down into river beds, the ford across the river layered with rocks and sealed with cement.

For several months of the year the crossings were dry, but during the rains, fording the rivers was always a moment of exhilaration. The engine note would change as my father wrestled the gears down to keep the engine revving high. He lined up on the ford, which was hidden under a smooth, fast-running sheet of brown water. Then came the sickening swoop and rush down into the water. The flood water hissed and drummed against the vehicle, and would leak in streams under the doors. Finally came the tilt and rise as the Land Rover pointed its stubby nose towards the sky, engine bellowing and exhaust burbling as the sturdy vehicle shouldered its way up out of the river. We dripped off down the road, our tyre tracks initially clear and dark on the sandy surface but then gradually lightening and disappearing completely.

Our first stop was at Bhande, a village just a few kilometres from the Mission where the church services were held in a school classroom. As the Land Rover pulled in, a boy ordered to watch for the arrival of the vehicle would be energetically "ringing the bell", which was in fact banging a length of steel rail hanging free from a tree with a piece of iron. There might be just a handful of people there to start with, but soon lines of people would flow in from all points of the compass, walking across the fields, often singing hymns as they came.

Sunday school met in the open air, a collection of wooden benches next to the massive purple bole of a baobab tree. The children, each dressed in the best that their household could provide, drummed, danced, and sang while vigorously doing the actions that went with each song. Stories were told from the Bible, by my mother and her group of older teenage trainees. They used flannel-graphs, felt-backed printed shapes that adhered to a background scene. My mother, with her artistic skills, took the figures and discreetly modified the unlikely Anglo-Saxon faces and hands of the biblical figures. Sometimes she could simply look up from the cartoon world of the flannel-graph and point to yokes, oxen, ploughmen, and sowers in the fields around.

She also travelled out from the Mission midweek to join in with the Bhande women's meeting, or *ruwadzano*. I would sometimes go too, especially when there was anything to celebrate, usually with mugs of smoky, lip-stickingly sweet tea and great slabs of bread spread thick with jam and Blueband margarine. There were games to follow. My favourite was Wackem, a game which involved hitting someone with a rolled-up newspaper. Dignified matrons and young teenagers alike joined in wholeheartedly until tears of laughter ran freely down their faces. The women's meeting was often a high point: it was full of joy, a moment of deep, expressive spirituality, an opportunity to talk together of tough lives and to discuss how the Bible spoke to those troubles – a powerful source of mutual support and solidarity.

The Hwesa women were the backbone of the rural economy, subsistence farmers toiling with the simplest of tools. They bore and raised children in poverty where water was carried kilometres from a well and darkness signalled an end to the day. Excluded from much of traditional religious practice, they responded readily to Christianity. Women in their thirties and forties, illiterate, with no formal education, who had never travelled beyond the visible horizon, begged to be taught to read so that they could study the Bible for themselves.

Women began to work together in caring for one another. An elderly woman, newly widowed and ostracized by the wider community, was troubled by the approaching planting season as she had no one to prepare her portion of land. Out of their own great poverty, the Christian women decided to put aside small amounts each week until they had enough to pay a man to plough her field. They told their friends and family about what they were discovering, prayed for them, spoke in tongues, healed, and exorcized demons. They became women with a new confidence and spiritual authority that until then had been denied them.

But often this new-found faith and freedom came at a heavy price. One Sunday, Mai Enesia found her husband waiting for her as she got home from church, hefting the heavy, braided leather thongs he used to hitch his oxen to the plough. When she refused to respond to his question, "Who is greater, Jesus Christ or me?" he thrashed her mercilessly. She lost an eye. Another woman, a traditional healer and source of income for her husband with her foretelling, decided to burn her divination tools after her encounter with Christ. Week after week she would return home to beating after beating. My parents mourned with those who suffered, and prayed for many in such situations. Yet the women held on in hope, and some were rewarded by seeing their husbands respond to Christianity too.

The conversion of husbands brought a range of changes. It often meant a replacement of drunkenness, neglect, and violence with respect and affection. Men remained sober, worked harder, generated income, provided more for their families, created opportunities for their children to receive an education, and gave their wives both time and attention. This renewal of the family often had a wide impact, transforming communities.[4]

The Griffiths family Sunday morning didn't end with the service at Bhande, though as children we often wished it did. Loading up again, we headed further into the bush. The road grew narrower and rougher. The vegetation on each side would tower over the vehicle. Our Land Rover was one of the handful of vehicles that would travel this road each week to and from Chifambe village, a very poor part of a very poor area. The school classroom had walls built out of poles, bound together with *rudzi*, or bark string. Thick clay was then layered onto the latticework and then was roughly thatched. There was a gap in the wall for a door, and the windows were simply spaces in the walls. The benches inside were ridges of dried mud. The interior was plastered with a mixture of clay and cow manure, the latter helping to reduce cracking as the clay dried. From time to time the schoolroom-cum-church was replastered, which lent a certain pungency to the atmosphere.

Outside was a massive fig tree which Paul and I would climb as we waited for people to arrive for church, my mother despairing but resigned to our increasingly dishevelled state as the morning wore on. The figs were sweet, but we learned to tear them open and inspect them first. A mouthful of fig previously invaded by a tiny acidic swarm of biting ants was not easily forgotten. Sometimes my father would preach, his Shona rich and rolling, although I could still detect mistakes from time to time. More often, though, my parents were there to support and encourage local leaders drawn from the community of believers.[5]

Back on the Mission on Sunday evenings, my father would head to the school to preach at the evening service that would be held there. Paul and I stayed at home with my mother, who would sing with us and tell us Bible stories. Together we would colour, cut out, and stick, or do whatever activity she had planned. When my father returned, he would get down on the small piece of carpet in our grandly named living room and we would fling ourselves on him. It was always "rugby": he would crawl forward to score a try at the edge of the carpet while Paul and I hurled ourselves on him, doing our best to stop him, while he gave a running commentary.

I started at the local primary school, one badly cropped blond head in a sea of black hair. But I was bored, and the teacher was uncertain how to help me, so I withdrew and went back to reading voraciously and playing in the hills. Needing an alternative, my mother enrolled me in School on the Air, which meant tuning in and listening to regular school broadcasts on the radio. I loved it, as I was able to combine it with my bush life.

Somehow I kept track of the time each day, and would tumble back into the house, dirty and dishevelled, find a drink, and then turning the knob of the big Bakelite radio set that sat on a trolley underneath the window, connected to an adapted car battery. It took time to warm up, and as I waited I ran my finger along the strip at the base of the speaker which showed where to tune the radio to receive an exotic collection of stations – Tangiers, Luxembourg, Moscow. As the valves heated up, the sound of voices came in, faintly at first, and gradually growing stronger.

Workbooks matching the broadcasts had been prepared and purchased in advance. The unseen teachers did their best to give their invisible students the feel of being part of a group, "Now class, let us turn together to the next page. Look at the picture there. Tell me what you see." Across the country, obedient children on missions, on mine compounds, and in farmhouses spoke their thoughts to unheeding radio sets.

My mother slid my completed workbooks into a canvas sack along with the library books I had finished reading and tied them up with thick cord. At the bus stop by the hospital, Simbisai flung the sack high, and the skilled conductor would snatch it from the air as he stood atop Mangondoza's bus. Somehow my workbooks found their way across the bush and into the large Ministry of Education building in Salisbury. The familiar canvas bags came back too, the work marked, trenchant or encouraging comments appended, and silver or gold stars stuck to the pages. Along with the workbooks would come a fresh batch of library books, and I was plunged into new worlds once more.

Once I went with my mother to an austere building in town, where the floors were shiny with polish and with long, echoing corridors. We meandered through a labyrinth of passages and then knocked on a door which opened on to a wide room, piled high with workbooks, cord, and the magical canvas sacks. To my surprise I was introduced to my School on the Air teacher – a small, greying, cheerful woman with a twinkle in her eye. Until then I had never really thought of her as a real person but simply as a voice which I could turn on and off.

Change was on the way as School on the Air reached the end of its usefulness. My parents were alarmed by the comments of a friend living in the city. At a children's party in town, Paul and I were completely lost, ignorant of what to do and how to behave in that company. The friend turned to my father and said, "You're going to have trouble with those kids as they grow up," pointing out that we were finding it hard to relate to children who were (nominally) from our own cultural background. This concerned my parents deeply. Although we felt much more comfortable playing with Shona friends than we did in "European" surroundings, they finally decided to send us to boarding school in 1973.[6]

Murewa Katerere was a man of character, a skilled driver, and nephew of Chief Katerere. Living in Katerere, we were at least five hours travel away from the capital Salisbury – if all the bridges were open and not too many sections of road had been washed away. Travelling took a lot of time and energy, and my parents were busy people. So we were entrusted to short, stocky, gentle Murewa who would be going into town anyway for cement, hinges, nails, timber, uniforms, cutlery, stationery, and all the thousands of items that were needed to run an enterprise as big as the Mission had become. It was a challenge to clamber into the open back of the big five-tonne Ford truck – front door open, on to the lowest step, scramble up the curve of the front mudguard, grasp the grill at the back of the cab, and swing daringly over into the truck bed. Our favourite spot was standing right behind the cab, clutching the grill, with the wind rushing into our faces.

The truck was loaded. A diesel generator broken beyond the ability of the Mission mechanic to repair it, a littering of gas cylinders (acetylene for the workshop, oxygen for the hospital, and propane for the kitchens), and worn or broken medical equipment was lashed into the back. Around and in between these sat people: sick children listless and crying in the arms of their parents, referred to the huge red-brick Harare Hospital by our medical staff; local men who lived and worked in factories or companies in town. They piled on rough, hairy jute sacks of maize; fat, purple sticks of sugar-cane; lumpy bags of pumpkins; and clacking pods of baobab fruit – rural riches to supplement their town diets.

The road wound up a steep escarpment out of the lowland valley in which the Mission lay. Turning my head away from the drop to our right, I fixed my eyes on the jagged, striated wall of rock rushing past on the left. Once we were over the top and the fearsome drop-off to one side of the road was behind us, I could relax and enjoy the trip.

Murewa was a source of security to us, a solid, dependable, kind individual, someone we treated with respect, knowing of his relationship both with the local chief and with our parents. Suddenly, despite the excitement of the trip, I was overwhelmed by the realization that we were heading away from home and that our parents were not there. I began to weep. Someone on the back of the truck banged on the roof and Murewa slowed, pulled over to the side of the road, and stopped the engine. The silence seemed so deep after the roar of the engine and the rush of air. We were gently lifted off the truck bed and passed into the cab to sit between Murewa and his driver's mate. Paul and I leaned into each other and into him, seeking comfort as Murewa started up and pulled away into the hot afternoon.

* * *

Insecurity was slowly growing as insurgents began to filter into the country. Roadblocks became a feature of life on our long journeys into boarding school. Oil drums linked by poles with a big painted "STOP" on both sides would be placed across roads, compelling vehicles to draw up so that the occupants could be subjected to identity checks and searches by the authorities.

The first time I saw a white soldier, he was standing at one of these roadblocks. As we drew level with him, Murewa brought the lorry gently to a halt, and to our surprise there was no exchange of greetings, no clapping of the hands in polite respect, no enquiry as to how the day had been passed as we had grown up to expect. Instead there was a single word bellowed in through the window of the cab, "*Chitupa!*" This was the identity card which, theoretically, all citizens were meant to carry, but in practice were usually only demanded from black Rhodesians. Murewa fumbled his rather tattered document from his top pocket.

Then the soldier caught sight of Paul and me. His look of astonishment and horror bordered on the comical. Two small white children apparently alone in the middle of a host of black passengers on the back of a truck in a "tribal trust land" beggared belief. He angrily questioned Murewa and then turned to us directly. He asked us where our parents were and why they allowed us to travel with a truck-load of *kaffirs*.[7] Didn't our parents love us? An unsettling sense of his barely suppressed anger remains with me to this day. Paul and I remained silent and frightened in the face of his rage.

Our meeting with the white soldier was a clash of world view and life experience. The members of our missionary team lived among Shona people, whom they saw through the eyes of their faith-shaped world view as brothers and sisters. Their black colleagues were skilled teachers, nurses, laboratory technicians, pastors, and evangelists in the wider community of rural peasant farmers. In contrast, many white Rhodesians knew no languages of the black peoples of the same country and only met or mixed with those who were lowly domestic servants, labourers, or (as in this case) potential threats to "the best standard of living in the world". Frustrated with our confused and timid silence, the soldier eventually turned away in disgust, and with a dismissive wave of his hand freed Murewa to pull away. But that sense of being pulled apart between two worlds, of being caught between two millstones grinding against one another was only just beginning.

Late in the evening, Murewa would drop us off at the Mission-run boarding hostel, located in the less affluent south-eastern part of Salisbury. The hostel held about thirty-five children from across Southern Africa. The Canadian boarding parents greeted us and helped us carry our luggage to rooms we shared with three or four other small boys. Dazed by the roar of the engine, our skins stinging and sensitive after hours under the sun, hair thick with dust, our eyes red and running, we stumbled to bath and bed and then cried ourselves to sleep. The excitement of the journey was over. The school term would begin the next day. Home was an eternity away. Thirteen weeks apart at the age of eight was an incomprehensible span of time.

The early days of each term I could get through. It was the nights that were hard. I loved to be in the bush, loved to be at home, loved my parents, loved the familiar and safe. But for the first week or so of every term, I sobbed into the darkness. If I woke during the night, I cried myself to sleep again. Looking up to the dark ceiling overhead, I would plead with God to end my misery by taking me to Himself. I would squeeze my eyes tight and wait, but the next breath would come, and then the one after that. My mother kept a letter from me, written rather quaintly just after I went to the hostel for the first time: "We are settling in nicely but Paul is a bit sad. Mummy are you sad too a bit? Never mind there are some kissis at the bootom for you and daddy. I hope you like them. Paul sends all his love so do I. We miss you very much… PS keep in toch."

There were advantages to my new-found existence. Visiting the bathroom in the middle of the night, which was indoors and had a light that worked all the way through the night, was so much better than visiting the long-drop outside by torchlight. Drinking fresh milk rather than the stuff made from powder was another delight.

For the first time my school companions were all white and

all English speaking, although some felt more comfortable with Afrikaans or Portuguese. I quickly discovered that very few of them spoke any Shona, although some spoke Chilapalapa, an odd mix of Zulu, Afrikaans, Shona, and English. I discovered words I did not know before: words like *munt*,[8] *hout*,[9] *piccaninny*,[10] *nanny*,[11] and *umfazi*[12] were sprinkled through conversations. I discovered a world of attitudes and feelings that I found completely alien and that I was unprepared for – all derogatory of the black people I had only related to as fellow human beings. I discovered young white children addressing grizzled older black men as "boy". It was all so strange.

Not long before starting boarding school, I had been sitting on the steps of my father's office early one morning, looking out at the day and talking with him in Shona. Then I'd said to him while plucking at the skin on my arm, "Dad, let's talk this language now," meaning English. I didn't even have the words for racial categories. So struck was my father by this that he included it in a letter home to his parents. But it seemed that the attitudes inculcated by my family were aberrations in my new life, far from the rural area where I had grown up.

My father would not allow me to take Afrikaans as a subject at school even though everyone said it was easy to learn. He told me to put my name down for French, which would be more useful in the wider world. Shona was not offered, which I was disappointed about as that was something I would have done well at! That was a language which would really have helped with mutual understanding. How different Rhodesian history might have been if all white children had been required to learn one of the majority languages of the country. Worse still, Shona was despised by my new classmates. Afraid to be different, I concealed my ability to speak Shona and so began to lose it.

The tension between black and white created internal strain for me, caught among worlds. Rhodesia was a racially divided country. Race was the key issue, the elephant in the room, the shibboleth that determined how you stood in line, who you were, how much you earned, where you lived, how you farmed, where you went to school, who you fell in love with, even who your friends and neighbours could be. Although it seemed as if it was a simple black and white issue, the more I learned the more knotted and snarled it became. There were mixed-race communities, "coloureds" – or, much less politely, "goffles". Asians figured too, as Indian storekeepers and Chinese restaurant-owners, but it seemed they were not really part of proper society either.

But just to be white was not enough. There were complex shadings of acceptability there too. If you were Jewish, you wouldn't be allowed to forget it. Afrikaners were considered slow and stupid, the butt of hundreds of jokes. The Portuguese were too smooth, overly concerned with their looks, inept and cowardly, giving up their empire in Africa too easily. Even the British-born weren't good enough – soft, poor at sports, easy to push around. Once you'd started down the road of dividing people based on their race it became an endless, loveless, barren road that left you travelling on your own.

RUSHING WIND

Next in importance to freedom and justice is popular education, without which neither freedom nor justice can be permanently maintained.

James A. Garfield

Like giant beaks, the whirling picks pecked neat holes in the baked red soil. Clouds of dust eddied up beneath shuffling feet and punching steel tools. The evening sun was beginning to sink behind the mountain range to our west. A pool of shadow crept forward, stealthily swallowing up the valley in the twilight. The toiling, grunting workmen were powdered with bronze that clung to sweaty faces, thickening eyelashes, and clogging noses. Beneath their flailing arms, the ground began to open, splitting into sharp-edged trenches into which they jumped, steadily cutting deeper into the earth.

There was a sudden yell. The steady, rhythmic beat of the digging dissolved into a scuffling scramble as the trenches magically cleared of diggers. Circling cautiously along the edge, I looked down. One wall of neatly dug trench had suddenly crumbled, unleashing a shower of leathery white eggs the colour of dirty cream onto the feet of the worker. One of the eggs had split, and a tiny serpent writhed in the ruins of an underground nest. One brave soul jumped back down and crushed the head of the snake under his heel. He piled the eggs together at the edge of the trench and began to pack the nest with soil, steadily rebuilding the wall of the trench that was being dug for the foundation of a new building. The pile of wrinkled, rubbery eggs shifted and trembled with the slow coiling of the young snakes within.

As a young boy, it was a matter of amazement to me how a space in the bush would be cleared, lines would be marked out with string, and then, almost before I knew it, a classroom or a dormitory would rise from the ground. I tolerated boarding school, doing my duty, obeying the rules, surviving the strangeness. But I lived to go home for the holidays, to feel the dirt between my toes, back in a familiar integrated world, basking in the warmth and love of my parents and the endlessly interesting life at Katerere. Delighted to be included, I roamed the Mission station, gravely walking alongside my father as he oversaw the building work. The staff team of missionaries and national teachers was growing. The achievements of the students meant an increasing demand for limited places. So the school had to expand.

* * *

In 1967, my father took over as the principal of the tiny, new Emmanuel Secondary School in the north-eastern mission station at Katerere. He taught maths and Scripture, the ever-dependable Cath Picken took on English, and my mother undertook music and the extraordinary subject of French. Initially, the school only covered two years, preparing the students for the government Junior Certificate public exam.

With half the student body gone home for the Easter holidays, the remainder of the students were so few they could all squeeze into two Land Rovers for an outing to the Nyangombe River on Easter Monday that year. Crashing and bouncing down a gravel road battered by torrential rains brought even the Land Rovers to a standstill. The students piled out, willing hands lugging stones to repair the road so that the journey could be completed. Enthusiastically, my father led the larking and the games on the sandy banks of the roiling, brown, rain-swollen river. In the Mission church the day before, he had preached on the resurrection of Christ. In response, four of the students had made a profession of faith. The care of mind, body, and spirit were all in view.

During the mid-year school holidays, in June 1967, seminars in Umtali had been led by two Brethren Church leaders, South African Denis Clark and Scot Campbell McAlpine, who did much to pioneer charismatic renewal in the English-speaking world with an emphasis on prayer, deepening relationship with Jesus, and simple church structures. My parents attended and my father then took Mufundisi Chiwara, his dear friend, mentor, and colleague, from Penhalonga to hear the two men speak.

Chiwara was encouraged by the teaching and also had a fresh experience of the Holy Spirit, and spoke in tongues. Travelling up to Katerere for a visit, Chiwara preached with fervour, and five students stayed behind to make professions of faith. The headmaster of one of Elim's primary schools had hidden the fact that he had two wives. His polygamy came to light at the same time. Polygamy was a reality that the nascent church in the area was wrestling with. It was not the fact that he had two wives as such but his hypocrisy that was seen as wrong. My father saw these all as part of the move of the Holy Spirit: a new depth of experience of God, a renewed warmth of relationship among believers, the conviction of wrongdoing, and people coming to saving faith for the first time.

Energetic, passionate, and full of life, my parents crammed their days with hard work, giving themselves unstintingly to the people of their adopted country. Their working week focused on the school: teaching, administrating, building, marking. Despite long hours at school each day, their time after hours and at weekends saw them busy working at Bhande and Chifambe churches, this time not among the young elite but with the rural poor.

Year by year they saw a trickle of Hwesa people come to faith. Two teenage boys walked from Bhande and asked to see my father because they wanted to become Christians. At Chifambe, some girls just eleven years old or so wanted to repent. This took considerable courage, because the area around Chifambe Village was strongly influenced by the *mhondoro* spirit medium Diki Rukadza who was implacably opposed to Elim Mission and all its activities. A few weeks after their conversion they were full of questions after the Sunday service. Of particular concern was what they as Christians were free to eat in their village. "It seems they mean to be real," wrote my mother.[1]

A baptismal service was held in the mountains behind the Mission in the Manjanja, the "Stream of the Lion Spirit", when twenty-five people were baptized, including eleven students from the small secondary school. Three short times of prayer were offered to those seeking to be filled with the Holy Spirit. My father recorded in his prayer newsletter, "In the first at least six were baptized in the Spirit almost immediately... by the end of the third seventeen had been filled with the Holy Spirit... It was just like the Day of Pentecost as they spoke in varied but distinct languages as the Spirit gave them utterance... A new note of praise has been introduced into the school." He added, "Please pray as I continue to teach about the gifts of the Spirit and of service."

The rains of 1967 had been scanty. Crops reaped by the

villagers were negligible. Precious money had to be used to buy the staple food that many normally reaped from their fields. For months the sun beat down incessantly on the arid countryside, turning dead grass black. By Christmas 1968, owing to the delay in the onset of rain that year, the walk for water was becoming longer and longer as streams and wells dried up.

Finally it rained – and how it rained! Awoken in the night, befuddled with sleep, I plucked at the sodden sheet covering me, bemused and unable to understand why water was falling on my head. Swinging my feet over the edge of the bed I stepped into a pond. The door swished open and, clutching a torch, my mother came in to reassure my brother and me. The thatch on our little house had dried and shrunk in the prolonged months of drought and was now allowing the rain to pour in. Muddy water spurted from under the back door, swirling through the house and eddying around our beds. Outside in the drenching darkness, my father was vigorously wielding a shovel, digging a trench to divert the storm water running off from the hill behind our house.

The grass roof rapidly absorbed water and, plumped up again, kept most of the following storms at bay. Myriads of insects appeared, biting generously and leaving us itching. Our bites turned septic, so Paul and I were soon painted liberally with gentian violet and decorated with strips of sticking plaster. Great clouds of flying ants rose from their turret-like nests in the ground, a rich bounty for birds that swooped and snapped. Along with our friends Jaime Mudondo and Andrew Mukwewa, the sons of teachers at Munjanja Primary School, my brother Paul and I reached into the buzzing swarms to collect hundreds of the strange creatures, which would be fried and eaten.

The church work at Bhande had been a source of concern for my parents. Although there were about fifty children coming along each week, only a handful of adults attended. Most came to church wearing charms and amulets, part of traditional ancestor worship. My parents highlighted this as a matter for prayer in their regular letters home, and they began to see shoots of new life at Bhande.

In the ensuing two years so many came to faith that a baptismal service was held and Communion took place. At a river near Bhande, seventeen teenagers took the very public step of baptism, indicating their desire to follow Christ. One was Nisbert, who had been terribly deformed by polio and was only able to shuffle around by walking on his hands while dragging his withered, twisted legs behind him. My mother found his courageous choice to be baptized deeply poignant. Unable to walk into the river for himself, he had to be totally reliant on strong arms to lift and carry him, to plunge him under the water, and to carry him out of the river in front of all the congregation, as well as others who had gathered out of curiosity or to mock and jeer. Local leadership had emerged, despite early anxieties about a lack of men, and three men were being considered for leadership.

Rather than meeting in a schoolroom, a church building was going ahead after permission had been granted from both the District Commissioner and the chief. People were growing groundnuts to sell to raise funds for the new building. One woman had set aside part of her fields, and others came to help cultivate the land for this purpose, despite the searing heat.[2]

Emmanuel Secondary School continued to gain a good reputation. But the teaching team needed to grow, a theme reiterated in the regular prayer letters.

In a small, frequently vandalized Elim church in Huddersfield, Peter and Sandra McCann met and married. A superb teacher, Peter was impossibly chaotic at managing daily life, but Sandra's practicality compensated for this, mixing common sense with good humour. Responding to an appeal for qualified teachers, the McCanns arrived in Katerere in mid-1970 with their toddler son Paul. Peter McCann, as a chemistry graduate, took over science teaching, and Sandra began to develop the library.

Before the end of the academic year in 1970, twenty-five students were baptized in the Manjanja. As my father commented in a prayer letter, the scorching heat, the seemingly endless hours of marking into the night, the struggle to fund the running of the school, the headaches of staffing, the challenges of managing building projects "seemed worth it all that Sunday afternoon as these students publicly declared their faith in Christ".

My father hoped to double the proportion of girls in 1971, and was aiming to have at least one-quarter of the school made up of girls within three years. That involved a commitment to opening up boarding facilities for girls in 1971, to enable female students to come from a wider catchment area. This implied extra teachers and, at the end of 1970, former student Paul Makanyanga returned to Katerere as the first trained pastor, having completed his studies at Rusitu Bible Institute.

By the end of the first term of 1971, quite a number of the new intake of seventy-two students had made decisions to become Christians. My mother was cautiously optimistic: "We think of it as forty who have at least taken a step towards Christ. It is impossible to know how many have actually entered the Kingdom," she wrote to their supporters in their April 1971 prayer newsletter. They called for people to join them in intercession: "Please continue in prayer for the work among the students. We feel it is strategic in these critical days of Rhodesia's history."

Our playmate Paul McCann was injured by a fragment of wood driven deep into his foot in 1971. It became infected and wouldn't be dislodged. Eventually, Dr Brien decided that to avoid the risk of the infection spreading up Paul's leg, the wound would have to be explored under anaesthesia. Peter and Sandra agreed, and so Paul went into the operating theatre at the Mission hospital.

As Mary Brien started to administer the anaesthetic, Paul suddenly and unexpectedly had a cardiac arrest. Cecil and Mary worked on him, their desperation growing as their interventions failed to restart the little boy's heart. After nearly an hour of frantic effort, they had to admit defeat and declared Paul dead. Peter and Sandra were flooded with grief at the totally unexpected news that their precious boy had died during what should have been a routine procedure.

Paul's funeral service was held in the Elim Church on the Mission compound. Crowds came from villages across the valley to attend. Peter and Sandra paced slowly, weeping, hand in hand behind the small coffin of their only child as it was carried up from the church to be buried in the hills behind the Mission. Sandra wrote home to her parents with details of the funeral service, which included the hymn "God holds the key of all unknown, And I am glad". She described her very deep emotions at the loss of her son, then wrote, "It will mean a lot to the Africans that we have buried Paul in their soil. This is now a part of Rhodesia that is ours and now a foundation stone has been laid… which cannot be removed."

Later in 1971, my parents took a year-long furlough, returning to the UK. Realizing he needed to continue to develop professionally, my father started a Diploma in Education at University College London's Institute of Education, ranked first in the world for education. We lived in Clapham, and each day he made his way to the grand art deco building of Senate House in central London.

Paul and I found the unknown relatives we were taken to meet rather daunting; it felt as though they were all exclamations and enthusiastic embraces. We visited a succession of dreary church halls filled with smiling people we didn't know in places we had never heard of. Our local school was welcoming, but the whole family found the transition from rural Katerere with its rich network of relationships to anonymous urban London very demanding.

Once again, my father seized every opportunity he could to learn and to share his faith. Despite having just arrived, he became president of the Christian Union at UCL. He quickly realized the potential of reaching out to students from around the world who were coming to the United Kingdom for training and wrote an article for the *Elim Evangel* on the issue, entitled "The World at Your Door". He earned a sufficiently high grade in his diploma to qualify for entrance on to a Master of Arts degree course. But he put his studies on hold for another five years and took us back to Rhodesia.

After a demanding year of intense study, hospitality, and travel across the United Kingdom to dozens of Elim churches to give over and over an account of the mission work funded and prayed for by those churches, suddenly my parent's furlough year was over. We sailed from Southampton on the *Pendennis Castle*, along with a brand new tropicalized Peugeot station wagon for the Mission. The voyage was two weeks of enforced rest and recovery for my parents, which they desperately needed.

Now five and seven years old, my brother Paul and I enjoyed the children's menus, swam in the pool, and laughed uproariously at the slapstick comedy of the "Crossing the Line Ceremony" put on by the crew as "King Neptune" came aboard as we sailed across the equator. In the playroom, I found a small ship's wheel, mirroring the ocean liner's wheel in the bridge overhead. In front of huge windows that looked out at the vast ocean that stretched to the horizon, I stood at the wheel and steered, a hundred fantasies dancing in my head. The days spent out in the emptiness of the glittering sea awoke a sense of the numinous in me, a longing for God, young though I was.

Arriving home in Katerere, we found that Emmanuel Secondary School was now more than 200 students strong, and taking pupils through four years of education to their O Levels. Pleased by most developments, my father was disappointed, however, that there were only thirty girls among the students. But he wrote home in the December 1972 prayer newsletter, "We are seeing many decisions to follow Jesus in the hospital, school, and church work; please pray for a deepening intimacy with God among all the Christians, including us missionaries."

Not long afterwards, Mary Fisher arrived from the Welsh valleys. Slim, with long red hair and a beautiful singing voice, Mary's degree in maths and her years of studying theology at London Bible College brought further depth to the team. As soon as she arrived, my parents whisked her off to Kambudzi Church twenty-five kilometres away, where sixty eager young students were gathered for a Bible teaching and witness weekend on the theme of the Holy Spirit.

Missionaries and students alike slept on mats on the floor of the church, eating the local staples of *sadza* and *muriwo* together.[3] Unconcerned by her recent arrival, my father got Mary to open the camp, and she spoke on "Who is the Holy Spirit?" By 6.00 a.m. on Saturday (starting early to avoid the heat), "The Holy Spirit and Witnessing", the second session, was under way. The young people were then split into small groups and dispatched on foot into the surrounding villages for the next six hours to put into practice what they had just learned!

In June 1973, my father was asked to provide his vision for the school work to the Missions Board. He wanted to expand the school to 280 students, seventy in each year up to O Level, by January 1975. The proportion of girls was still too low and he planned to address this. By 1976, he aimed to see a sixth form opened, with fifteen arts and fifteen science students. He wanted to continue to recruit black graduate teachers from the University of Rhodesia, creating a multicultural teaching team and moving towards a fully African staff. But it wasn't just about numbers.

He laid out the broader context in four main goals. He wanted to see Emmanuel Secondary School developing as a centre of educational excellence that would draw in students from across the country, while giving them an opportunity to hear the gospel, come to faith, and be well discipled before scattering across the country again. It would prepare future church leaders both in Katerere and further afield. The school would offer a service to Christians in both Katerere and Penhalonga, as a place where they could send their children for an education in a Christian environment. Finally, my father envisioned the school developing students' potential, improving their prospects, enabling care for their families, "and so a means of fulfilling some of the social implications of the gospel," he wrote.

The students called my father *Mudhara* ("old man"), but not to his face. Running the school could be challenging at times, as a student recalled: "We used to have students' complaints over meals. The most resented meal was *sadza* and powdered milk. We boycotted the meal and *Mudhara* had to be called. He came to the school dining room to address us. Before he did, he ate a chunk of *sadza* and drank the milk. He explained that due to the low school fees the school charged to enable everyone to afford them, it was difficult for the school to afford better meals. One of the students laughed as if to suggest *Mudhara* was just bluffing. *Mudhara* was furious. He landed a clenched fist on the student, saying, '*Iwe mwana iwe*' ('You naughty child!') The whole student body laughed, saying, '*Mudhara anopenga*' ('The old man is furious'). The student body talked about it for many months later and nothing was held against him."

In 1974, my father requested funding from the Beit Trust for some of the school buildings. True to form,[4] Sir Alfred and Lady Clementine Beit[5] made the long journey out from Kensington Palace Gardens in London to our remote area, keen to see how their funds might be used. They were shown around by Thandiwe

Sithole and George Charamba, the head girl and head boy, who impressed the Beits with their articulacy and confidence.

My mother was in a panic about what to serve this fabulously wealthy couple for lunch, especially when she discovered she had been let down yet again by our temperamental paraffin fridge and the cream she had planned to use had turned sour. Eventually she plumped for something very simple. Clementine Beit slurped her tomato soup with great gusto, to the surprise and delight of my mother. The grant was made.

* * *

On 9 November 1974, Ephraim Satuku, my mother's star student from nearly fifteen years previously, was ordained in the Manjanja Church on the Mission station. It was a grand occasion and the church was packed to overflowing. Following the service, a long, twisting, colourful column of people snaked up into the hills behind the Mission to gather on the banks of the Manjanja River. Fifteen young people from the area were baptized on the same day, while people clapped, danced, ululated, and sang.

The following morning, we walked to the building site where new science laboratories were going up. My father stopped suddenly in the doorway of one of the half-completed labs. One crate was standing on its end, for all the world like a pulpit. Wooden crates had been dragged into a semicircle in front of it. Inquiry showed that the previous afternoon, a small group of students had met in the half-finished laboratory for several hours to pray. But it was not an isolated incident. Completely unknown to the missionary team, a spontaneous student-led revival movement had been gathering pace within the school for months. Earlier in the year, in May 1974, a number of students had experienced visions of spiritual renewal in the school. They had not shared these widely but had begun to pray earnestly that what they had seen would be realized in the life of the school.

Their prayers were answered when, in November 1974, there was a spontaneous outburst of spiritual activity among the students. God began to move, filling them with His Spirit, one by one. Then one Monday, ten students were praying in a group behind the laboratory. The blessing of God came upon them and nine were filled with the Spirit. Some prophesied, and the secret wrongdoing of others was revealed. Three of the other students confessed to possessing witchcraft charms, and then destroyed them in a bonfire on the football pitch. Another two confessed to stealing, and made restitution. A great concern came upon the believing students for their non-Christian friends, and they began to speak to them about getting right with God.

My father wrote home in his December 1974 prayer newsletter: "Speaking personally, we have never seen God work like this in all our Christian experience, and our prayer and desire is that it will continue and spread to the other people in our churches. All this has been happening in the midst of final examinations! But people seem to be more than coping. Please pray that the revival fires started will not go out… but that fire will be taken by the students to their homes and various outlying churches, and that next term, they will be fanned to a great inextinguishable blaze so that Rhodesia might be spiritually prepared for the uncertain days ahead."

The girls in the school noticed that a number of boys, previously marked out by their aggressive sexism and overweening arrogance, had changed markedly. On coming to faith they became gentle and pleasant, and (much to the surprise of the girls) joined the clandestine prayer groups. The great emphasis on prayer continued, as did a sense of conviction for wrongdoing. Students even travelled for several hours to bookshops in Umtali, from which they had stolen textbooks, to confess, ask forgiveness, and pay for what they had taken. The school library also benefited as stolen volumes, previously smuggled out, were returned with heartfelt apologies.[6]

But some students were insisting that only those who spoke in tongues were true believers, while others were concerned by the content of some of what was described as prophecy. Controversy and argument brought confusion. My father took up the challenge of teaching on this in school assemblies. A student recalled, "He helped us gain clarity on spiritual gifts and to realize that whenever God is at work, the devil is there to steal, kill, or destroy."[7]

Students had become very active in sharing their faith with their contemporaries in the school. However, not content with this captive audience, small bands of students began to trek to the nearby villages over the weekends, walking sometimes for hours in the dust and the heat. They conducted open-air meetings, going from hut to hut, talking to anyone who would listen, eager to share their faith with people in the area.

The missionary team saw it as a simple sign of blessing from God but, with hindsight, it seemed much more. It was preparation for what was to come. The revival of 1974 led to infiltration across the Katerere area by young people, in small groups, with a driving passion for change, seeking out the farming folk of the rural areas, and yet willing to endure hardship. There were echoes of this attitude and approach in the infiltration that would begin less than a year later. And yet that infiltration would be so different in its impact on the area, and indeed on the school itself.

* * *

Far away in Lisbon, the "Carnation Revolution" had taken place in April 1974. Portuguese troops, tired of fighting and dying for an empire overseas, had risen up against the dictator Salazar. Hastily, and without ceremony or due preparation, Mozambique, part of that Portuguese "empire" where a war similar to that in Rhodesia had been raging, gained its independence from Portugal within a year, on 25 June 1975. Control of the country had been handed to the Frente Para a Libertação de Moçambique (FRELIMO),[8] the armed nationalist group. The new nationalist government agreed to host guerrilla bases for those fighting for control in neighbouring countries. There was a scramble to move Zimbabwe African National Liberation Army (ZANLA) bases from Zambia and Tanzania into a newly welcoming Mozambique.

Early in June 1975, just before Mozambican independence, my parents daringly took sixty-three O Level pupils 300 kilometres through central Mozambique to camp on the beach in Beira. There was a friendly welcome from the FRELIMO troops, who were already in effective control of the country. The missionary team did not fully grasp at the time the political and military implications of Mozambican independence. Suddenly, more than 1,200 kilometres of Rhodesia's eastern border with Mozambique was under the control of a newly independent black government, which was sympathetic to the nationalist aspirations of black Rhodesians. Little did my parents realize then that within weeks, hundreds of children would be fleeing from Rhodesian schools into guerrilla camps in Mozambique to be trained there and return to fight in Rhodesia.

Rhodesian news reports reported growing concerns from government and parents alike, as senior pupils absconded from secondary schools and found their way on foot into Mozambique and Botswana. A brooding sense of threat was heightened on Friday 25 July 1975. The *Umtali Post* reported that the Senior Assistant Police Commissioner, Protecting Authority of Manicaland Province, had imposed a draconian curfew on the border area under Emergency Powers. No one in the area in question was allowed to move more than fifty metres away from any dwelling between the hours of 6.00 p.m. and 5.00 a.m. The order named twenty-three missions and schools to which this would apply, including Elim Mission. Violating the curfew would result in two years in prison for the perpetrator, or a Rh$200 fine (£3,700 today – a colossal sum for a peasant farmer).

Despite the curfew, nine students disappeared from Emmanuel Secondary School. The first to go was a girl in Form 3 who had pleaded for a place in the school just a few months before. Two boys followed her but were caught just before the border near Umtali and interrogated. The police appeared at Emmanuel Secondary School and a Form 4 boy was arrested. He was from the area where the two boys were caught and had been drawing maps for them. Four other boys and one of the African teachers were arrested on a second visit. My mother wrote in her diary, "They do not realize or perhaps do not care about the heartache they are causing their parents and relatives. Two went back to their homes demanding more money for uniforms and school fees saying the Principal said they had got to have it – and then just went off. Parents and relatives have been here – mothers weeping."

When the exodus of potential guerrilla recruits to newly independent Mozambique began, some schools lost more than 100 pupils. One school was left with only seven students. But only nine students left Emmanuel, which my parents ascribed to the "salt of the earth" influence of many Christians. But after the excitement of Mozambican independence, everything seemed to return to normal by the end of the year.

* * *

At the end of 1975, a year after my father had found the crates strangely arranged in the laboratory, a baptismal service was held by the Manjanja River, the jungled banks crowded with people. Perched on a knoll high on the bank and leaning against a small tree that curved over the river, Paul and I watched my father waiting in deeper water as the students waded out to him one by one. Suddenly an older man, carrying a heavy stick, stepped towards us. With an oath, he violently struck the branches of the tree we were leaning on. The heavy green coils of a large snake fell into the water. The student about to be baptized shot with alacrity from the water, with a great panting and thrashing, while my father followed at a more dignified pace!

All but one of the thirty-one students had come to faith since arriving at the school, a number responding to the witness of other students – three through the head girl, Thandiwe (meaning "beloved"). Among that group were a brother and sister who came to faith on the same evening. Nearly all had been in the school for a number of years, although one had started that year. The details on his application form had stuck in my father's mind as the prospective student had described himself as "pagan"! The student prayer cells had continued throughout the year – bringing blessing and godly influence to the school.

One Saturday afternoon while I was home for the Christmas holidays, an army lorry rolled to a stop close to where I was watching the schoolboys play football. A number of heavily armed troops in camouflage jumped from the back, and a curious crowd gathered. These were days of innocence when combat fatigues and weapons provoked interest rather than fear and horror. An officer gave a short talk, then I was fascinated to see the soldiers pass their weapons into the crowd. I pressed nearer to touch a gun too, but just as I was reaching out, with an oath, one of the soldiers leapt into the crowd, retrieved the weapon, and unloaded it. The "hearts and minds" exercise would have failed if a member of the crowd had accidentally shot someone!

As dusk fell, the officer gave an order. One of the soldiers turned to face the mountains, raised a machine gun to a firing position, braced himself, and pulled the trigger. There was a heart-stopping, ear-shattering roar. The muzzle of the weapon flickered and flashed with fire, rounds of glowing red tracer racing away into the gloom, smashing into the mountain a kilometre away and scattering up into the darkened sky. It was a true spectacle, imprinted indelibly on my memory.

Like the Maxim gun demonstration seventy years before, the object was to inspire respect among the locals for powerful weaponry, tools of authority, and control owned by these agents of the minority government. There were gasps of surprise and astonishment and murmurs of admiration from the crowd pressing around me. The demonstration had its effect – for the moment. But it was another sign for those with eyes to see it that all was not as quiet, as peaceful, or as orderly as it seemed. Not everyone was playing by the rules.

The year of 1975 held a final sting in the tail. On 31 December we went out to Salisbury airport to welcome the longed-for reinforcements of double science graduate Phil Evans with his wife Sue and children Tim, Rachel, and Rebecca. Phil had earned an MSc, an MPhil, and a teaching diploma by the age of twenty-six. No ivory tower academician, he had worked in a concrete factory, on a farm, and with a fast-food delivery service. Sue was a qualified secretary who had cooked in an all-night food factory to keep the family supported while Phil studied. An appeal for graduate teachers for Rhodesia had coincided with Phil completing his degree, advice from a trusted mentor to choose teaching, and a challenging article on missions which both Phil and Sue had read.

They decided to send in an application to the Elim Missions Board. "I have always been available for God's work," Phil wrote, "but I have waited for direction."

Sue added, "We made our lives available to God, and He wants to use them now. This is the way God has chosen for me and not one I would naturally choose myself. I have put many questions and problems to Him concerning this call and He has answered in such a way as I could find no reason why I should not go to Rhodesia."[9]

Eager to meet this new family, at the airport we scanned the faces of the passengers who were appearing in varying states of dishevelment and emotion. In knots and groups, in rushes and pauses, the travellers walked out to their various welcomes. The crowd in the arrivals hall steadily thinned, but there was no sign of our new team members. Increasingly concerned, my father persuaded a guard to escort him into the immigration hall, but he found no sign of the Evans family. An immigration officer said they were in a holding room and would be flown back to England that night. The family had been refused permission to enter Rhodesia.

My father drove back into the city to seek an urgent interview with senior immigration officials. Pleading for the Evans to be allowed in, my father begged that they be given short-term entry while the issue was dealt with. Not even told the reason why the Evans were refused entry, my father angrily burst out, "Is this Moscow – or Nazi Germany?" The cold attitude of the immigration officer turned to ice. My father was stonily informed that the office was closed for the New Year holiday, and the interview was abruptly terminated.

Back at the airport, my father persuaded officials to allow him and me to visit the Evans family in their holding room. He told them he had done all he could but had failed, and the entire family were to be put on the next plane and flown back to the UK that night. Sue Evans' response etched itself on my father's memory. "There's some mistake," she said, face furrowed with bewilderment. "We must stay. God told us to come."

My father asked Phil if he had any idea why his completed immigration forms might have provoked such a reaction. Phil responded that he had found a question on conscientious objection to military service a struggle to answer. Although not a conscientious objector in principle, Phil's answer to the Rhodesian authorities was that he would refuse to bear arms in the Rhodesian conflict. My father agreed that Phil's answer was probably the reason for Rhodesian immigration to refuse entry. Inwardly, my father despaired of the decision ever being reversed.

An immigration team arrived in the room and we had to leave. Escorted to the plane, the exhausted Evans family spent another sleepless night travelling back to the UK. On arrival in London, Phil and the family were held by the British immigration authorities until an Elim International Missions Board representative had met with the South African Airways pilot and guaranteed payment for the family's return flights.

Despite my father's misgivings that Rhodesian immigration would never reverse their decision, after gathering for prayer, the missionary team felt that no stone should be left unturned. Although the denial of any official explanation made addressing the issue problematic, visits to Government Education Officers, to the Chaplain General of the Armed Forces, and to a Cabinet Minister ensued.

Astonishingly, by February 1976 permission was secured from the immigration authorities, and in March the Evans family had an uneventful entry into Rhodesia. Driving the 240 kilometres north-east from Salisbury to Katerere took several muddy, hot hours crammed in the Peugeot station wagon. Dense, towering cumulonimbus clouds reared high into a soaring expanse of sky. The dirt track meandered through thick bush, green and fecund after the fat months of the rainy season. From time to time the wilderness opened out to left or right, a cluster of fields around the round, thatched huts of a peasant farmer's homestead. The newly arrived family had much to absorb and adjust to.

Phil and the two older children were quick to make Elim Mission home, especially Tim, who loved the rough roads and travelling around in open trucks and Land Rovers! Finding even the Mission compound with its widely spaced buildings scattered through the trees and orderly routine so different to all that they had left behind, Sue took time to adjust to their new life. "It is still quite hot and sticky here," she scribbled in one of her first letters home. "The insects are unbelievable. If you stand still anywhere for more than ten seconds you have ants crawling over your feet. Everything has to be covered all the time and you have to check your clothes carefully for 'things'." But Sue's warmth and sensitivity led to relationships of trust with local people. Very early she sensed an undercurrent of tension despite assurances that all was quiet in the area, and wrote home that there was a lot of military coming and going along the road that led past the Mission, "but we haven't seen any guerrillas yet".

Just five weeks after the Evans arrived, in April 1976, we were due to set off on a trip at the end of the school term. My mother had been chronically unwell, was still weak and thin, and my father was worried. She needed a detailed medical review. My parents were going to be involved in leading a Scripture Union camp for young people down in Bulawayo – something of a busman's holiday for them both. A number of other staff members were away and the compound was quiet. Phil Evans had agreed to take charge while my father was away.

But just as we were about to drive off, as my father was having a final word with Phil, a police Land Rover pulled up. Together the police officer and my father walked out to the sports field in the baking sun. There they were clearly visible to any watching eyes, although nothing could be heard.

My brother and I whined while my mother sat, staring fixedly through the windscreen. The conversation was animated and long. Phil was beckoned to join in. Then my father strode over to the car in his purposeful way. The engine clattered into life. My parents communicated with each other in the code that parents have. Nothing made sense to Paul and me, but obviously there was surprising news for my mother.

The policeman had come to tell my father that a large group of

ZANLA guerrillas were thought to have crossed the Mozambican border and to be in the Katerere area. There were a limited number of options available for the missionary team. Immediate withdrawal based on such scanty information wasn't really an option. Armed response was incompatible with the aims of the Mission. That left staying put, seeing how things unfolded, and responding as developments took place.

Concerned by the news, my father wondered aloud about staying. The policeman did not feel that anything would happen, and told my father that he couldn't simply stay on the compound forever. Phil urged my father to go to speak at the Scripture Union camp so as not to let them down. Reluctantly my father agreed to go, as long as the news of possible incursion was passed on to Matron Joyce Pickering, anticipating that the guerrillas might look for medicines, and to the principal of the primary school Pious Munembe, and to Pastor Ephraim Satuku.

Finally we pulled away in a cloud of dust, sweating on the blue vinyl seats, wheels rumbling on the stony road as at last we began the long trek to Bulawayo.

THE BLIND KILLER

In war, the first casualty is truth.

Aeschylus

It was April 1976. Accompanying the darkness, the silence rushed back in as the "duh-duh-duh" of the generator slowed to a stop. As they rose to their feet from their prayers for safekeeping, Phil and Sue Evans were startled by loud banging on the door of their kitchen. Together they fumbled their way to the kitchen and pulled open the inner door, but left the outer screen bolted. Through the wire mesh they glimpsed grim-faced men in battledress. Stin Gumbo, a national teacher, had led ZANLA guerrillas through the compound, and they had picked their way quietly through the still night to the Evans' house.

The guerrilla leader described his group as freedom fighters who had come to liberate the people of Zimbabwe. He explained specific grievances: forced cattle-dipping, compulsory contour ridging, carrying of identity cards. Nothing made much sense to Phil, after just seven weeks in the country. Behind Phil, Sue slipped away through the dark house where an unmarried colleague was sitting with her sleeping children, Tim, Rachel, and Rebecca. The children were woken and, in their groggy state, were wrapped in sheets and thrust into the dusty space under the beds by their mother, where they fell asleep again. "Look after my children," whispered Sue to her frightened colleague. "Stay with them and pray. If they shoot us please take my children home to England."

As she rejoined her husband, she heard the leader say to Phil, "We've come to tell you what to preach."

Phil responded firmly, "We don't preach politics here but the good news of Jesus Christ."

To Phil's surprise the guerrilla commander said, "I used to believe what you believe. I was a Methodist preacher once. I prayed for the liberation of the African and God didn't answer my prayer, so my trust is now in this." He raised his AK-47 rifle with its distinctive curved magazine. That opening exchange led to a conversation that went on for two hours. The guerrilla leader was passionate about the inequalities that he saw in Rhodesia. Phil said he had initially been refused entry to Rhodesia because he would not fight. This struck home. But despite the apparent rapport, at the close of the clandestine meeting there was an instruction with a chilling warning. There was to be no reporting of the guerrilla visit to the Security Forces or they would return and kill Phil and Sue.

As the guerrillas moved away, Phil could see that they were heading for the nurses' houses. He tried to open the door and go after them but Sue clung to him. "Don't go Phil. They'll think you're on your way to report them to the Security Forces. You'll get shot. Please – let's pray that God will keep Joy and Joyce safe!" As they knelt together on the floor, Sue lurched forward and vomited, overwhelmed with fear.

Joy Bath's dog was barking so loudly that Joy, dazed with sleep after a busy day, fumbled her way out into the darkness in her nightie, determined to find the dog and let him have it. To her surprise, Stin was standing close to the dog. "Hello, Stin, what are you doing here in the middle of the night?" said Joy, a feisty young nurse with a pert face and cheeky manner.

"There are some visitors to see you," said Stin, as a shadowy group materialized around them.

"What a time to come!" retorted Joy.

To Joy's surprise, Joyce Pickering, the diminutive, no-nonsense, warm-hearted hospital matron was there too, and she was trembling. The section leader introduced himself as a freedom fighter. "This year, 1976, is the *Gore ye Gukurahundi* – Year of the People's Storm," he said.

Joy listened politely, but when the speech seemed in danger of going on, she became impatient. "Hurry up and finish what you have to say. I need to get back to bed. I've had a busy day delivering babies!" Fortunately, the guerrillas retained a sense of humour and took Joy's comments in their stride.

She had to accompany them down to the hospital where they provided her with a list of medicines they wanted. A spirited Joy complained that it was very unethical to give out medicines without seeing the patient. The guerrillas told her they had their own medical personnel. Before they melted into the darkness the threat was repeated, "Report and we kill you."

Only afterwards the reality of what had just happened hit Joy and she began to shake. Together she and Joyce read Psalm 91. Joy started but then broke down in tears as she read, "Under his wings you will find refuge; his faithfulness is a shield."

Her father, visiting from the UK, picked up the Bible and read on: "You will not fear the terror of the night, nor the arrow that flies by day."

After praying together they went back to bed. Typically, Joyce couldn't sleep, but Joy plunged immediately into deep slumber.

The next day, without my father's leadership, out of reach as he was at the camp in Bulawayo, and without consulting local church leaders, the entire missionary team withdrew from the area. Years later, Joy commented on how the lack of discussion between missionaries and black leaders before taking such a dramatic decision demonstrated a failure of trust. But the ongoing years of war where black Christians and white missionaries suffered together would bring new depth and dimensions to that trust and those relationships.

The team met together in Salisbury with my father and mother on 1 May. Elim Rhodesia Field Director Ron Chapman was there from Umtali. Very concerned about the risks to young, single women in their twenties like Joy Bath and Mary Fisher, to mothers like Sue Evans, Sandra McCann, and my mother, Ron made it clear that no one was under any compulsion to return unless they were personally convinced it was the right thing to do.

Using the same Bible reading notes, a number had found the Bible reading for that day both reassuring and challenging: "Peace I leave with you; my peace I give to you; not as the world gives do I give to you. Let not your hearts be troubled, neither let them be afraid… My people will abide in a peaceful habitation, in secure dwellings, and in quiet resting places… He makes peace in your borders."[1] Shopping had already been done. Preparations had been made. It soon became clear that the decision to return was unanimous.

The meeting refocused on managing risk. On their return to the Mission, the unmarried workers were to be within the walls of a family household by nightfall. Whenever there was a call to the hospital at night, a man was to accompany the nurse to the hospital, wait while the work was carried out, and then return with her. Tim and Rachel Evans, the two older Evans children, would start school in Salisbury. The firearms on the mission compound, an antiquated .303 used for killing cattle from the school herd and a .22 for snakes, were both to be handed in to the police. The missionary team were to be cautious in their dealings with the authorities, and would conduct any meetings with members of the army or police in public view.

There was a palpable sense of relief that the immediate crisis appeared to be over, that the growing threat had been acknowledged and openly discussed, and that some basic policy decisions were in place. The missionary team travelled back to Katerere in time for the Sunday services.

On 2 May we received chilling news that the group of ZANLA guerrillas who visited the Mission had been caught. A Rhodesian Army patrol had engaged the ZANLA group in battle near the Gairezi River on 28 April 1976, the day after their visit to Elim Mission.[2] Six guerrillas were killed in the first contact and four others in running engagements over the next few days. Another six guerrillas were captured, including the group leader, and sentenced to death for possessing arms of war by a Special Court[3] sitting at Inyanga.[4]

Phil Evans was powerfully affected by his meeting with the section commander. A man rather like himself, he was passionate and committed but had taken a radically different direction. Phil tried to make contact with him but was prohibited from doing so as the section commander was on death row. Eventually Phil poured out his thoughts and feelings into a letter, reminding the guerrilla of the truths he himself must have preached of the forgiveness of God, of the love of the father for the prodigal son. Finally the news came that the section leader had been hung on charges of terrorism. Phil never heard whether or not he received the letter.

Deeply concerned about the killing and capture of most of the group that had visited the Mission, my father feared that the survivors would believe the missionaries were responsible for revealing their presence to the authorities and would return to the open, vulnerable Mission compound in killing mood. In fact, my father had taken the difficult decision to let the police know what had happened. But he discovered that someone else had got there first. After the guerrillas had visited his village close to the mission, a local man had cycled up the escarpment to the police camp three kilometres away. He had reported the presence of the armed men and claimed the reward. Within days, the informant was dead himself, killed by others in the community infuriated at what they saw as betrayal of *Vakomana Vedu*, or "our boys".

The unmasking of the informant within the community and his extrajudicial killing would have come to the attention of the surviving guerrillas. This incident had probably spared the missionaries from being killed themselves. It was one of the first twists in the tangled moral maze that my father and his colleagues were to be drawn into. A dreadful dilemma faced both missionaries and civilians in the growing conflict: they could comply with the law which required citizens to report the presence of guerrillas; yet if they did, they faced horrific retribution at the hands of the guerrillas: beatings, torture, and summary execution. Alternatively, they could keep quiet and face discovery by the authorities, trial, and long prison terms or deportation.

Avila, the Catholic Mission sixteen kilometres north of Elim, was an example of how badly things could go wrong. Priest in charge Father Peter Egan was put up against a wall and mock-executed by a group of ZANLA guerrillas in an attempt to frighten him into cooperation. He was deeply traumatized by this, reported the incident to the Rhodesian authorities, and then had to flee to Salisbury to avoid being killed by vengeful guerrillas, thus ending his ministry at Avila. A heavy-handed Rhodesian army response took place, with arbitrary beatings and interrogations of mission nurses, teachers, and priests. The army eventually commandeered the entire Mission complex and turned it into a military base.

Of course, the Elim missionaries had a third option. They

could withdraw. But they did not believe that God had given them permission to withdraw from danger when those they were called to serve in the name of Christ were suffering as the first flames of armed conflict began to flicker.

Education was seen as critical, to grow and develop young Christian leaders to be salt and light as they inherited the nation. My father wrote for the *Elim Evangel*,[5] "Students come from up to 300 miles away and from many different backgrounds. Very few are Christians on arrival and many are from heathen homes. They are hand-picked, drawn from the best ten per cent academically of those who entered primary school. So we see our work as strategic – winning souls for Christ and training potential future leaders."

Elim's medical services were in heavy demand, especially as government medical services and other mission hospitals along the north-eastern border had closed. And as for the church work, with the conflict came new spiritual opportunities as old ways of life, old sources of security, were tested and found to be wanting by many.

A few weeks later the Rhodesian Security Forces were tipped off that a ZANLA section would pass through the Mission complex. A heavily armed contingent of Rhodesian troops slipped down from the base camp under cover of darkness and took up ambush positions among the Mission buildings one night. The group of guerrillas did pass through without making contact with anyone on the Mission, but inexplicably the Rhodesian men did not open fire.

When my father was told by a friendly policeman about the ambush that had been laid, he was enraged. A battle on the premises could have resulted in the deaths of Mission personnel and serious damage to buildings and equipment, and would have meant the end of the team's work in the area. ZANLA commanders would not have believed that the ambush was laid without tacit cooperation from the missionaries. He extracted a promise from Rhodesian commanders that no such action would be planned again while the Mission remained open and in operation in service of the people.

In fact, the promise of "abiding in a peaceful habitation" that many of the team had read and taken to heart on that sunny May morning was kept over the long, frightening months that were to follow. As the war raged around the Mission, it was never again visited by ZANLA guerrillas, to the knowledge of the missionaries.

The arrival of that first group of guerrillas presaged a rapid acceleration in the rhythm of the war. A new threat began to emerge, a blind, merciless threat that spared no one.

It was Sunday lunchtime in May or June of 1976, and through her kitchen window, Joy Bath saw army vehicles driving into the hospital compound. A young army officer leapt from the lead truck, asking for urgent medical help for the civilian victims of a landmine explosion. My father drove the old Peugeot 404 station wagon, with Joy sitting next to him, medical equipment on her knee. He had refused to travel inside the military vehicles, trying to maintain a visible distance between mission and military, in an attempt to avoid militarization of humanitarian involvement.

They drove along a narrow, single-lane dirt track, choking on the dust kicked up by an armoured truck in front of them. Another truck followed as they threaded their way between kopjes, across dried-up river beds towards Kazozo village. Just outside the village, they came upon a scene of devastation. An ancient Ford truck belonging to a local shopkeeper had hit an anti-tank mine buried in the soil of the road approaching a bridge. It was smashed, lying on its side like a crippled beetle. The driver was breathing his last. A young mother lay dead, her body shattered, her toddler still pitifully suckling at her breast.

While the escorting troops fanned out, creating a security cordon around the destroyed truck, Joy rapidly assessed the wounded. She tersely instructed a young man with fractured ribs who was making a great deal of noise to stop moaning. She bypassed a woman lying unconscious with her legs bent up the wrong way from mid-shin, her wounds full of dust and ants. Joy started with a barely conscious man who had a huge gash in his inner thigh and had lost a huge amount of blood. She skilfully inserted a drip which my father tied to a tree while Joy tended the man's terrible injuries as best she could before moving on to others. A soldier brought a Coke over, which Joy shared with the terrified, dehydrated toddler, who drank most of it.

The "wap-wap-wap" of a helicopter steadily drew nearer. It touched down nearby in a flurry of dust and dry grass. The gunner ran over with a stretcher, and the man with the leg wound was loaded into the Alouette[6] helicopter gunship. Joy pressed into the gunner's arms the orphaned two-year-old wrapped in her blanket. The chopper lifted off again, the gunner cradling the child behind his Browning machine guns.

The ground troops were grumbling, concerned that the helicopter landing would have signalled to any guerrillas in the area that the military were there. Yet my father and Joy worked on steadily, the anxious troops maintaining a perimeter, nervously fingering their weapons and urging speed as the afternoon wore on. Cleaning and splinting the legs of the unconscious woman came next, and finally the broken-ribbed youth was attended to. The helicopter returned, and this time the pilot hurried over. "The doctor sends his compliments to the nurse for a first-class job." Joy's dusty, sweaty face, drawn with the tension of hard work under battlefield conditions, cracked into a smile. The remaining wounded were loaded, and then the helicopter was gone. Hastily, the troops withdrew to their trucks and escorted Joy and my father back to the Mission before nightfall, leaving the wrecked vehicle to rust there for years to come, a vivid reminder of the lives taken and ruined by that one mine.

Earlier that day, Phil Evans had driven down the same narrow track in a two-tonne open-backed truck loaded with people on their way to take a church service. As he approached the bridge, inexplicably he had lost control of the vehicle. It had slid off the road and through the thick sand to one side as Phil had wrestled with the steering wheel to get the truck back onto the road. The very point at which he had lost control and gone off the road was where the mine was buried. He and his passengers had been spared.

Joy heard later that the young man with the cracked ribs that she had assessed and passed over for initial evacuation had also ruptured his spleen and died later in hospital of internal blood loss. This deeply upset her as she felt responsible for choosing who went on the helicopter first. The event had a traumatic impact on both nurse and teacher. For months afterwards both Joy and my father were still having nightmares, reliving the scene of appalling human suffering. Years later, when Joy was back home in Wiltshire, she wrote to tell my parents that whenever she heard a helicopter go over, she was plunged back into intense images of the past, the hammering sound of the helicopter blades reminding her of the terrible injuries she had seen during days of war on the Mission.

Informed of the deteriorating security situation in Kambudzi, my father knew that a weekly clinic was held there by nurses who travelled out from the Mission hospital. He discussed the situation with the medical staff and finally told them (with a self-confessed touch of cowardice) that they would need to take the final decision on whether to go or not. With great sweetness and a cheeky grin Joy responded, "Peter, we'll keep on running the clinic if you get us there!"

Shortly after this, memories of the horrors they had seen just weeks before came flooding back as principal and nurses drove down another narrow track to Kambudzi. They anxiously looked for signs on the road – recently turned earth, signs of sweeping to obliterate tracks – but saw nothing. On the return journey, they were followed down the road by an army truck. Suddenly, with an ear-splitting roar, the truck behind them reared violently and the air filled with swirling, arid, choking dust. My father had driven over a landmine, yet somehow the tyres of his vehicle had not triggered the detonator. The army lorry, with its wider tyres, hadn't managed the same feat. The troops strapped inside the mine-protected vehicle were unharmed apart from shock, perforated eardrums and a fractured coccyx. But it was a shattering reminder of the proximity of death and injury.

At that stage of the war, both the Rhodesian Army and ZANLA guerrillas were wrestling with different challenges. The Rhodesian military could deploy only about 1,500 combat troops on any given day to cover a country three times the size of England. They developed methods to overcome this, such as the rapid delivery of elite troops by air to an established contact with their enemy. The Rhodesian Army was innovative, well trained, well armed, and well supported with artillery, armoured support, and air cover and, critical for morale, a well-developed medical support team.

On the other hand, ZANLA had the advantage of numbers, but seemingly little else. Their lines of supply were long and all their equipment and ammunition had to be hand-carried over the border of neighbouring countries. They had minimal medical supplies or support. They had no artillery (apart from the occasional mortar tube or recoilless rifle), no armoured vehicles, and no air support. For these reasons they found it difficult to sustain a prolonged firefight. Other methods were needed, and the guerrillas quickly learned that the landmine was a potent tool to deny access to areas they wanted to control. They realized that rapid movement of troops across vast areas was essential to the Rhodesians with their limited numbers. And so they set about disrupting or denying that movement.

The landmine,[7] a squat round container about the size of a biscuit tin, packed with explosives and originally designed as an anti-tank device, was a highly effective guerrilla weapon. It did not require heavy guns, elaborate training, or fire control systems, but only a spade and the mine itself. Landmines lay below the narrow dirt roads networked across the countryside, more accurate than artillery shells. They were safer to deploy as they could be laid and left without risking battle. They gave the Rhodesian Army the huge headache of finding a handful of landmines in thousands of kilometres of road while avoiding the loss of lives and vehicles in that search.

For the Rhodesians, being under sanctions meant that replacing or repairing mine-damaged vehicles ate into dwindling stocks of foreign exchange. Vehicles could be off the road for months. Being injured or seeing comrades killed in a landmine explosion, without being able to see or engage combatants from the other side, was deeply distressing and frustrating, and undermined morale.

The Rhodesian military responded to this threat by intensifying efforts to find and kill porters carrying mines across the border. They tarred roads, as this made mines more difficult to lay. Engineers worked to develop ways of detecting and removing landmines. Finally, methods were devised to protect drivers, passengers, and vehicles in the event of a mine detonation.

From a guerrilla point of view, landmines could be used to kill and wound enemy combatants, to slow down troop movements, and to isolate garrisons by cutting roads, all at relatively low risk. The use of landmines became more and more frequent, even though each mine weighed nearly ten kilograms and had to be carried by guerrilla fighters moving on foot across immense distances.

While the landmine was a useful weapon of war for the guerrillas, its indiscriminate nature had an appalling effect on civilian vehicles, as Joy and my father so agonizingly discovered. In addition to the terrible human cost of each explosion, the danger of travel quickly impacted mission work.

The Mission's five-tonne truck was at risk as Murewa continued to ply the route to Salisbury for supplies. My father had become an expert buyer of *mombe*, or cattle, and kept the school supplied with fresh meat. The boarding school needed more than a thousand meals a day and, despite the school gardens, the school cattle herd, and the fields round about, the school still needed regular resupply from the capital city. There was also a network of primary schools in the area surrounding the Mission whose teachers had to be visited, supported, and paid.

The seventy-bed hospital supplied meals to some patients (although usually a relative was asked to cook for their sick family member in the common kitchen provided). The network of schoolrooms also doubled as clinics, and these had to be resupplied with drugs and equipment regularly. Staff from the hospital went out on clinic days to support local health workers.

All the missionaries had full-time roles in teaching or medical care. But they also gave themselves fully to the church work in the area. Each weekend they fanned out across the Ruwangwe Valley, sometimes attending two or three different churches on a single day. All of this travel took place on the same narrow dirt tracks that the Security Forces travelled, and which the guerrillas had begun to mine.

Collecting missionary children from boarding school also became fraught with tension. Returning to school after the holidays in the Mission's ancient Ford Prefect, my father drove us past Rhodesian Army engineers who were sweeping the gravel road for mines. On the return trip the following day, the engineers flagged him down to tell him they had recovered an anti-tank landmine from the road just after we had driven past them. The mine itself had been "boosted" with explosives packed around the mine casing to increase its destructive power. Our tyre track had passed directly over the landmine, but the mine had failed to detonate.

The missionaries met to discuss the impact of the landmine campaign on the work of school, medical services, and church outreach. So seriously was this new threat taken that two members of the Elim Council in the UK flew out to Katerere to discuss the issues.

Each missionary wanted to continue to serve the local people, to keep spiritual, medical, and educational services running at that critical time. Again the decision was taken to reduce risk rather than avoid it. The missionaries were required to draw up wills, and were asked to include what should be done with their bodies should they be killed. Joy Bath wrote to her parents to discuss this, recognizing what a hard question she was presenting. Their response was to support whatever course of action she chose. Joy decided that if she were to be killed, she would "rather be buried in Rhodesia, to keep costs down"!

'Mine-proofing'[8] was carried out on the Mission's five-tonne truck, to reduce the chance of death or injury if the truck were to hit an anti-tank mine. Armour plating was placed inside the wheel arches to direct the blast up and away from the truck cab. The tyres were filled with water to reduce heat and dampen the blast. Heavy rubber conveyor belts lined the floor of the cab, and sandbags were placed in the bed of the truck as protection from shrapnel. Six-point seat belts were bolted into the truck frame to hold the occupants of the cab firmly in place.

Motorbikes were purchased. Travelling the roads on these reduced the chance of detonating mines. The pressure required to activate an anti-tank detonator was as much as 400 kilograms. A much lighter vehicle may not detonate a mine. In addition, there were only two narrow wheels on one side of a bush track rather than four.

Amid much laughter, several of the team learned how to ride a motorbike, at the cost of a number of nasty scrapes and cuts. My father wrote to Paul and me at our boarding school, teasingly describing my mother's riding skills: "Mummy now uses the Honda to go to Bhande, whizzing along at twelve miles an hour – it's so difficult to keep up with her if you are not a very fast walker!" The team were able to keep working with churches scattered across the area at reduced risk using the bikes.

But for the hospital and clinic outreach, a different solution was needed. The very seriously sick and critically wounded had to be transferred either to the Mission hospital from clinics or from the Mission to the larger government district hospital in Inyanga, ninety kilometres away on winding dirt roads. How could this be done safely?

In mid-July 1976 my father negotiated with the Rhodesian Army to buy from them a very unusual vehicle: a modified Land Rover, or "Rhino". Built specifically to counter the anti-tank mine threat, the body was an armoured steel hull, like a boat sitting on the chassis of a Land Rover, with roll bars encircling the hull.

My father took his family for a test drive. We faced each other on rock-hard seats[9] along the length of the vehicle, strapped in with shoulder harnesses. We stuffed cotton wool into our ears to protect our eardrums from any potential blast, and crammed crash helmets onto our heads. In an explosion, being thrown around in an armoured vehicle, twisting and turning in the air or on the ground, and banging one's head against the rough steel plating was potentially lethal.

With a grunt, my father slammed and locked the heavy, white-painted armoured doors. Finally, he strapped himself in behind the thick, green-tinted windscreen of bullet-proof glass that distorted and twisted the view, straining the eyes. If the vehicle hit a mine, the blast would be deflected outwards by the steel hull. The vehicle was designed to roll over to one side or the other with the occupants still safely strapped in. Stretchers carrying casualties could be strapped down on one row of seats or the other. Our Rhino was repainted white with red crosses on the side. Red lettering spelled out along the sides of the ungainly vehicle that it was an ambulance.

In this vehicle the nurses continued their clinic visits. The mine threat to the functioning of the Mission work was reduced even though it couldn't be eliminated. So on Sundays we still went to church but no longer riding in the cab of a Land Rover, or hanging on the back, enjoying the freshness of the wind in our faces and the beauty of the landscape rushing past. Instead we were strapped into our seats, our feet resting on sandbags, with cotton-woolled ears and crash-helmeted heads, cocooned within the Rhino's white steel walls.

On 19 June 1976, a series of meetings and consultations were held on the Mission, bringing together missionaries and local people, both Christian and non-Christian. The challenges of the security situation were addressed openly, with missionaries listening closely to the assessment and advice of their national colleagues. Although church leaders made it clear that they wanted the presence of missionaries, they also emphasized that a continued foreign presence placed local people in the dangerous position of being advocates for and protectors of white people to the growing numbers of guerrillas in the area. Mistakes made by the missionaries could cost local believers dearly.

Recommendations were made by local people to reduce the risk for everyone. Mission personnel were asked not to identify too closely with the Rhodesian Security Forces by inviting them into their homes or travelling in military vehicles, but rather to meet with them only in public. Some of the missionaries still had weak language skills which hindered relationships. Local people knew that the rifles held by missionaries had been handed in, and it was critical that the missionaries did not rearm.

In response, the missionary team agreed that each missionary would work on improving their Shona language skills, as this would enhance relationships with local people. Anything that suggested clandestine contact between missionaries and the Rhodesian military would be avoided. My father pointed out that any contact made with the Rhodesian military was largely on behalf of the local people, in order to enable services to continue. His thinking on this was accepted by the local people.

Pastor Ephraim Satuku spoke forcefully, explaining the need for a joint executive who would be responsible for both church matters and institutions. He expressed concern about the imbalance of control, insisting that more black involvement in leadership of the churches was needed. My father pointed out gently that more local men were required who were faithful mature Christians. The need for a new constitution fully owned by the local church was discussed, and it was agreed that work would begin immediately.

Open and frank exchanges to air grievances, concerns, and fears led both to a noticeable reduction in tension and to a deeper rapport and trust. Ephraim led a Communion service which was marked by a profound repentance. Colleagues black and white returned to their homes with a sense of thankfulness. But the hammering, menacing rhythm of the war in our area was about to become louder and more urgent.

HAMMER AND ANVIL

Discipleship means allegiance to the suffering Christ, and it is therefore not at all surprising that Christians should be called upon to suffer.

Dietrich Bonhoeffer[1]

Rearing hundreds of metres into the air, the colossal granite dome of Sanhani Rock loomed over the surrounding plateau. Eroded along ancient lines of weakness that formed as the granite cooled aeons ago, the rock's massive curves were cracked and shedding massive boulders. Beneath its shadow lay Sanhani Church, an outstation ten kilometres south-west of the Mission. Joyce Pickering, the mission hospital matron, supported the church work among the people in the Sanhani area.

One Sunday morning in July 1976, she arrived to find almost no one there: the young people were all missing. Concerned, she asked those who were there about absent individuals but received only muttered, evasive replies. Heart sinking beneath the brooding shadow of the giant rock, she looked out across the dry, brown plain, the air above it shivering in the heat. A sense of threat menaced the quiet land.

Later that day, my father was told of a very sick young boy who required an emergency operation that couldn't be performed at the Mission hospital. The boy desperately needed to be transferred to the district hospital in Inyanga, ninety kilometres away. Despite the danger of landmines and the rapidly fading light marking the approach of the curfew, Mission maintenance man Roy Lynn[2] courageously volunteered to drive the boy and his father.

In view of the risk of Roy either being ambushed by guerrillas or being shot as a curfew breaker by the army, my parents went up to the police camp[3] to see if it would be possible for the child to be evacuated by the military. Surrounded by high fences, the camp comprised low, green-painted buildings huddled along the rocky top of the escarpment, giving a wide vista across the valley below and into distant Mozambique. There were slit trenches, and a central dugout in which was piled stores and ammunition.

As they stood in the camp, waiting for an answer, four helicopter gunships roared overhead, low and fast. Just a few kilometres away a battle was taking place between the Rhodesian Army and ZANLA guerrillas. The contact, in local military parlance, was clearly visible to my mother from the escarpment ridge. "Fireforce", elite helicopter-borne troops, had been flown in from a distant air base. She could see a guerrilla seeking cover behind a baobab tree as a gunship circled it.

There was an air of excitement. Soldiers and police were gathered at the radio hut, listening closely to the terse, staccato exchanges between the circling "K-car" command helicopter, "G-car" gunships attacking the guerrillas from the air, and troops fighting on the ground. My father could hear the strain in the young voices screaming from the radio speakers, making themselves heard above the whine of aero engines and the whip-crack of cannon and gunfire. "I'm firing, I'm firing.[4] I've got a hit. He's going down. I got him." The men listening roared their delight, as if it was a sports commentary.

A helicopter detached itself from the battle and swung back towards the camp just a minute of flying time away. As it touched down, it was immediately obvious why it had returned. The young gunner had been hit by ground fire, shot through the head, and killed.[5] The celebratory atmosphere was immediately doused. The young airman's body was gently lifted from the aircraft and laid in a Land Rover to be taken to the airstrip and flown out after the battle.

The next helicopter in was carrying a ZANLA guerrilla who had surrendered. Already hooded, he was dragged out and carried, one man to each of his limbs, like a sack of maize. He was thrown to the ground and a furious wave of soldiers, grieving the death of their comrade, broke over him in violent anger. The prisoner was repeatedly kicked in the face. The situation was getting out of hand as soldiers began running towards the fracas from across the camp, presumably to join in the abuse. A pistol was drawn and placed against the prisoner's head as he lay bleeding, unarmed, and prostrate on the ground.

Standing on raised ground just metres away, my father was unable to remain silent. He shouted out, remonstrating with the troops and pleading for the captive's life. Immediately a soldier standing next to him rounded on him, yelling, "They killed my brother." Then, from the hut close by, a policeman burst out to sprint down the slope towards the melee. Dropping his shoulder, he charged into the pistol-wielding would-be executioner and sent him flying. Rescued from being shot out of hand, the prisoner was carried to one of the tents, away from the angry soldiers. The police officer later told my father that the prisoner gave useful information about guerrilla numbers and intentions.

Shaken by all she had seen, my mother drove back to the Mission as dusk began to fall. Joy Bath told her that a third helicopter involved in the battle had landed at the Mission helicopter pad. Soldiers had disembarked, ready for trouble.

When they saw that the landing zone was clear, a badly wounded soldier was carried from the helicopter into the Mission hospital. Joy and her colleagues had worked to stabilize the injured man, until a medevac plane arrived from a major base at Mutoko, north-west of the Mission, to remove him.

My father stayed on in the base camp with Roy Lynn and the sick little boy and his father, still hoping they would be able to get the child to a surgeon. A military plane touched down at the airstrip close to the Mission to evacuate the Rhodesian dead and wounded. My father rode down to the airstrip in the back of the police Land Rover alongside the dead body of the gunner, to ask for a place for the sick boy. But the plane was full of wounded from the battle that afternoon, and the boy had to be returned to the Mission hospital for the night.

Early the next morning, a helicopter touched down at the hospital again. On board was a twelve-year-old girl who had been shot through the arm and then caught in a grenade blast during the battle, her back terribly torn by shrapnel. Badly wounded and unable to move, she had lain bleeding in the bush all night. Troops sweeping through had found her as they looked for weapons, documents, and bodies.

The military plane returned later in the day, and finally the boy was evacuated for surgery, alongside the little girl. My father was able to track down her parents, who were beside themselves with fear, and let them know that their daughter was alive, that she had been found, and where she had gone.

Guerrillas had appeared in Sanhani Village that Sunday with a gramophone. The latest in local music had begun to float through the hot, sultry, dusty air. Nothing much happened in the remote rural areas, and the boys were star-struck by the guerrillas. The girls came to giggle and to watch, and to submit bashfully to invitations to dance, and so had been missed at church by Joyce, who had been puzzled by the absence of young people.

But the guerrillas had been seen and reported. Battle was joined. In terror, the young people scattered into the surrounding vegetation as the air around them suddenly hummed with violent steel bees. A number of ZANLA guerrillas had been killed or captured during the ferocious afternoon battle that my parents had witnessed. Some had escaped, so Rhodesian army units had lain in ambush all night, expecting movement and hoping to catch their enemy as they attempted to regroup under cover of night. There was the crackle and rustle of bodies moving through the brush, the sound of urgent whispers carrying in the silent stillness; the shooting began again. In the morning, the bodies of those caught in the ambush, lying in the "killing ground", could be seen and identified. They were not guerrillas attempting to regroup but "six girls and a boy", my mother mournfully noted, some members of the Mandiza family who were known to my parents. They died while trying to find each other and their way home after the thrilling party had dissolved into a vicious maelstrom.

The battle at Sanhani was one of the first major incidents in the area, but was merely the lighting of the touchpaper as the war exploded into the region. Inyanga North Tribal Trust Land, right on the Mozambique border became a major battleground as ZANLA guerrillas began to cross into the remote, previously neglected region in large numbers.

Two days after the battle at Sanhani, a helicopter roared low over the school and landed within a few metres of the school hall. Assembly was under way, led by an enthusiastic Youth with a Mission group with musical and acting skills. But the assembly had to be temporarily abandoned as the students poured out to see the helicopter, still a novelty at that stage of the war. On board were four girls who had been wounded during a battle at Chifambe Village, just twelve kilometres north of the mission.

At the hospital, Joy Bath and Joyce Pickering worked rapidly with their team of nurses. They had to evacuate the male ward to make room for the large number of female casualties coming in, all having spent the night lying injured in the open after the battle the previous day. Several were in severe shock and Joyce had to do cut-downs, cutting open the skin of the legs of the girls to insert intravenous drips into their collapsed veins. Joy talked to the girls who were conscious as she examined them, inserted drips, and cleaned their wounds.

They were staring, bewildered, still in deep shock. Having started out to draw water, pots on their heads, the girls had been laughing and chattering. It had seemed like just another day. But suddenly a battle had erupted around them, out of nowhere. As the girls had huddled in a group, terror-stricken, a rocket-propelled grenade fired by guerrillas hit the stony ground next to them and exploded, wounding them all, many by pieces of flying stone.

During the day, six more wounded civilians came into the hospital, some brought by military helicopter and others, found injured in the bush later, ferried in by bicycle or in wheelbarrows. Three dead bodies were also brought in, two teenage girls and a man.

The image of one girl's injuries was seared into my mother's mind as she was lifted off the helicopter by the school. The teenager had been found dragging herself on hands and knees away from the carnage in her village. She must have been standing, paralysed with fear by the horrific scene unfolding around her. A projectile of some sort, perhaps shrapnel from a cannon shell fired from a helicopter gunship, had caught the back of both her feet and neatly removed both heel bones, leaving her Achilles tendons exposed and unattached. She was included in the official statistics under the designation of wounded while "running with terrorists", the euphemism used by the Rhodesian government when reporting on civilian casualties caught in crossfire in the presence of guerrillas. It seemed shockingly inappropriate, a euphemism too far.

Despite the high numbers of civilian casualties, no ZANLA guerrillas were captured or killed. The section commander was wounded, his hat found later with a bullet hole in it. He was spotted from a gunship overhead, frantically tearing up his documents as he was carried away into hiding by his comrades. The documents were later recovered and pieced together by an intelligence team.

The following Sunday, my father went with Mary Fisher to Chifambe Village, still devastated by the week's fighting, only to find that a local leader had announced there would be no church service. But on hearing the vehicle, several people hurried up to sing and pray together. The Christians of Chifambe poured out their stories of the fighting the previous week to Mary and my father.

The all-out contest for control of the people had begun abruptly two weeks earlier, in early July, when ZANLA guerrillas executed the Rhodesian government-appointed village headman at Chifambe, the village where we went to church each Sunday. Headman Manjezi was also killed by ZANLA for "taking money from the people". My mother speculated that this money was fines taken by headmen from local farmers for not contour ridging their land, an unpopular government anti-erosion measure needed to prevent land degradation.

The local store and grinding mill were robbed. The guerrillas also abducted one of the grinding mill employees, a fifteen-year-old boy. At that point in the war, ZANLA was extremely short of manpower, and abduction was a ZANLA policy to gain recruits.[6] The guerrilla section searched for another government employee, but he was away. So they beat his wife Berita, shot the family cow, two goats, all the chickens, wrecked the house, and abducted a teenage boy who was working there. Because of the killings and robberies by the guerrillas, the attempt to deny services, and to drive off or kill government employees, Rhodesian Army patrols had been stepped up in the area. The Chifambe Village battle with its heavy civilian toll was the result.

In the south-east of Rhodesia, in early October 1976, guerrillas lined up a group of workmen who were putting up a fence round a protected village and machine-gunned them, killing twelve.[7] One of the men was local and his body was brought back to Katerere. My father and Ephraim Satuku went to his funeral, where my father spoke. There was a palpable sense of fear during the ceremony. Not even his mother cried for him, unheard of in a culture where people very vigorously and publicly expressed their emotion. Her son had been killed by the guerrillas, and weeping would be a sign of her displeasure at their action.

Students from the school, among them Barnabus Kuzaza, Joseph Mashenu, and Gibson Mabambe, and led by the school head boy Paul Ngadze,[8] had gone out beyond the Mission precincts with Phil Evans to cut wood for the school kitchens. Dropping them off, Phil promised to return an hour later. On his return, Phil was disconcerted to see bundles of wood scattered in the undergrowth but no sign of axes or students. One student, captured a few weeks later by the Rhodesian Army, told his interrogators that he had slipped away from tree-cutting for a few moments for an illicit cigarette. ZANLA guerrillas had appeared and forced him across the border as a recruit. He claimed not to know what had happened to the other students.

A long concrete bridge across the Inyangombe River had been built, opening up a shorter way – just four hours on the road – from Katerere up to the main Mutoko road and into Salisbury. The guerrillas attempted to blow it up in October 1976. I directed my father as we edged our way round the massive fissure they had blasted in the concrete. The guerrillas didn't make the same mistake twice, and soon rendered the bridge unusable.

My parents called in at the military base to talk to Mel Hughes, a friendly policeman, on their way into town to see Paul and me at school. Mel said that the Duza Bridge on an alternative route out of the area had also been blown up. He showed my father a note found at the scene, "Down with Smith, down with Kissinger, down with helicopters, down with Christ."[9] My father told Mel he planned to cross the bridge. "Impossible," said Mel. "The only way across that bridge is by bicycle." My father's bold response was to tell Mel that he believed in the power of prayer.

Arriving at the scene, my father wondered if he had been rash in what he had said. There was a gaping hole in the centre of the bridge. My father had heavy planks in the back of the truck and rigged up a rough repair. Everyone got out and my father drove, one set of tyres up on the intact parapet of the bridge, the other on the planks. They cracked ominously but held. My parents got through – that time. My father sent a mischievous message back to the police camp: "Tell Mel that prayer works!"

Ridiculed as guerrilla activity frequently was, these were not mindless, random acts. A strategy was emerging. Other bridges in the area were blown up too, cutting access roads across the mountains into our lowland area. Only a long winding dangerous road, very close to the Mozambique border, remained regularly open. Guerrilla control and monitoring of movement in and around the area was steadily taking effect through a combined approach of bridge destruction and mining roads.

The guns fell silent in July 1976 at the end of the school term. Guerrillas wanted students boarding at Elim to get home safely, and so they stepped down their campaign. The big Chingaira buses arrived, revving their engines and hooting. Skilled conductors rapidly loaded the roofs, piling them high with black steel trunks, battered cardboard suitcases, and multicoloured holdalls. Excited faces smiled, arms wildly gesticulated from every window, and exhausts belched choking black smoke as the drivers pulled away from the premises. The high floating voices of the song leaders rang from the vehicles, giving the first line of the song before the spine-tingling moment when the rest of the singers thundered in with the bass. Rather blandly, my mother jotted in her diary, "The students went off happily."

My brother Paul and I made our own journey in the opposite direction to the school buses, ecstatic to be leaving town and returning home to the bush. We celebrated Paul's tenth birthday with a *braai* (barbecue) under the tree by our back door joined by our "uncles" and "aunties". I baked Paul's birthday cake and made apple crumble. His candles flickered in the warm, velvety darkness. Tim Evans, Paul, and I listened to records and danced, our antic gestures mercifully hidden in the night while the grown-ups sat and talked around the glow of the fire. The Mission community was at peace, but around us the night was anything but peaceful.

As the political struggle for control grew more and more intense, often the Rhodesian Army's counter-insurgency tactics resulted in recruitment for the guerrilla cause. Sometimes guerrillas would cynically provoke what they guessed would be a heavy-handed army response to convince wavering or hostile villages to give them their allegiance. On 20 and 21 October 1976, an army patrol passing through the battered Chifambe Village stopped to question villagers about the presence of ZANLA in the area, which they denied. Yet while the questioning was taking place, a section of twenty-two guerrillas was hidden in a group of huts about fifty metres away from the patrol. Suddenly the guerrillas opened fire and withdrew. One civilian died and one was wounded during the short, sharp engagement. As reprisal, the Security Forces burned every hut in the entire village, even though the army patrol were unharmed. The villagers were in an impossible situation, ground between the remorseless cogs of two military machines.

Renzva, a Mission worker from Chifambe Village, lost his home and all his property in the fire. The police arrived at Elim Mission and took him away for questioning. My father went repeatedly to the base camp to ask for Renzva's release, but it only came after Renzva had been held for several days in the wire "pens" there. It was obvious when my father finally secured his freedom on 3 November that he had been badly beaten. Renzva's four sons witnessed the burning of their family homestead and all their belongings. Their father had been violently assaulted by the Rhodesians while in their custody, before his release without charge. The young men predictably responded by going "across the border" into Mozambique to join ZANLA.

At the end of August, we were still on our school holidays when, before dawn, our windows rattled as a colossal series of explosions was heard. The terrified nurse assistants on night duty at the hospital ran to Pastor Satuku's house for refuge. The Rhodesian military base just three kilometres away was coming under sustained attack by more than ninety ZANLA guerrillas. Rocket, mortar, and heavy machine gun fire poured into the base from a ridge to the north of the camp and overlooking it. Twelve of the fourteen military vehicles on the base were rendered unusable in the thirty-minute onslaught. Owing to a shortage of sandbags in the base and the rocky terrain on the escarpment ridge, each explosion's effect was multiplied, sending stone as well as steel splinters slicing through flesh and bone. Of the thirty men on the base, twelve were injured, some critically. All survived, but many were left brain-damaged, paralysed, or blinded.[10]

The guerrilla campaign had initially focused on creating a "semi-liberated area", closing roads with mines and blown bridges, gaining the cooperation of the local people through persuasion or violence, gaining new recruits through abductions, interrupting government services by killing or driving off government employees, and sometimes being caught by Rhodesian Army patrols and brought to battle. Now they had taken the war to the army. As a result of the attack on the base, the relatively inexperienced army units there were withdrawn within a week and the base returned to police control. The attack on the camp marked a growing confidence among the guerrillas.

* * *

On the Mission, there was growing confidence too among the local pastors and leaders, not in a demonstration of firepower but in an emerging realization of where God might be leading the local church. My father led a regular men's group on a Saturday morning where more than twenty men would come together to look at the Bible and talk through the issues of the day, followed by a meal.

Intense discussion followed my father's presentation on indigenous church on 6 November. A vision of a self-governing, self-supporting, self-propagating community of followers of Jesus Christ among the Hwesa people was coming into view. Together, the next steps were hammered out towards a full transition of leadership from missionary to national. The contrast between the violent struggle for political control, audible and visible on a daily basis all around them, and the sense of partnership and brotherhood within the church was stark.

A letter arrived from Thandiwe Sithole, former head girl who had started her state registered nursing training at one of the teaching hospitals in Salisbury. My parents were delighted that Thandiwe had enclosed Rh$6.00[11] from her first pay packet to support the ongoing work at Bhande Church.

But Sunday 7 November dawned with a massive explosion that rattled windows across the Mission. It turned out to be a "boosted" mine detonated by Rhodesian engineers who were led to the mine by a ZANLA prisoner. My mother was both shaken and grateful. The mine had been placed on the road we were to take to Bhande Church later that morning.

The evening of Friday 12 November came and, as was their custom, my parents went to eat with Pious and Evelyn Munembe. Other colleagues joined them there. They talked over the events of the week, discussing their implications. Then they spent time in prayer – for themselves, for one another, for students and staff, for the churches, for the people of the area, and for the war-torn nation. Before closing, my father led his colleagues through a simple Communion service, the broken bread and poured-out wine a reminder of the sufferings of the Lord whom they followed. They found that this weekly celebration of the Lord's Supper together gave them a sense of proportion in all that surrounded them. They were reminded that their own Lord was no stranger to violence, to hatred, to racist conflict. He had not avoided the darkness but entered it to redeem and transform it. So they parted from each other, walking home into the dark, heartened and encouraged.

Saturday 13 November 1976 dawned hot and dry. My mother was up early and walked to the school to join in the Scripture Union meeting where about 150 students had gathered to sing, pray, and read the Bible together. As the meeting drew to a close, booming across the sunlit, still expanse of the plains stretching out before the Mission came the distinct sound of automatic gunfire from the north. Then a few minutes later the throbbing of helicopters and roar of rocketry, fired from a Lynx[12] aircraft circling overhead, meant that a battle was under way within a few kilometres around Kazozo Village.

My father headed for the hospital to warn Joy that casualties would probably be arriving. On the road leading into the hospital compound he met the first casualty, just coming out of the battle zone under his own steam. He was a black member of the Rhodesian Army, a veteran of the Rhodesian African Rifles who had fought in Malaya years before during the Emergency there. Animatedly he described how he had been ambushed by guerrillas, separated from his unit, and pursued through the bush by six guerrillas for seven kilometres who had fired rocket-propelled grenades at him. He had a spectacular bloodstain on his shirt, where a piece of shrapnel from one of the grenades had hit him in the chest. Keeping a cool head, he had shot and killed two of his pursuers.

Despite the deteriorating security situation, my mother travelled out to Bhande school that day to judge an inter-primary singing competition there. The first group of children were merrily singing when suddenly the door burst open and a white soldier, a member of the Internal Affairs unit, came staggering in. My mother and the soldier stared at each other in mutual shock. A hush fell in the classroom, broken only by the great heaves and gasps for breath from the wild-eyed, blood-spattered soldier, a sudden fierce irruption of camouflage and weaponry into a tranquil scene. It was a deeply surreal moment: the soldier emerging from a scene of extreme violence and bursting into a classroom full of bright-faced, enthusiastic young singers facing their judges and carolling merrily.

The fighter was emotionally shattered, having just experienced his first taste of combat. He had been driving on a routine patrol through the bush, when there was a loud clang. He looked to his left, and to his horror his black colleague sitting at his side in their armoured vehicle had been instantly killed by a rocket-propelled grenade that had penetrated the canvas roof of the vehicle and passed through his chest without exploding.[13] The world flared up into a vortex of noise, a hail of fire being directed against the steel sides of the vehicle. Bullets penetrated the engine compartment, crippling the engine. The vehicle coasted to a stop. The soldier had returned fire and then jumped from the stricken vehicle to run twelve kilometres through the bush, pursued by guerrillas most of the way. That frantic dash had brought him into Bhande school.

My mother stood up and led him from the room, away from the now frightened children and out to the Mission truck. He flung his arm over the side of the vehicle, pulled off his glasses, and laid his head down on his arm, weeping. "They've just killed my mate," he sobbed over and over again. Blood ran from both his ears, his eardrums damaged by the din of battle. My mother offered him a seat in the vehicle to rest, but he staggered off in the direction of the village store just a few metres away to find something to slake his thirst.

The Mission driver Murewa who lived nearby came hurrying up to my mother, and she asked him to take the soldier to the Mission hospital. However, the soldier asked to be taken straight to the police camp, a request that deeply concerned my mother, as she was afraid of placing Murewa in a difficult position – being seen with a member of the Security Forces in the Mission vehicle entering the police camp. But a verse came to mind: "So then, as we have opportunity, let us do good to all men,"[14] and my mother reacted in compassion, despite the complexity of the situation. She went back to the singing competition while Murewa drove the wounded, distraught soldier to the police camp. A little later, as my mother looked through the window of the classroom, she saw a convoy of military vehicles going past. Within an hour they returned, towing the soldier's crippled vehicle, the body of the District Assistant still inside. Local people grieved for him: he was a man with a good reputation for serving the community.

That same Saturday afternoon, despite the sporadic clashes still underway, my father went with Ephraim Satuku to visit a man dying of tuberculosis at Mbiriyadi Village, eight kilometres away. As they talked together, the man clearly and emphatically reaffirmed the faith he had professed a few weeks before with

Pastor Satuku at Elim hospital. The following day he died, "passing into the presence of the Lord", noted my father.

Early Sunday morning, my father was struck by a passage from the book of Ezra, where Ezra, the leader of a group of God's people travelling through hostile territory in the Middle East 2,500 years before, had written, "I was ashamed to ask the king for a band of soldiers and horsemen to protect us against the enemy on our way; since we had told the king, 'The hand of our God is for good upon all that seek him.'"[15] Later, Ezra could say, after passing safely through that dangerous terrain, "the hand of our God was upon us, and he delivered us from the hand of the enemy and from ambushes by the way". Thoughtfully, my father stored the passage away in his mind.

That Sunday was a day of celebration, despite the intense warfare all around. Pastor Satuku baptized more than twenty new believers. My parents went out to Bhande Church, where very few appeared for the Sunday service, afraid to walk through the fiercely contested battlezone that the area had become. That night at the school, more than fifty students came to the prayer meeting. A first-year boy approached my father, trembling, and confessed to stealing five dollars from him, by having deceitfully claimed it twice. He paid it back on the spot. Many stayed on after the meeting, praying and weeping before God, concerned about their ability to stand firm in their faith in the intensity of the conflict and their fear of threats made by many guerrillas at that time regarding the fate of those who followed the "white man's God".

Joy Bath hurried up to find my father on Monday evening. A woman was in obstructed labour and unable to deliver her tenth child. She needed urgent transfer to Inyanga District Hospital some ninety kilometres away for a Caesarean section or Joy feared she would rupture her uterus and both mother and baby would bleed to death. But unplanned travel along the Inyanga

Road was potentially lethal. Bridges had been blown up, mines were laid continuously, police and army had been ambushed, and white farmers closer to Inyanga had been killed. The guerrillas had made it clear that any vehicle moving at night would be presumed to be military; they had already attacked several, firing just above the headlights well before a vehicle could be identified.

There was only half an hour of daylight left for a two-hour daylight trip, and travelling at night would take longer. Mission policy that my father had helped draw up said that Mission vehicles should never travel at night. But two lives were at stake. The passage from Ezra suddenly came to mind. My father didn't want to go to the police camp and ask for an escort, given what had so forcefully leapt off the pages of his Bible. He had the impression that the police would have refused an escort anyway. Both my parents were at peace as they walked together up to the truck that was being loaded with the stretcher bearing the woman in labour. A relative scrambled in too, to keep the woman company, and promptly lay down to take advantage of the meagre cover afforded by the low steel sides of the truck bed.

Joy and my father clambered into the cab and drove off into the gathering dusk. Suddenly, they came over the brow of a hill and there was a sudden intake of breath for Joy. Below them it looked as if the darkened world was ablaze, fires spread as if there was a giant battle spread across the valley. My father saw that it was simply the remains of fires set to burn off the stubble in the fields. Despite the danger, they drove for hours through the night, the only vehicle on the road, and arrived safely. The woman delivered her child at the district hospital. My father went straight on to Inyanga police that night and they radioed through the news of the safe arrival to Ruwangwe Police Camp just three kilometres from the mission as reassurance for my mother. But the police at the base refused to drive to the Mission to tell her because they thought it was too dangerous!

All that was going on around my parents they saw not as a signal that they should withdraw because the situation was dangerous. Rather they saw that a witness to the gospel of Christ was needed all the more among the violence, fear, and sudden death that was so much a part of everyday life for rural people at that time.

* * *

A few days after that demanding weekend, my mother was awoken by the heat in the bedroom. Pulling back the curtain, she looked down the gentle slope and out across the valley below her, watching the first rays of the sun colour with fire the distant mountain peaks across the Mozambique border. Although already very warm, she thought ruefully, "As soon as the sun hits those peaks it will be hot… hot all day!"

After a hasty dawn breakfast she went down to the school to invigilate the final O Level exam. The temperature kept on rising until it was over 40°C. Through the quivering air, the crackle of gunfire carried across the valley. Minutes later, the heaviest air traffic that my mother had yet seen roared low overhead. Rhodesian Dakotas carrying paratroopers and helicopter gunships headed in the direction of the Inyangombe River close to the Mozambique border.[16] She longed for the British O Level examiners to know the conditions under which her students had taken their exams: extreme heat, gunfire, and already one of the circling helicopter gunships had two dead bodies dangling beneath it, clearly visible through the classroom window. She sighed, turning back to her roomful of students as they completed their work, and then left the exam room to prepare for the Form 4 party to close the year.

Despite the fighting nearby, that same afternoon my mother and Sandra McCann climbed on my mother's little motorbike and went to the women's meeting out at Bhande, where fifteen of the local women had gathered. They sang and danced together, and women's leader Mai Helen spoke above the throbbing of aircraft roaring low overhead all afternoon and the distant rumble of ordnance. The women knelt, black and white side by side, the Shona tumbling from their lips as they poured out their hearts to God, the sounds of battle bringing urgency to their prayers.

The following morning, my father went up to the base camp to retrieve the mail. The police had taken on the task of moving mailbags around as bus services ground to a halt because of mines and robberies. On the ground inside the wire perimeter, an appalling sight met my father: a neat line of eighteen stark naked bodies, many with gaping wounds and shattered limbs, young men killed in the intense battle that was raging nearby. Special Branch operatives were moving from corpse to corpse, photographing and fingerprinting them one by one. Recoiling from the macabre scene, he looked away, only to see two captured guerrillas, locked in the wire "pens" nearby, able to see all that was being done to their erstwhile comrades.

Later that day, the police rounded up people at the stores and took them to the camp to dig trenches, put the bodies in, pour fuel over them, and set them alight. My father caught the police trying to take Form 4 students who were waiting for the bus, and stopped them. At the time my father didn't know what the police wanted labour for, but he was disgusted when he found out. He wanted to raise a complaint about the use of civilians for such a gruesome task. Mission driver Murewa Katerere, the nephew of the local chief, talked him out of it, afraid of reprisals.

The previous night, a four-man Rhodesian Army patrol, probing forward after the fighting of the previous day, had engaged with what was thought to be a final handful of guerrillas. At least one more guerrilla was killed, but suddenly the patrol had found themselves outgunned. One patrolman died[17] and another was seriously wounded. In fact, the patrol had stumbled across a group of more than 200 heavily armed guerrillas. A Rhodesian reaction force had been hastily assembled to respond to an escalation of guerrilla attempts to take full control of the area by capturing the large Rhodesian army base at Inyanga.

The third day dawned, and still the fighting continued in what would become known as the Battle of Inyangombe. My mother saw five different types of plane and three different types of helicopter, a sign that the Rhodesian Security Forces were pouring massive resources into this battle. From time to time the ground shook and the air split as the air force dropped 1,000lb bombs into the battle.

To my mother's horror, Ephraim Satuku came to tell her that members of the Chikumbinde family had been caught up in the fighting. Richard Chikumbinde had been my mother's student years ago at primary school. My mother had been there at Bhande Church when as a teenager Richard had wanted to repent one Sunday and had come to faith. He had married a Christian girl and they had settled down at Gande Village just a few kilometres away. Together my parents went out to Richard Chikumbinde's house. Brokenly, Richard told them what had happened.

His wife and his daughter-in-law had gone to fish at the Inyangombe River, when they heard a plane overhead. Something fell from beneath it,[18] and suddenly the bush around them flared up in a roaring inferno. The two women ran in panic from the fire, straight into an army unit waiting for the blaze to flush out guerrillas. The army didn't hesitate but promptly killed them both. Richard's wife was decapitated, such was the firepower that caught and killed them.

There was silence as my father and mother absorbed the impact of the story. There were few words that could be said in the face of such horror. Together, they knelt and wept with Richard Chikumbinde, sobbing in anguish before God.

The weekly women's group out at Bhande became a source

of strength, a point of sanity in a world gone mad, a support group for those caught up in a maelstrom of blood and steel. But at the same time my mother could hardly bear to hear some of the stories. A number of the women's group were among those rounded up by the police to bury the bodies of dead guerrillas. A police lorry arrived at the village and they were ordered to get in. At the base camp they were kept waiting with no idea why they were there. Mai Maria got down on her knees and began to pray. Ordered to be silent by the police, she was made to cook food for the forced labour team. The group of women listened to Mai Maria in hushed silence as she told her story. She had cooked and fed the forced labour detail as they dug graves for, burned, and buried thirty-eight young men in those trenches. Her voice trembled and broke as she gave thanks to the Lord for bringing her through what she had found to be a dreadful experience. The Battle of Inyangombe had lasted for six days.

It was sobering to hear of the murder of three Roman Catholic missionaries in Lupane on 5 December. Acknowledging the danger, my mother wrote home, "We continue to look to the Lord who has told us not to flee! We believe that we have seen an unprecedented advance in the church work during the year. The African church now has a constitution. They have an executive committee and are taking more and more responsibility. We thank God for those who during the year have joined the Lord's army and are truly born again."[19]

Elim Mission was now far behind the front lines, deep in territory largely held by the guerrillas. The battle for the area had been lost by the Rhodesian Security Forces and by the state. Agricultural services, district administration, communications, public transport, and the network of stores were all largely closed down or greatly curtailed. No alternative administration or services were put in place by the guerrillas, even in a limited or rudimentary fashion. On 2 December, Elim Mission received news that the Roman Catholic Mission of Avila had been closed down. Only Elim Mission still provided health services, and the primary and secondary schools continued to run.

Missionary-led churches were under great pressure but astonishingly, bravely, the missionaries still scattered across the area each Sunday. My mother puttered from village to village on her motorbike with one of her Shona friends, Rhona, visiting friends and families that she knew, praying with people, sharing from the Bible, talking about expectations for the coming harvest, and nibbling roasted peanuts, even as military vehicles rumbled past. Increasingly, the army and police would only enter the area in large numbers or by air, while remaining in well-fortified garrisons. ZANLA guerrillas, through their use of landmines and selective demolition of bridges, increasingly controlled access to the district.

Across the country, it became apparent that for those living in rural areas where guerrilla infiltration occurred, traditional power structures had been turned on their heads. The work and safety of missionaries living in war zones was based on the quality of relationships with local people. Where this was poor, they could be denounced to the guerrillas. For the Elim missionaries, long years of medical and educational services in the area and the growth of many deep personal relationships with local people through the church work led to good standing within the rural community. So the ground was well prepared to allow the missionaries to continue to serve, despite the conflict.

* * *

My father went up to the base camp trying to find out which roads were safe to travel on, in the tornado of violence still sweeping the area. In the wire pens where prisoners were held, he spotted Willard Sagwidza, a schizophrenic well known in the area for his erratic behaviour. Willard had an untended bullet wound. My father insisted on his release and took him down to the Mission hospital.

Increasingly, even as local people acted as advocates for the missionaries to the guerrillas moving into the area in larger numbers, so my father "gave himself fully to the local people, representing them before the Security Forces", in the words of a visitor from Elim headquarters in the UK.[20] As local people became his advocate to the guerrillas, so he became an advocate for the local people to the Security Forces. Both missionaries and local Christians, caught between the pounding hammer and the unyielding anvil, actively sought out men of goodwill and compassion in the opposing armies, men who could be negotiated with.

One day in late February 1977, my mother was out with the women's group at Bhande when Mai Gracia Tsengerai, related to Harry Tsengerai who had helped the Briens years before, came through the door, flung her arms around my mother, and began to sob uncontrollably. Earlier that day, her teenage son John had been seized and beaten severely by the army before being thrown into the back of a truck and driven off. She was afraid that he would be killed. Her husband had been arrested and so badly beaten that he could not walk. Mai Gracia herself had been knocked down and kicked in the mouth by an army boot. The family had been accused of cooking food for ZANLA guerrillas, which they had denied.

In response, my mother found some men to help and drove them down to the Tsengerai homestead, finding the semi-conscious Baba Tsengerai, Mai Gracia's husband, lying on the ground before his door. They gently lifted him into the vehicle and took him to the hospital. My father, furious at the illegal way in which the family had been attacked, took Mai Tsengerai with him up to the police camp. She was terrified on entering the camp, afraid that she might be beaten again, but was greatly comforted to have a moment with her son, who was being held in the wire pens. Mel Hughes, a senior police officer, negotiated with the army but couldn't arrange for John to be released immediately. Meanwhile, in the hospital, Joy realized that Baba Tsengerai's injuries were beyond their ability to treat, and so my father drove him the ninety kilometres to Inyanga District Hospital.

The Bhande women's group met a week later. Mai Tsengerai was there, full of joy and deeply thankful for my father's negotiation with the police. John had been released, as Mel Hughes had promised. The women began dancing and singing together, embracing my mother, and praising God.

But the war crashed on, gathering an increasingly lawless momentum. In late March, agonized parents from Chowa Village brought two distressed teenage girls into the hospital. While walking from field to home they had crossed the path of Rhodesian soldiers on patrol. The girls had run and locked themselves in their huts, but the soldiers had followed them, ordered them out at gunpoint, dragged them into the bush, and gang-raped them. Joy Bath treated their injuries and then came up to our house to see my father. Enraged by Joy's grim testimony, my father reported the crime, with the parents' permission.

My father took the girls, along with their parents, up to the base camp, where the girls were shown a selection of weapons in order to identify the guns they had been threatened with. Then the entire company of soldiers were called out on parade and, in what must have been a terrifying ordeal, the girls had to walk up and down the line of men and pick out the individuals who had carried out the assault. In an act of tremendous courage they unhesitatingly pointed out the men. It was confirmed that the men had been on patrol in the area at the time. The soldiers were arrested, placed under guard, and transferred to Inyanga. My father later arranged transport for the families to the District Court in Inyanga where they saw the men prosecuted and jailed.

Through events such as these, my father had unwillingly become not just an advocate for the local people but also the conscience of the local army base, a thorn in their flesh. There was ambivalence towards him. Charming as he was, many Rhodesian army troops warmed to him as an individual. One or two he became close to.

But others called him a *kaffir-boetie*, combining a deeply offensive word for black people and the Afrikaans word *boetie*, or "brother". Young Rhodesian troops on the back of their military trucks leaned over as he rode past them on his motorbike and spat on him. They believed that the Elim missionaries provided shelter and food to the guerrillas as well as providing them with information on Rhodesian troop movements.[21] But, unknown to the young soldiers, my father was doing what he could to save their lives.

My father had developed good relationships with many key people in the area. He was respected for leading a team willing to stay in a dangerous environment for the sake of their faith and to serve the people. Many local people knew very well what was happening during the hours of darkness. Guerrillas themselves would pass details to trusted go-betweens who would make sure my father knew about some landmine placements for the benefit of those working at the Mission.

The possession of such information immediately created a terrible dilemma for my father. He was acutely aware of the many other vehicles using the roads, including the Rhodesian military. How could he withhold details of landmine placements if that might mean serious injury or death for young Rhodesian soldiers? They might be combatants but they were also fathers, husbands, brothers, and sons, all seen by my father as made in the image of God. In addition, he would break the law of the land if he did not pass on the information.

On the other hand, the guerrillas had military objectives in placing those mines. Was he weakening the guerrilla cause if, through his action, a Rhodesian military vehicle was spared? Might that mean that he was making a small contribution to prolonging the bloodshed? More personally, if he passed on information to the Rhodesian forces, even in a clandestine way, this might soon become apparent to the guerrillas. He ran the risk of being killed or seeing his colleagues killed, either directly by the guerrillas as reprisal or because his sources dried up and a Mission vehicle detonated a landmine. His dilemma was just one of many faced on a daily basis by rural people caught up in this civil war. Right or wrong, he decided that his first objective was to save life, and so he found a way to pass on details of landmine placements when he knew of them.

Daily, in those sombre years, agonizingly difficult decisions had to be made, not just by my father but also by many others. They were years of secrets and silence, shadows and darkness, corrosive and pervasive fear. They were years of violence and bloodshed, blood crying from the ground from every corner of the country. They were years of betrayal and lies, of sundered families, bitter hearts, and blighted lives.

My parents and the missionary team working with him did not embrace the military pursuit of the nationalist cause, nor did they support the Rhodesian government in their supposedly Christian war against Communism. But the stance of neutrality chosen by the missionaries was neither passive nor disengaged. As they lived in the complex world of a civil war, they bravely chose to walk the third way, the way of the cross, seeking to live with integrity and authenticity, wanting to demonstrate a different quality of life and hope.

In early 1977, my mother recorded in her diary that there had been ten landmine detonations in the area in fourteen days. Next to this grim entry, she scribbled, "O Level results arrived: excellent! 27 of 51 had a Division 1 pass." Despite the challenges of living and working in an area visibly and audibly engulfed in violence, the school campus was an oasis of calm, and the students were continuing to achieve the grades they needed.

* * *

On 11 February 1977, my parents travelled to Salisbury to collect a new missionary nurse, Wendy Hamilton-White. Slim and with striking good looks, Wendy had graduated from Trinity College, Dublin, before working in London, first as a social worker, subsequently with disabled children, and then as a matron in a boarding school. Her experiences had led her in the direction of nursing, and she qualified SRN from the Nightingale Training School at St Thomas' Hospital in London.

Wendy had come to join the team to relieve Elim Hospital Matron Joyce Pickering for a year. Her introduction to the realities of life in the "operational area" of Rhodesia was abrupt. At the point that they turned off the tarred road in Inyanga onto the dirt track that led down through the bush towards the mission, my father handed round the cotton wool for my mother and Wendy to stuff in their ears and crash helmets to go on their heads. The truck cab was reinforced with steel plates and everyone was strapped in securely with shoulder harnesses. It was pouring with rain and the going was very slippery. As they drove down the road, they came across an army unit guarding a wrecked "Hyena", an armoured military vehicle that had detonated a mine a few hours earlier. They weaved their way in and out of several mine craters still surrounded by debris where other vehicles had been blown up. Wendy seemed to take it all in her stride in a very British way!

The day after her arrival, Wendy travelled with Joy in the mine-proofed Rhino to take a clinic together at Chiwarira. The rain was still pouring, and on their return journey, the Rhino stalled in a rapidly rising river. Joy could feel the force of the river lifting and moving the heavily armoured vehicle downstream.

Baba Jim, who had been driving, tried to get out but was nearly swept away by the raging water and they had to drag him back in. There seemed nothing that could be done.

Joy crossly thought that she had been saved from death by landmine. She had been spared in her encounter with guerrillas. Was she now to drown in a river? In fear, the nurses burst out in prayer. Then Wendy suggested praising God. Joy thought to herself that it sounded very good and spiritual but she didn't feel that there was much to praise for. Reluctantly she joined in, and before long they noticed that the water level was falling. Rescue was finally effected three and a half hours later! After a harrowing first two days in her newly adopted country, Wendy's reading that night was deeply comforting "When you pass through the waters, I will be with you; and through the rivers, they shall not overwhelm you."[22]

Wendy had come out in the nick of time to support Joy while Joyce had a much-needed home assignment. In contrast to the secondary school children who came from across the country, the hospital and church work was focused on the people of the area.

Elim Hospital had a capacity of about seventy beds, although often patients were only on their beds for ward rounds and medicine distribution. Many preferred to sleep under their beds, comfortingly familiar as most people used a sleeping mat on the floor. Evelyn Munembe worked alongside Joy and Wendy, Evelyn being particularly skilled at midwifery. Orderly Leonard Katerere ran the laboratory, and there were eight Red Cross nurses who were trained in the hospital.

Wendy joined the early morning service held each day in the open air for the staff and any patients who wanted to come along. Bible woman Mrs Mudangwe would frequently lead.[23] Relatives wandered along, sitting on the veranda to listen to the singing and overhear what was taught from the Bible. Mornings were busy with queues of outpatients, ward rounds and antenatal checks, but by lunchtime the hospital was usually quiet again. The patients' relatives would be cooking *sadza* on open fires in the kitchen area, where chickens pecked self-importantly, yellow dogs slept in the shade, and someone's small herd of cattle wandered through the hospital grounds, grazing as they went.

Every fortnight, Mission Aviation Fellowship pilots flew their tiny Cessna planes in low circles over the hospital, the sign that they were bringing in a doctor. Wendy grieved the absence of a full-time doctor, the operating theatre lying redundant and unused even as lives were lost. "A little boy was brought to us with an abdominal stab wound. He had been gored by *mombe* (cattle). The IV infusion we managed to start quickly blocked. He was in shock and our efforts to get another drip up failed. We lost him in the early hours of the morning."[24]

Upset as Wendy was about being unable to save the sick or injured who did somehow get to hospital, many more died at home, unseen casualties of the war's impact. Before the war, a network of clinics across the area was serviced by the nursing team twice a week, but this was reduced to monthly because of the risk of landmines. The transport network provided by the tough ubiquitous rural buses had stopped. Emergency cases that could not be handled by the nursing staff had to be transferred to Inyanga in the mine-proofed ambulance Rhino, a dangerous undertaking for the small team.

Regina Coeli Hospital was forty-five kilometres away. After that it was the large government hospital in Inyanga, ninety kilometres away.[25] Although there was much that could not be done under the pressure of the war, the hospital staff chose to persevere. Those patients who could, walked many kilometres. Some arrived on the back of a bicycle, or were pushed in wheelbarrows. Keeping the hospital open in the area was serving people and saving lives by shortening dozens of journeys.

* * *

Despite the relationships that had been built and the respect that had been shown to the missionary team's policy of neutrality by both sides, the missionaries struggled with the unrelenting burden of life in a war zone. My father captured the issues in a letter he wrote to the Provincial Director of Education in 1977. He described a palpable sense of isolation "behind the lines" for his colleagues. No buses were running, no mail was getting through, no light aircraft could land, and no resupply was possible without running risks or enduring losses that were increasingly unsustainable. All around, every day, there were the sights and sounds of combat. In addition, despite the relationships that existed between the missionary team and the Rhodesian Security Forces on one hand and through the local people and ZANLA commanders on the other, that understanding could be very fragile.

Even as the missionaries advocated for local people with the Rhodesian Security Forces, so black Christians in the area advocated for the missionaries with guerrillas. Unknown to the missionary team, Ephraim Satuku made arrangements to meet with ZANLA guerrillas. He took with him the Elim constitution on which black and white leaders were working together for the guerrillas to read, so they could see the desire to serve.[26] Some guerrilla groups might have contained some members sympathetic towards the Mission, but there were also other groups passing through who felt no such sympathy either for missionaries or for their own people.

Black Christians found themselves walking a precarious path, under intense scrutiny by the community as well as ZANLA guerrillas, facing unwelcome and often violent pressure from the Rhodesian police and army while seeking to maintain the "unity of the Spirit in the bond of peace"[27] with their white brothers and sisters. In mid-November, Isaiah Simbi, the church leader at Bhande, while walking through the bush on his way home from church, was accosted by three local men who told him the guerrillas would not like him going to church. Two mocked him for the Shona New Testament he was carrying in his hands. Frightened but determined, Isaiah told them that if he threw the Bible away it was like throwing God away, something he was not prepared to do. The men sneered at him, claiming that ZANLA had said that Jesus Christ was a white man and that those who went to church were "sell-outs" or collaborators. It was a powerful, threatening word to use, which still causes a cold shiver, not only for the implications of betrayal which lie behind it, but also for the memory of the inventive and varied ways in which "sell-outs" and those accused of such suffered before dying.

Soon, all churches in the area faced a sifting process of open opposition and indirect threat, whether linked to white missionaries or not. The Christian community was being winnowed to reveal a faithful handful.

Kambudzi Village lay south-east of Elim Mission, nested in the heart of steep hills and approachable only by roads that cut through narrow passes and crossed multiple rivers. In 1973, spiritual growth in the village had been sparked by a mass gathering there for a convention. The village headman had come to faith. The local people were glad to have built their own church in Kambudzi, with a clinic and primary school.

The community of faith at Kambudzi was led not by a missionary but by Ephraim Satuku, who had carefully prepared his flock for the hard times he foresaw, teaching them to meet in homes if there was reason to be afraid and openly in the church building when things were more secure. By mid-1977, other churches across the Ruwangwe plain had closed down completely, but Kambudzi remained open, the believers there plumbing war's dark depths, experiencing opposition and persecution but holding on in faith.

A GREATER DANGER

There's nothing easy about real forgiveness... When you want so much to carry out vengeful actions but you refuse them in an effort to forgive, it hurts. Why? Instead of making the other person suffer, you're absorbing the cost yourself... true forgiveness always entails suffering.

Tim Keller[1]

I leaned over daringly to round the bend on the rough bush track. Pebbles jumped and clacked beneath my tyres, skittering off to thud softly on the roadside. Exhilarated with the rush of speed, my brother whooped with delight on the pillion behind me. The low-pitched thumping bass of my father's big motorbike alongside us underscored the tenor refrain of our smaller machine. Sharing our excitement, Tim Evans grinned widely across the gap between us, his arms wrapped around my father.

The day before had been Good Friday, and people had poured into church. Tim, Paul, and I sat on long wooden benches wedged in among a mass of humanity as close to the front as we could get. Oblivious to the heat radiating down from the tin roof above us as it creaked and groaned beneath the sun's glare, we were captivated by the realism of a Passion Play put on by the Emmanuel students.

In the sleepy heat of Easter Saturday afternoon in April 1977, the low-flying Dakota had thundered over the Mission like a great ungainly crow. Turning slowly in a great sweeping curve, the military aircraft had settled ponderously to earth, disappearing behind a distant curtain of trees. Curious to find out what was going on, my father called us to join him as he rode to the airstrip a few kilometres away.

Rolling to a stop, we found the Dakota parked just off the end of the gravelled runway. Faces streaked with camouflage paint, a picket of heavily armed Rhodesian troops squatted beneath its shady wings. The soldiers were members of an elite rapid response unit flown in from a distant base, and not familiar with the area. As they stared sullenly at us in the breathless afternoon, they offered no greeting. The unspoken question of how we came to be unarmed and unharmed in such danger hung uneasily between us in the stifling air.

Expansive and charming, my father eased the tension with a few words of greeting and a joke. Eventually we were allowed to scramble inside the metal skin of the aircraft and explore its echoing interior. The afternoon sun streamed in through the square windows, the light turning the bare steel seats lining the ribbed sides of the plane into bowls of silver and shadow. Their occupants had been parachuted into a nearby battle.

The throbbing of a helicopter gunship grew louder. Ducking back out through the aircraft door, we jumped down onto the dusty airstrip. Turbine engine whining, the Alouette gunship touched down gently, flinging dust and dry grass in every direction. As the blades unceasingly chopped the air, a heavily laden armourer ran up to fling coppery coils of ammunition on board. As the door gunner wrestled with the heavy belts for his twin Browning machine guns, the chopper tilted forward as if in salute and raised a few inches above the dirt strip. The gunship slowly gained altitude and we followed it with our eyes, back down the long flat valley bottom. Other gunships were swinging and twisting above the savannah. Ferocious volleys of fire pouring into the bush below reached us as a muted, unwarlike popping. Paratroopers had already jumped all around Kagore Village. The helicopter gunships were circling, giving air support to the ground battle.

Death came that long, hot afternoon to seven guerrillas, killed in battle. Rhodesian troops would describe the afternoon's reckoning in callous military slang as "seven floppies slotted".[2] The nickname for dead guerrillas came from the slackness of their bodies, the way that heads drooped and swayed as the bodies were collected from the battlefield, carried or dragged to trucks or heaved into nets that were slung beneath helicopters to be taken to base for the body count and search for documents. Three guerrillas were captured. But two Rhodesian soldiers had also been killed.[3]

Twilight raced forward to engulf us as the sun dropped behind the ridge of mountains behind the Mission. Droning overhead, loaded with exhausted men, the Dakota lumbered westwards towards the far-distant base the Fireforce troops had come from. We turned for home and I raced along, enjoying the cool rush of wind after the scorching stillness of the afternoon. My father rode up close beside me. Taking his approach as a challenge, I opened the throttle to leap ahead. Eventually he caught me, yelling furiously and gesticulating wildly to slow down. When we got home he complained about my reckless riding to my mother, who added her words of discipline too.

Although just twelve years old, I recognized the irony in my father's concern about my excessive speed of fifty kilometres an hour instead of the stipulated forty. We had just spent an afternoon among the trappings of war, as spectators on the field of battle, deep in fiercely contested guerrilla country. Yet there was also something quietly reassuring about parents continuing to shape behaviour and uphold boundaries despite the abnormality of life outside our walls.

That evening, Paul and I rode on the back of the motorbike with our father, winding up the escarpment to the base camp above the Mission for a *braai*. Of course, it was dangerous to move at night, and to enter the base camp was always a risk, not because my father was afraid of the Rhodesian troops but because it might be misinterpreted by the guerrillas. But he was a sociable, gregarious man who loved being with people, and he couldn't resist the opportunities both to laugh and to share his faith. We sat around the fire in the open air under the rich canopy of the starlit sky, meat bubbling and spitting on the steel ploughshare disk sitting on the flames. The soldiers kept their weapons close at hand but the atmosphere was relaxed. One of the young soldiers showed Paul and me how to open bottles of Coke (or beer) without an opener. The talk and the laughter went on late, my father in the thick of the conversation, telling jokes and recounting stories.

As the evening wore on, the discussion became more serious. Young men who had been in battle that very afternoon, who were facing serious injury or death on a daily basis, wanted to ask questions about the meaning of life, about whether God existed, about what happened after death, about how to relate to God, whether it was possible to be forgiven. Lulled by the rumble of men's voices, Paul and I were nodding by the fire long before the conversation ended.

We rode home sleepily through the cool night on my father's motorbike, with Paul slumped over the tank in front of my father and me clinging on behind, sternly ordered not to fall asleep and fall off! Back home, Paul and I clambered into our pyjamas and then, clutching our bedding, we all stumbled through the darkness to the Evans' house. There we would sleep under one roof with other families and unmarried women, so we were all together if the worst should happen. Crowded into a small house as the missionary team was, I was delighted to be on a mattress on the floor in the same room as my parents with my brother beside me. Paul and I whispered to each other in the darkness until a curt word from my father ended our conversation.

It seemed only a moment later that there was the sound of a match strike flaring into light. Groggily looking up from my mattress, I saw my father climbing into his clothes and talking in low urgent tones to my mother, who was sitting up on the bed, lines of anxiety scored on her face. My father was on his way to the hospital to accompany one of the nurses called to attend to an emergency. That night he was called at 9.40 p.m. and returned at 1.45 a.m., then slept for only an hour before being called out again for another two hours. The demands of caring for his team and managing the situation had become a twenty-four hour, seven days a week task for my father. The strain was immense.

* * *

Seen through boyish eyes, the years of war brought unexpected excitements. It wasn't just the armoured vehicles to church, the motorbikes to ride on – but something more. "You should see the road to Inyanga! I was on it in the Rhino two weeks ago," my father wrote to my brother and me in March, once we were back at school. "It is so full of landmine craters that you could mistake it for the moon. We have decided not to use the Inyanga road for the time being. Our bread is getting very stale, though, and we are now eating stuff nearly two weeks old. It's not so bad if the crusts are cut off and if it is toasted and smothered in Marmite and jam and curry!"

Tim and Rachel Evans, my brother Paul, and I travelled

every six weeks between our boarding hostel in Salisbury and our homes in Katerere. So many landmines were being laid that Mission Aviation Fellowship flew us home for the holidays in their robust, high-wing, six-seater Cessna 210. MAF pilot Gordon Marshall was very thrilling to fly with. A former fighter pilot with the South African Air Force during the Korean War, Gordon would forget that he was only flying a Cessna. He would send his plane plunging down to get a closer look at an animal or to tightly circle a rocky outcrop so we could see it better. Coming in to land on the football pitch, he frightened my mother by approaching so low that it seemed as if he would hit a stone wall that marked the far end of the pitch. Hitting the throttle with split-second timing, he "blipped" the engine, hopping the wall, only to settle immediately on the far side to gain as much "runway" as possible for landing!

In February 1977, Gordon flew in a courageous young BBC reporter, Brian Barron, into the Mission. Barron reported to camera as he stood by the side of the Elim Hospital Rhino, with a vista of the mountains behind him. The reporter focused on the landmine issue which had stopped buses running, describing how Elim had bought a Rhino in order to keep church and ambulance services going. He emphasized the isolation of the Mission and that Elim missionaries had deliberately not sought government protection, but avoided carrying weapons, and this allowed them to continue effective ministry in the area. Barron had just come from Karanda Mission Hospital which had taken a very different approach, being transformed into an armed and fortified garrison, but seen as protected by and therefore aligned with the Rhodesian political system.

Barron went on to interview my father as students played volleyball behind him, the sweep of the Ruwangwe Valley across to the distant mountains of Mozambique completing the backdrop.[4] My father said he was aware of the incursions of ZANLA guerrillas pouring across the border from newly independent Mozambique. He mentioned the presence of the police and army very nearby. Barron asked a challenging question: "Would you be afraid if ZANLA came in to the Mission again?"

My father shrewdly responded, "I would be afraid if anyone came to our house in the middle of the night with a gun, even if it was a Welshman!"[5]

But Barron also heard my father reiterate the policy of not bearing arms, emphasizing that this would hinder his team's witness. In an apparently naive statement he said, "We have simply come to tell people about Jesus Christ." My father's approach of "telling people about Jesus" had led in some interesting directions. In his classical evangelical world view,[6] he believed it important to see people transformed through belief in Jesus Christ and then see the world put right through energetic action by those transformed individuals.

From a working-class Labour background in south Wales, my father was certainly no blind supporter of the status quo. He and other missionaries had seen the writing on the wall. They were aware of the aspirations of the young people they worked with on a daily basis. They had worked alongside local people, spoken the language, sought to meet them as equals, and through relationships of trust had heard how change was desired and longed for. They were often more keenly aware than the average white Rhodesian of the progress of the war as it unfolded around them. They were busy telling people about Jesus Christ, but within the broad parameters of that simple expression were also working hard to prepare young black Christians to be well positioned in a post-independence government.

As the intensity of the conflict flared, so the room for the "man in the middle" to manoeuvre between hammer and anvil continued to narrow. On 31 March, my father heard the news that Michael Pocock had been arrested on charges of "harbouring and assisting terrorists". Pocock, tall and softly spoken, was the Principal of St Mary's Mission School, an Anglican secondary school and one of Elim's closest neighbouring schools, about forty kilometres away. The next day, my father went to see him in jail in Umtali. Despite hostile questioning and hindrance by the prison guards, my father persisted, eventually helped by the prison governor who was a deacon in Umtali Baptist Church. Giving Pocock apples and Corrie ten Boom's *The Hiding Place* to read, my father heard Pocock describe how relieved he was to be in a prison cell. The terrible strain of managing his school in a combat zone was finished, so Pocock was sleeping well and able to eat more heartily than he had for months, despite being charged with a crime that carried the death penalty.

Two weeks later, Nicholas McNally, Pocock's lawyer, requested that my father testify at Pocock's trial on Monday 18 April 1977. Pocock was to be jointly tried with Carmelite Father Lawrence Lynch from Mount Melleray Mission. Pentecostal, Catholic, and Anglican experienced solidarity in this season of testing, despite their denominational differences. Over the weekend, the leadership team on the Mission met to pray together for my father as he prepared to testify.

As my father drove along the road to Inyanga on his way to the trial, just near Dumba's Store he caught sight of something lying at the bottom of a huge landmine crater. Scrambling down from the truck, he looked over the steep, crumbling crater's edge to see two ruined corpses slumped in the bottom of the crater. Retching, he stumbled back from the scene of horror and pulled away towards the nearby police camp to report what he had found.

Two villagers had tried to take advantage of the large government bounty offered for information. They had passed on details of guerrilla numbers and movements to the Rhodesian authorities, becoming collaborators, or "sell-outs" – the word that had so frightened Isaiah Simbi. In a tight-knit rural community, someone found them out and betrayed them. In turn, the sell-outs were tried in a makeshift guerrilla court. Found guilty and sentenced to death, the two men were dragged to the edge of one of the massive craters blasted in the dirt roads by anti-tank mines, and shot more than 115 times. Their shattered bodies were tumbled into the crater, the symbol of the power of the guerrillas.

My father went straight from a bloody, stinking reminder of the summary judgment that awaited those seen by the guerrillas as cooperating with the government to face the powerful weight of the state's anger towards any who were seen as cooperating with the guerrillas. It was a terrifying illustration of the dilemma in which so many in rural Rhodesia found themselves, caught between the hammer and the anvil.

The trial took place in a crowded Umtali court. In a scene redolent with irony, the main witness for the government prosecution was a ZANLA guerrilla. Wishing to surrender after an altercation within his section, the guerrilla had gone to Michael Pocock's house and forced him at gunpoint to call a Rhodesian Army base. Michael was to tell the army in advance that a guerrilla was there who did not want to be killed but to surrender. Army units arrived and, after a tense confrontation, took the guerrilla away for interrogation. The guerrilla had then revealed that his platoon had visited St Mary's Mission on more than one occasion, demanding food and supplies. One night heavily armed guerrillas had even joined in a school dance, jiving and twisting among the students. The bloodbath that would have resulted if the Rhodesian Army had ambushed the guerrillas during the dance didn't bear thinking about.

My father gave evidence for Pocock's defence and then was cross-examined by the prosecutor. He referred to the visit by ZANLA guerrillas to Elim Mission a year before, the report that was made, the guerrilla platoon being caught and a number killed by the army. Then my father had endured an agonizing wait for retribution until the guerrillas had killed someone else who was known to have informed. His bitter experience meant he spoke from the heart, clearly articulating the dilemma that was faced by missionaries living in "operational areas". Afterwards, the Anglican bishop congratulated him, and Carmelite nuns and priests expressed their gratitude for his willingness to stand with them. Pocock and Lynch were given three and a half years in jail, and subsequently deported.

Returning from the trial two days later, my father saw the bodies still rotting in the landmine crater. The stench was overwhelming. He heard from those living nearby that after the execution the guerrillas had ordered that no one was allowed to touch, to mourn for, or to bury the men, an unspeakable punishment in spiritual terms for the people of the area. The proper ceremonies could not be carried out, and thus the spirits of these two would be doomed to wander the earth forever as *ngozi* instead of becoming part of the pantheon of ancestral spirits gathered round each clan. Relatives of the two dead bounty seekers were desperate to bury the bodies and to illicitly carry out at least some of the necessary rituals, but they could not be seen to be disobeying the guerrillas or the same swift, crude justice might fall on them also.

My father went to the police camp to raise the issue again, to ask them why the dead bodies of two human beings remained on grotesque public display within a distressed community. He explained why the people could take no action themselves. He pleaded for action. So the police sent a detail out to the village the two men came from and rounded up people "at gunpoint" to dig the graves. For the relatives, this came as a double relief. At last the bodies could be buried and, owing to the element of a very public coercion, the families were protected from guerrilla retribution.

* * *

What was feared finally came upon us. The news came first to my mother through a radio message from the police in Katerere patched through to the phone of Audrey Greenshields, our host in Salisbury while my parents snatched a few brief days of respite during the school holidays.

Setting off at 6.00 a.m. on 9 May 1977, on a regular resupply trip to Salisbury in preparation for the start of the new school term, the Mission truck, driven by our friend Murewa, had detonated an anti-tank mine near Chikore School twenty kilometres from the mission.[7] Someone had been killed. The injured were being flown out by helicopter to Harare Central Hospital.

We were meeting my father in a bookshop and I wanted to break the news to him myself. I ran ahead along the long ribbon of hot pavement in the bright heat of the midday sun, bursting into the shop's cool dimness. My father was standing in a corner, reading, and lowered his book to see who was clattering in so noisily. A broad grin of welcome spread across his face as he saw it was his son. Suddenly, I didn't want to tell him, didn't want to be the one to wipe away his smile and end the peace of his few moments lost in a book. I stammered out a few sentences about going to find my mother together and that she had some news to pass on to him.

Still unaware, he made his few purchases and chatted merrily to me as I glumly trudged alongside him. Looking up, he saw my mother coming towards us and shouted a cheery greeting. With a few deft sentences my mother told him what we knew, and instantly, as I knew it would, his holiday mood vanished and a grim look came over his face. Together we were hurrying for the vehicle and then racing to Harare Hospital.

In the dim coolness of Harare Hospital I looked at Murewa but didn't immediately recognize him. His face was purple with bruising, filthy with diesel and dust. He was bewildered and unsure of where he was. Tears of pain had cut runnels through the dirt caked on his cheeks. Every movement he made brought a hiss of pain and fresh tears. There was a strange smell about him, the sharp odour of high explosive. We were told by the doctors that Murewa had broken his back. My father sat beside his bed, crushed to think that he might never walk again

Murewa was deeply distressed. Afraid of being caught in a burning vehicle, his driver's mate Daniel Sanhani had refused to be strapped in, despite Murewa's pleas. The blast had thrown Sanhani through the cab's steel roof, and his body had been found twenty metres away in the bush. Just two weeks before, Ephraim Satuku had spent time with Sanhani, pleading with him to get right with God. Sanhani had abruptly ended the conversation, telling Pastor Satuku that he would wait as most of his life was still before him and he would return to the issues when he was older.

Ronias, a young lad standing on the back of the vehicle, had been thrown clear and survived. The shock wave of the explosion had travelled through the steel truck frame and shivered the bone of his right leg to fragments, leading to its amputation.

A few days later I went with my father to the workshop where the Mission truck had been towed by the police. Together we looked at the blackened, shredded front section of the truck. The cab roof and the windscreen had been blown right off. My father didn't have the heart to photograph the wreckage. A pessimistic mechanic materialized by our side – sanctions, shortage of parts, chassis alignment problems – the list of issues and the time frame for expected repairs made my father blanch. New vehicles were expensive and very scarce. It was not just the replacement of the truck that was needed but also a solution to the challenge of resupplying the Mission along precariously dangerous routes.

As our brief turbulent break drew to a close, during an apparently chance conversation my father heard that Eagle

School, an elite prep school close to Umtali in the Vumba mountains, had been vacant since 1976. The same day he read a report in the newspaper. Facing similar issues to Elim Mission, Bonda Mission had moved their school from a rural area into an empty convent in Umtali. Intrigued, my father made further inquiries about Eagle School. On hearing his interest, the secretary of Eagle's board exclaimed, "You are heaven sent!" having previously tried to interest both police and army to take the school over, without success.

Eagle School was a sprawling campus of fifty hectares, more than 1,600 metres above sea level and just twenty-two kilometres from the eastern border city of Umtali. Crucially, there was only a very short section of dirt road which linked the school to a tar road, sharply reducing the landmine risk. Landmines were difficult to bury under a sealed road surface, as the disturbed surface would be easily spotted. The campus was reported to be beautiful, with playing fields, tennis courts, an open air stage, and a swimming pool surrounded by woods and gardens.

* * *

On Tuesday 17 May we drove up as a family to Umtali to visit Eagle School. The huge kitchens were dark and empty and forbidding, the swimming pool had turned iridescent green and was choked with pearly chains of frogspawn, and the neat layout of the grounds was blurred beneath luxuriant unkempt high grass. Silence brooded over an abandoned campus intended to be alive with young people. But the beauty of the crags surrounded us with wonderful views whichever way we looked, out across the whole of the Zimunya Valley and the mountains beyond. Paul and I revelled in the excitement of visiting what my father said might be our "new house". We turned on the light switch in the middle of the day just to enjoy the sight of the light coming on, the marvel of parquet flooring and a fireplace against the mountain chill, our own rooms instead of sharing, and just possibly not needing to be away at boarding school any longer but coming to live at home with Mum and Dad. What a world of possibility Eagle School presented!

One hundred and fifty kilometres away in Katerere, dusk was falling as a troop of soldiers on horseback galloped on to the Mission.[8] Rhodesian Grey's Scouts, a mounted unit, rampaged throughout the compound. A small knot of horsemen rode up to Joy's house. When she came out to find out what was going on, they brusquely demanded coffee. Roy Lynn came home from his workshop to find his kitchen full of men in camouflage. The Scouts burst into an evening meeting being run by Mary Fisher. Rushing through the corridors of the school, armed men crashed through doors into classrooms full of students doing their homework, frightening them terribly. Mai Chaka, trying to prevent the mounted infantry entering the courtyard leading to the girls' quarters – an area of the school that not even my father would go into – was brushed aside as the men, uncouth and crude, went into each girl's room "looking for terrorists". Eventually they withdrew as night fell, leaving the entire Mission complex in a state of shock. My father protested vigorously to the police at the base camp above the mission. The member-in-charge was very apologetic, calling the Grey's Scouts troopers "animals". More than just inter-service rivalry, there were signs of deep disquiet in the police about the way the war was being prosecuted by branches of the military.

On 2 June the missionaries met to discuss the possible move of Emmanuel Secondary School to the premises of Eagle School. Intense discussion preceded a unanimous decision to move the school. On 6 June the move was announced to the school, and a wave of excitement rippled through the student body. When my father said there was a swimming pool, the students burst into spontaneous applause.

The next day, my father went to the police camp to drop off the mail and was invited to join the troops for a Coke. Chatting to Rhodesian Army Intelligence corporal Frank Hamp-Adams, my father thanked him for his help in tackling the ill-disciplined behaviour of the Grey's Scouts. A small knot of Rhodesian servicemen sat in a semicircle on the edge of the escarpment with my father among them, the sun setting behind the men as they looked out across the Katerere valley, watching as dusk crept up each of the kopjes on the plain.

In the clear, peaceful evening, his chair tilted back, Frank took a sip of his drink and turned to my father to ask a straight question: "What's all this about being 'born again'? What could it possibly mean?" It turned out that Ian Bond, a friend of Frank's and a well-known Rhodesian rugby star, had become a Christian, something which had unsettled and intrigued Frank. As my father talked about who God was and pointed out what he saw as Frank's need of forgiveness and reconciliation to God through Jesus Christ, others scoffed then turned to other issues. But the young corporal, remarking that he had never heard anything like it before, remained very interested and warmly engaged as the conversation wound on well into nightfall.

Five days later, Frank Hamp-Adams picked up Headman Fombe from his village. As they drove back towards the base camp the vehicle hit a landmine. Headman Fombe, on the side of the vehicle directly over the landmine, was instantly killed. Thrown from the vehicle, the young soldier was critically injured when the vehicle rolled on top of him.[9] He died in the helicopter evacuating the injured. My father had known Headman Fombe for many years, and knew that Fombe had heard the claims of the gospel many times without responding. My father also recognized that there was an honest hunger for truth in Frank; he knew that Frank had a wife and young children, and grieved for their loss. In the quietness of dawn in the camp, in moments snatched from the bustle of daily life in an operational military base, in those final bloody moments hovering between life and death, had Frank turned in faith to Christ? The heavy weight of grief, the increasing numbers of lives lost of people they knew pressed down heavily on my parents.

* * *

The planned move to Eagle School hit an unexpected obstacle. The Elim Pentecostal Church Headquarters in the United Kingdom edged close to insisting the missionaries stay put in Katerere. An increasingly intense exchange of letters led John Smyth, a bluff, astute leader, to travel out from the UK to spend two weeks with the team in Rhodesia. He wanted a slow, unhurried visit to create space to listen, pray, and reflect. A visiting government doctor voiced the wisdom of this approach to Wendy Hamilton-White: "At least your Mission sends someone to talk to you – others just send a telegram." Smyth's willingness to invest time and to join the missionaries in their dangerous situation was warmly welcomed by the missionary team.

Bringing an outside perspective, Smyth saw that the Rhodesians were either fleeing the country or withdrawing steadily from the rural areas under pressure from the violence there while preparing to defend the cities. He jotted down, "There is no doubt that the [Rhodesian government] is no longer confident of victory and the [ZANLA] forces are winning the war of nerves. Their domination of the people is complete in the bush areas."

He recognized the pressures the rural church was facing: "A flourishing church work opened at Chiwarira and in another village closer to the Mission and this work has been closed because the local [ZANLA] commander has forbidden the villagers to attend… the station has the air of a besieged city."

Within forty-eight hours, Smyth saw the situation very

differently from within. The challenge of running the school with a single usable road, heavily mined and vulnerable to ambush, meant that resupply to the school was becoming impossible. Coyly, Smyth wrote, "There appears to be knowledge about when not to travel and so far this knowledge has proved reliable. The recent incident with the lorry was at a place outside the area."

As Smyth joined a meeting held to thrash the issues out, he quickly realized there were matters too sensitive to communicate in writing. Previous policy to create a completely black staff meant that new staff for the school would not be provided from the UK. But graduate black teachers would not come to the area, to face the danger of bush war or the uncertainty surrounding their jobs. Few schools were still operating in the area, and potential teachers knew this. They doubted the ability of Emmanuel Secondary School to remain open. In addition, applications were down despite the standard of education provided and the desperate shortage of school places across the country. Parents of new students from other parts of the country saw the area as too dangerous. There were not enough students from the immediate area round the school to keep it open.

Smyth realized that a decision to keep Emmanuel Secondary School in Katerere would in fact be a decision to shut the school down completely.

A second option was complete withdrawal to Eagle School of all Emmanuel Secondary School staff with a simultaneous transition of medical and local church work to national leadership. Local church leaders were unanimous in their support of this option. The presence of missionaries put them in considerable difficulty in the complexities of the war zone.

Rising to the challenge in the grinding pressures of war, Ephraim Satuku and Pious Munembe, among others, all graduates of the Elim schools, were embracing their responsibilities gladly. Black church leaders considered that the church would survive and possibly increase. Ephraim Satuku made it clear that the withdrawal of the missionaries would mean national Christians would take up their responsibilities, but while the missionaries remained present they would not. Smyth noted that because of war-related violent intimidation, anti-Christian propaganda, and breakdown in transport links there had been a diminution of the church work and "all hope of the future must be entrusted to the leaders [who] appeared to welcome the unexpected responsibility. The distinct impression was gained that they wished to prove something to themselves. There is the possibility that left to themselves the work will, after a time, expand in Katerere."[10]

Finally, there was the option of recalling all the missionary staff back to the UK, of withdrawing from Rhodesia completely. But the missionary team rejected withdrawal as a breach of a duty of care of Elim to the young people at the school who had entrusted their future to the staff. The record of the meeting tersely noted the conclusions of those present: "Withdrawal… would be an absolute rout… of Christianity and the gospel whose ambassadors fled in the face of trouble. The school does not serve the area. It serves Rhodesia. The children in the school must not be betrayed."

The decision to remain was not taken by people out of touch with reality or living in some state of perpetual divine serenity. John Smyth recognized the emotional impact that life in a combat zone was having. Those with children were not at ease, one taking sleeping pills to overcome night nerves. Mary Fisher was struggling with migraines. Sue Evans and Wendy Hamilton-White shared that they were frequently very nervous. The base camp above the Mission erupted at times with gunfire, as Rhodesian soldiers carried out target practice. Each time this happened, one missionary told Smyth, "the fear grips more tightly".

A former evangelist at Chifambe had recently passed on a chilling message that the missionary team were "destined to suffer dreadful things". My father was told by friendly contacts in the Rhodesian police that they had intercepted correspondence indicating that ZANLA guerrillas were about to send him a list of demands. However he responded would inevitably have severe repercussions. "In human terms," wrote John Smyth, "it is hard to forecast how long the station will last out." The courageous decision to refuse to betray their students and continue the school in a different location was taken by those very aware of their human frailty yet perceiving a divine call to persevere.

The missionaries recognized that the battle for control of the Katerere area was over. It had become a border transit point for ZANLA. But they were under no illusions that the move to Eagle School meant security. In fact, John Smyth reported that his colleagues "recognize that there is no safety in Rhodesia that can be guaranteed. They see that in Eagle School there may be a possibility of a greater danger." That they might be killed was frankly discussed among the team. They came to the consensus that they would continue to take what precautions they could and then trust in God.

The decision to move Emmanuel Secondary School to Eagle School in the Vumba mountains was taken. On 11 July 1977 there was a formal handover of churches, hospital, school buildings, houses, and all other infrastructure along with full responsibility for leadership, maintenance, and budgeting to a national leadership team, headed by Ephraim Satuku.

* * *

Just a few days after that historic moment a ferocious backlash came. On Saturday 16 July, Pastor Ephraim Satuku, a gentle, slight man and no match for anyone physically, was summoned to a clandestine meeting with a group of ZANLA guerrillas. He had been targeted by a member of the Elim Church who was a Red Cross nurse working at Kambudzi Clinic. She had been disciplined by the church leadership for stealing a watch, for withholding money paid to her by patients, and for causing divisions within the local church.[11] Furiously angry, she sought a local guerrilla group, claiming that Ephraim had forbidden her to give medicines to the guerrillas. Frightened, the village headman supported her allegations.

A summary court had been convened. During the proceedings, with great courage, Ephraim said that whatever the decision of the court he would continue to share the good news of Jesus Christ. Despite Ephraim's denial of the false charge, he was sentenced to death for refusing to allow Kambudzi Clinic to give the guerrillas medicines. He was stripped and laid on his back to be beaten to death with heavy wooden poles. As the execution was about to start, the guerrilla commander advocated for Ephraim, asking if he could be turned over and beaten on his back instead. He was rolled over and severely beaten.

Then one of the group rolled him over again and was about to start beating him on the abdomen in order to rupture internal organs and kill him. In another courageous act, the commander stood between the would-be executioner and Ephraim, saying that he believed that Ephraim was innocent. Astonishingly, the commander declared he was willing to die with the innocent victim if the beating did not stop. The accuser's husband, a teacher at Kambudzi School, was ordered by the guerrillas to load Ephraim into a wheelbarrow, barely alive as he was, and push him twenty-five kilometres on rough roads to Elim Hospital.

Ephraim was so badly injured that he would not be able to walk unaided for several months. Seeing Ephraim's terribly bloodied, battered body lying in a hospital bed moved my father to both sorrow for his dear friend and colleague and anger towards the woman who had lied to the guerrillas in order to exact her revenge on Ephraim. As he sat next to Ephraim's bed, my father told him that he would be writing to the Ministry of

Education to request a transfer for the teacher from Kambudzi. This would force his wife to leave as well, ending her involvement in the church and her troublemaking.

Yet Ephraim's response, whispered through swollen lips, was to plead with my father and ask him not to take that step. Instead he wanted to offer forgiveness to both the nurse and the village headman who had also falsely accused him. Stunned by Ephraim's response, my father felt deeply convicted. The student had become the teacher. Ephraim, through his desire to offer love and forgiveness to those who had wished him so much harm and had done him so much evil, engraved a lesson on my father's heart that he was never to forget.

Pinned to Ephraim's body slumped in the wheelbarrow had been a letter: "Forward with Revolution" was scrawled across the top, with "ZANLA Forces" printed neatly below. It was addressed to the nursing team at the Mission hospital. The writers referred to the nearly fatal beating as Ephraim being "taught a lesson [as] he was intruding in our affairs". In the letter, the nurses were asked to take good care of Ephraim, the guerrillas being aware that nurses might be afraid of assisting someone who had been so severely disciplined by them. There was a demand for the sum of Rh$100 (£1,300 in 2015) to be brought from the teachers at Emmanuel directly to the guerrillas after the Sunday service at Kambudzi the following week. It was signed simply, "From Comrades".

Together with Pious Munembe, my father went to the Kambudzi service the following Sunday. He did not collect money from the teachers but took Rh$100 with him from the Emmanuel School safe. He took the opportunity to preach. All seemed to go as normal and there were no new faces in the congregation. The service came to an end and people gathered to talk, but no one said anything out of the ordinary. Just as my father was climbing into the truck, with a sigh of relief, to drive back to the Mission, a hand was laid on his. He turned to see a youth, who simply told my father to follow him as there were some people who wished to see him. When Pious heard what was about to happen, he courageously declared that he would go too. Together, Pious and my father walked into the bush on a fearful journey.

Acutely aware of Ephraim's broken body lying in a hospital bed just a few kilometres away, smashed and torn a few days earlier by the very men they were going to see, my father and Pious picked their way along narrow dusty paths to a mountain some eight kilometres from the road. Finally, they were led into the guerrilla camp between Kambudzi and Masoso. As they came to a clearing at the top of a slope, they looked up and saw silhouetted against the skyline two sentries with their distinctive AK-47s held at half-port. There were a further twelve ZANLA guerrillas waiting for them in the camp. My father went up to each of them in turn, clapping in the traditional way and greeting each politely in Shona, and then sat down on the earth. The commander ordered my father to sit on a blanket, which he took as an encouraging sign.

My father explained why they had decided to move Emmanuel Secondary School to the Vumba. The questions came thick and fast for the next hour, some very awkward. A guerrilla asked why the Mission vehicles were mine-proofed. This seemed to him to be a sign of mistrust by the Mission personnel. Did the missionaries not believe that the guerrillas would make sure they got the message if and when landmines were planted? Breathing a prayer and thinking quickly, my father explained that sometimes patients, especially expectant mothers, had to be rushed to Inyanga in the middle of the night when it would be impossible for any warnings to be sought. This explanation seemed to be accepted.

Finally, the guerrillas assured the two men that no missionaries would be harmed if they stayed, but they understood the reasons

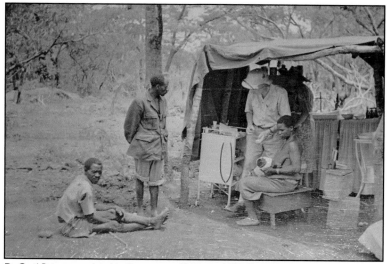

Dr Cecil Brien at work in his dispensary at Katerere, 1951. From this humble beginning would develop a 100 bed hospital and a network of surrounding clinics.

Dr Mary Brien stands at the door of the Briens' kitchen and dining room, which became an impromptu operating theatre!

A rendezvous that changed the course of their lives. Peter Griffiths and Brenda Hurrell meet in the Eastern Highlands of Rhodesia, 1961.

Surrounded by crowds of well-wishers, Peter and Brenda Griffiths walk joyfully to their wedding reception on 13 December 1963.

Paul Griffiths, Jamie Mudondo, Andrew Mukwewa, and Stephen Griffiths playing outside the back door in Katerere, 1969.

Paul and Stephen Griffiths perch on rocks being readied for yet more foundations as new classroom blocks rise from the ground at Emmanuel Secondary School, 1972.

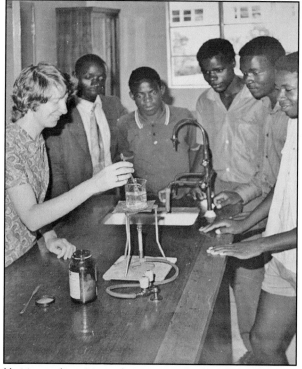

Musician, mathematician, and scientist, a smiling Mary Fisher demonstrates an experiment to her chemistry class in the peaceful days of 1974.

Philip, Suzanne, Timothy, Rachel, and Rebecca Evans about to leave for Rhodesia, 1975. Within twenty-four hours, they would be refused entry to Rhodesia and deported back to the UK.

The rain-greened Ruwangwe hills and neat thatched roofs of mission homes behind her, nurse Joy Bath cheerfully cares for a colleague's baby in the local style, 1976.

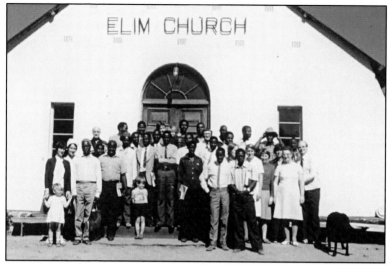

A crucial conference where missionaries transferred authority to their national colleagues in 1977. Ten of the thirteen missionaries and children visible in this picture would be murdered a year later.

As the war gathered pace, so civilians began to pay an increasing price. The wreckage of an Elim Mission lorry after detonating an anti-tank mine, 1977. Incredibly, everyone walked away – that time.

To counter the threat of landmines, my father bought an armoured vehicle from the military to be re-purposed as an ambulance. Nurses Joy Bath and Joyce Pickering pose in the "Rhino" in front of our house, 1977.

Science teacher and librarian Peter and Sandra McCann with their children Philip and Joy, 1977. The tragic death of their first-born, Paul, bound them closer to one another and the people they felt called to serve.

Arriving in 1977, nursing sister Wendy Hamilton White was the last to join the missionary team. She was immediately plunged into the intensity of the war, but responded with courage and faith.

Hospital matron Joyce Pickering and mission maintenance man Roy Lynn fell in love, marrying in 1977 and returning to serve in an increasingly unstable and violent Rhodesia.

Outstanding leaders, Pastor Ephraim Satuku and Headmaster Pious Munembe steered the church, hospital, and school work safely through violently chaotic and fear-filled days, 1979.

ZANLA guerrillas passing through Elim Mission on their way to the nearby Echo Assembly point during the tense days of the 1979 ceasefire, shortly before Zimbabwe's independence.

Now leading the Elim work across Zimbabwe, Pious and Evelyn Munembe reunited with Stephen Griffiths, 2016.

for moving. At that point the platoon commander asked if a collection had been taken up among the teachers. My father responded that he could not do that as it would cause the teachers to leave. He quickly added that he had brought the required Rh$100 with him that he had taken from the general school funds, but this left him with a problem. How would he record this in the accounts? As a Christian, he explained that he could not lie, but he also could not enter into his books, "Gift to the comrades".

At this, Pious seemed to get a little nervous and blurted out, "Give them Rh$50!"

One of the combatants who had been sitting on a tripod-mounted machine gun throughout the conversation came to my father's rescue, "If he can't fiddle the books for Rh$100, by the same principle he can't do it for R$50!"

The commander said quietly, "Well, I'm not forcing you, but we would like a contribution."

Astonishingly, my father responded, "Well, if you are not forcing me I'll keep the money!"

With that, they were ushered out of the group and the young *mujiba* who had led them to the camp took them back out through the bush again.

All this time, my mother was waiting in an agony of not knowing what was happening, all too aware of the very narrow escape from death that Ephraim Satuku had recently endured. All that Paul and I knew was that my father had missed his Sunday lunch.

* * *

The move from Katerere to the Vumba began to get under way. The first two lorry loads of equipment were safely delivered across 200 kilometres of demanding roads. Teacher Ian McGarrick worked with Phil Evans late into the night to load the truck with a third five-tonne load and then left at 7.30 a.m. on 22 July 1977, bound for Eagle School.

About 11.00 a.m. that day, while my parents were enjoying a cup of tea, there was a banging at the door. My father opened it and, to his astonishment, a filthy, blackened Ian, stinking of diesel and bleeding from the ears, staggered in. About twenty-five kilometres from Elim, the lorry had detonated an anti-tank mine.[12] The blast wave had ruptured Ian's eardrums. The front axle of the lorry was torn off, bursting the tyres filled with water and drenching those in the cab. Ruptured fuel lines leading into the engine beneath them had also sprayed out fountains of diesel. As the dust had settled in the stunned silence following the massive roar of the blast, so the dust had settled slowly down onto their soaking diesel-covered bodies, leaving them filthy. All strapped in, no one had been seriously injured.

Incredibly, the lorry had remained upright despite ploughing tens of metres down the road with its front axle blown off. Dazed and in shock, the first thing Ian had done after the blast was to quietly unbuckle himself, step out of the wreckage of the cab, and wander along the road and in the bush collecting the hundreds of letters scattered by the shredding of the mailbags caught in the explosion. Slowly, his senses returned and he set off to walk through the hot morning back to Elim.

Ian's confused collection of the mail meant a letter stained and splattered with diesel and dirt was eventually pressed into my hands. In the top corner was a four-cent Rhodesian stamp depicting a reedbuck. On a single sheet of paper, my mother had written a gentle letter, full of homely detail. The wandering family dog Scamp had come home the night before. Our toys were safely packed in trunks. Our books had been wedged into a bookcase and all loaded onto the very lorry that would carry her letter to the nearest post office. But that letter had never found its way into the postal system.

Somehow my father persuaded a recovery truck to come out from Umtali to recover the vehicle. The only way the driver would agree was with an army escort. In a hurry to get the job done, the recovery truck driver took up the tow then raced away. Excessive speed caused him to roll the Mission truck on the first bend. The entire cargo was ruined: school desks, beds, laboratory equipment, Sandra McCann's and Sue Evans' crockery, and all our toys and books, so carefully packed by my mother. The mine blast and the subsequent fiasco of attempted recovery meant tens of thousands of pounds worth of damage was done.

On Sunday 24 July my father went out to Sachiwo Church with Joy Bath and then beyond to meet Chief Katerere and tell him formally that the move was under way. School had closed three weeks early to enable the move to take place. My father spoke at school assembly on the morning of Wednesday 27 July. He took a text from Isaiah:[13] "For you shall go out in joy and be led forth in peace; the mountains and the hills before you shall break forth into singing, and all the trees of the field shall clap their hands." It was his last assembly before we left as a family for a furlough in the United Kingdom.

One of the boys stood up and gave my father a gift and made a short speech. "*Mudhara*, we are very sorry you are going. We love you. You sometimes scream at us but we still love you… Best of all, through you, many of us have come to know the Lord."

Three buses came on 29 July to take nearly 200 boarders to the city of Umtali from where they would disperse, making their individual journeys home. "The children left in high spirits," my mother jotted down in her diary, the sound of singing, laughter, and clapping coming from the vehicles, their joy echoing back from the surrounding hills as engines revved and roared and they pulled away under the midday sun.

The short column of buses had travelled sixty kilometres down the road when the road suddenly erupted under the first bus with an ear-shattering roar as it hit an anti-tank mine. Top student in Form 3, Leonard Bhunu, was hit by shrapnel, which sliced open a major vessel in his neck. In shock, Leonard flung himself down the steps of the bus and fled aimlessly down the road. Blood pumped from his neck, splashing across his clothes, great gouts raining down and raising puffs of dust in the road, marking his bloody staggering trail. Frightened, not knowing how to help, his friend Thomas Muripira ran with him. Finally, Leonard slowed to a drifting, faltering walk before collapsing onto the packed soil, blood pooling on the red earth. Cicadas shrilled as Leonard died in the searing afternoon light, with Thomas weeping and praying at his side.

Daniel Zvakona Bye, the school clerk's younger brother, also died where he sat, torn by flying metal. Jotham Munyarari lost his leg. The remaining students, some injured, poured, terrified and deafened, out of the bus onto the road. Horn blaring, the second bus roared on past without stopping, the driver pushing on through, alarmed faces peering out from the bus windows at the nightmare scene. The third bus pulled up. The driver, wearing a baby's bonnet on his head and apparently tipsy, roared at the students standing forlornly there, cajoling and forcing all to climb on board despite the fact that many were desperately frightened to do so.

But the guerrillas often planted landmines close together, hoping to destroy not only one vehicle but also any others that might attempt rescue. Just metres further on, the grossly overloaded third bus hit a second landmine. The front of the bus burst into flames, blocking the only exit. The blast trapped the driver, the inferno incinerating him in his seat. Waves of heat and flames roared backwards, licking at the students packed in the seats and aisle. But the explosion had also blown out every one of the bus windows. The young people, clamouring, shouting, and praying in the superheated air within the narrow metal confines of the bus, squeezed their way out through the windows, dropping on shoulders, heads, hips, and knees onto the hard gravel road below. Every student escaped from the burning bus alive, even Patrick Mandisodza, crippled by polio and unable to move as quickly as the others.

But all their belongings piled on the roof and in the aisles of the bus were destroyed. The mines had been planted after the buses had travelled down the lonely road to collect the students but before they returned along the same route. Supporting one another, limping along and carrying the injured, the students trudged to the abandoned St Mary's Mission not far away, formerly run by the deported Michael Pocock. There they found shelter for the night.[14]

As dusk was falling, the police brought news of the attack to my parents back on the Mission. My father lurched backwards on hearing what had happened. Such dreadful news was like a physical blow to him. Missionaries and staff alike spontaneously made their way to the church, which filled with the sound of keening and loud crying. "O God," called Mary Fisher, "how much more? We can't take any more." The broken sobs turned into prayer, with Mai Chaka leading and encouraging the people to sing as they wept before God.

Courageously, my parents got into a pickup truck and drove a long, circuitous route along the Mozambique border to Inyanga to get help from the Rhodesian Army to escort replacement buses in to the abandoned school to bring the students out. When my parents arrived at St Mary's with the buses, food, and a military escort, many of the students cried to see them, and gathered round to tell their stories. The young people climbed on the buses which turned for Umtali, where they were met by Christian folk Gerald and Annette McCullough with food and blankets.

Unaware of the news, the Byes were waiting for the buses, joyful at the prospect of seeing their son Daniel again, only for their joy to turn instantly to grief as they learned of his death coming home for the holidays.

Together with Lieutenant Colonel Peter Browne, officer commanding the Fourth (Manicaland) Battalion of the Rhodesia Regiment, my father travelled back to the scene in a convoy of military trucks. The devastated hulks of the two buses lay close together, silent on the deserted road. A litter of broken trunks, torn suitcases, exercise books, school reports, papers, and clothing lay scattered about the dirt road and into the bush on each side. Hurriedly, my father worked alongside the troops to collect all that they could, loading the jumbled assortment into the vehicles. Official identification of the bodies of the two students killed in the first blast was needed, so my father said he would do it. The body bags were opened and my father looked down at Leonard Bhunu and Daniel Bye. In that bleak moment, he held on to the promises of God, solaced by knowing that both young men had made professions of faith in Jesus Christ during their time in Emmanuel Secondary School.

Having seen the students safely delivered to Umtali,[15] having met with and sought to bring comfort to the grieving parents of Daniel Bye, and having made arrangements for the transport of the bodies of their students, my parents wearily clambered back into their pickup truck to return to the Mission. But after the intense activity of the day and the long hours on the road, they were unable to complete their journey before dark and had to stay in a hotel. They went for a walk around the edges of a mountain lake, attempted a game of snooker, and enjoyed a meal together. Poignantly my mother recorded, "The Lord gave us a little time of luxury and relaxation."

Over the months to come, when school resumed, teachers were to describe how the bus explosions resurfaced again and again through vivid descriptions in students' English essays, the violence depicted in art classes, and unpleasant physical symptoms were reported by survivors to Wendy, who was working as the school nurse. Some found a deeper meaning in their traumatic experience. Student Patrick Mandisodza wrote to my parents, "Christ showed me at the landmine incident that death can come at any time so we must be prepared and waiting in faith."

* * *

The school's five-tonne truck having been destroyed by a landmine, the rhythm of the move could not be maintained in time for the school to reopen in its new location at the start of term. My father decided to hire a removal company, but they agreed to help only if a Rhodesian Army escort was provided for their enormous trucks. Lieutenant Colonel Peter Browne offered to personally lead the military escort in the final move.

Those early days of August 1977 were a frenzied flurry of packing. A single massive move meant hundreds of beds, desks, chairs, cupboards, laboratory equipment, and thousands of textbooks all had to be readied for loading. The households of all the teachers also had to be moved to Eagle School. Several loading points were chosen across the Mission, and veritable mountains of cargo began to appear at each as houses, classrooms, school kitchens, and boarding hostels were emptied.

My mother went out to Bhande Church on that final Sunday in Katerere. Isaiah Simbi spoke, choosing Luke 21:17–19 as his text, "*Uye muchavengwa nevose nekuda kwezita rangu. Asi hakungatongoparari ruvhudzi rwemusoro wenyu. Mukutsungirira kwenyu wanai mweya yenyu.*" "You will be hated by all for my name's sake. But not a hair of your head will perish. By your endurance you will gain your lives." The women gathered round my mother after the service, praying fervently for her.

Attending the main Manjanja Elim Church, my father stayed on the Mission. Ephraim Satuku, still frail and weakened by his beating, had been helped into church that morning. My father had been asked to preach on the story of Paul's final message to the church at Ephesus, "And now, behold, I am going… constrained by the Spirit, not knowing what will happen to me there, except that the Holy Spirit testifies to me that… afflictions await me. But I do not account my life of any value nor as precious to myself, if only I may finish my course and the ministry that I received from the Lord Jesus, to testify to the gospel of the grace of God."[16] Weeping as he heard my father speak, Ephraim left the service, overcome with emotion.

Peter McCann left for the Vumba, leading a small party driving a pickup truck, the old Mission Land Rover and the white-painted armoured Rhino, all packed with as much as they could carry. The huge Glens Removals lorries and trailers rolled on to the Mission with four military vehicles accompanying them, as agreed. They were dispatched to the loading points across the Mission, and my mother marvelled at the skill of the removals teams, rapidly dismantling the great heaps of furniture and equipment and stowing them compactly inside the great trucks. Rhona cooked vast steaming bowls of *sadza ne muriwo* for the sweating teams of men, black and white working alongside one another.

As the dusk grew dense, the packing slowed to a stop. Not all was loaded but there was no more room. Ephraim and Winnie Satuku, Wendy White, Pious and Evelyn Munembe, Phil Evans, and my parents met to eat together and to pray. Uncertain of his ability to control his emotions, Ephraim had asked my mother to share from the Scriptures after the dishes were cleared from the table. She picked up on themes mentioned by Isaiah Simbi the previous Sunday, where Jesus had offered reassurance to his disciples in the face of persecution.

In the wavering glow of the bulbs, flickering in time with the distant chugging of the generator, my mother reminded the small group of friends, those she regarded as her brothers and sisters in Christ, to look up, to remain steadfast, to watch and pray. Capable and privately emotional as she usually was, she struggled to hold back her tears as she looked around the table at the faces she knew so well.

In an echoing, empty house, every movement noisy, my parents, Phil Evans, and Wendy Hamilton-White tossed and turned on camp beds. No one could sleep. Early the next morning, my mother's precious piano was embedded in mattresses and wrestled into its reserved spot. The removal trucks crawled up the escarpment to the police camp above the Mission and waited for the military escort to join them.

As a final sting in the tail, my father saw Ephraim's brother David Satuku and his friend Albert Fungirai being held, awaiting interrogation in the wire pens. He went over to talk and pray with them while the military vehicles were readied. Colonel Browne summoned my parents and Wendy to ride in his command vehicle at the front of the convoy. Soldiers held their rifles as steps to help the women climb up the high-sided military truck. With one hand on his revolver, Colonel Browne shouted, "Mount up!" and the convoy was under way.

The pace felt dreadfully slow for my parents, atop the lead vehicle. Would they detonate a landmine? How would an ambush come? Would they even see the steel fingers of bullets feeling their way towards the target? Maybe without warning, the windscreen would suddenly star and shatter as the first rounds smashed into the vehicle, into flesh and blood and bone.

Overheating, one of the removal vehicles juddered to a halt. Soldiers spilled rapidly off their trucks, fanning out to set up a protective perimeter. A fan belt had broken, and Wendy offered her tights as an emergency repair. Then one of the giant removal trucks, towing a trailer up a long hill, ground to a halt, unable to climb the slope under the load. So the trailer was unhitched, a towrope fashioned, and a military vehicle inched the trailer to the top of the hill.

It took six hours to travel the first ninety kilometres, to Inyanga. Before nightfall, the entire convoy had safely arrived at Eagle School in the chilly heights of the Vumba. Students working for their school fees during the holidays descended on the trucks, rapidly unloading them into houses and classrooms. As the shadows grew long, so the vehicles were away in good time to reach Umtali before dark.

Still on the Mission, Phil Evans made sure that the remaining cargo which would not fit into the trucks was secured. Bunch of keys in hand, he went around the secondary school, ensuring that doors and windows were locked, then placed the keys in Ephraim Satuku's hands. Phil had four hours of hard riding ahead of him, heading for the capital city, back to Sue, Tim, Rachel, and Rebs who were preparing to meet his mother, coming for a long-awaited holiday in Rhodesia with her family.

Leaping onto his powerful motorbike and cramming his helmet onto his head, he gunned the motor then raced off, dust spurting from beneath his tyres. Long after he had roared past, the powder-fine dust trail marked his path, hanging in the still hot air above the Katerere plain.

EAGLE SCHOOL

Let it come – not what will, for there is no such thing – but what the eternal thought wills for each of us, has intended in each of us from the first.

George MacDonald[1]

A dark, brooding canopy of trees enfolded the winding ribbon of road that climbed steeply south-east from the frontier town of Umtali up into craggy granite mountains. So often shielded in swirling cloud, the Vumba mountains derived their name from the Shona *bvuma*, or mist. Like giant serpents glimpsed in the cool jungle twilight, creepers hung from the soaring boughs far overhead. The thick, luxuriant undergrowth of ferns and mosses was constantly slick, moist with the leavings of the mist and alive with the rustle and quiver of small, secret living things. Frilled, coloured fungi sprouted in terraced curves from crumbling, rotted boughs. Fine driving rain swept in delicate curtains drawn across peaks more than 1,800 metres high.

The peace of the misty mountains enfolded Emmanuel Secondary School as teachers and students began to settle into their new setting. Although the complex was already high, four mountain summits looked down on it: Maduma in the west, Lion Rock to the north, Camel's Hump to the south-west, and the Vumba's highest peak Castle Beacon to the south-east. Most of the hundred-acre estate was coarse mountain grass, with a valley and stream on the south-east side which was thick with jungle.

There was no military camp nearby. No thunder of artillery could be heard. There were no helicopter gunships thudding through the sky. From the school gate there was just a kilometre and a half to the tarred main road, so there were no distant, ominous thumps of detonating anti-tank mines. The district was not contested as Katerere had been. The sense of being at war seemed to dim and grow distant in that ethereal, remote, lost world.

And yet behind the mists, amid the cool air tinged with the unfamiliar raw smell of damp earth, there were scenes of frenetic activity. Missionaries, staff, and student helpers had to force their aching limbs and exhausted bodies back into action. The colossal job of packing up and moving a secondary boarding school across 200 kilometres of war-torn terrain was now reversed – in addition to restoring a school complex that had been abandoned to the elements for two years. Ivy-clad buildings had to be freed from their green shackles, and feral grounds tamed and brought to heel. The sombre, darkened kitchens with their dusty, congealed ranges were scrubbed and sanitized and brought to fiery, roaring life. Beds were reassembled and, together with mattresses, bedding and lockers were crammed into three dormitory blocks. Desks and chairs scraped and clattered across cement floors as silent, bare compartments slowly turned back into classrooms ready for lively, eager learners. Science laboratories had to be conjured out of what was available.

Improvisation and ingenuity was the order of the day as my father and his team turned a preparatory school for small boys into a secondary school for teenagers. All the missionaries also had to unpack and move into their own quarters at breakneck speed. Members of staff surrendered their weeks of well-deserved leave to throw themselves into the second part of their colossal task, ready for the start of the September term. It was a demonstration of commitment and service to the young people in the school, a determined act of obedience to the God who had called the team to the work they did.

My father shook Paul and me awake in the diffuse cool light just before dawn. Befuddled with sleep, we stared up at his smiling face. "Come on boys," he said, "let's go to Israel today!" As the move to the Vumba was brought to completion and leadership of Emmanuel Secondary School handed over to Phil, so my family were free to go on furlough.

My father was going to complete his Master's degree at the University of London. It was time to renew our relationship with the extended family Paul and I barely knew. My parents wanted to report back on the past five years to the individuals and churches who had supported our family financially and in prayer.

But we were to start with a long-anticipated two-week visit to the Holy Land. Sights of the teeming, narrow exotic streets of the Old City of Jerusalem, the solemn hope of the Garden Tomb, the stark desert fortress of Masada, and the rolling beauty of the Galilean hills fascinated and transported us. My parents seemed to shed years as the immense burden of leadership, the constant background strain of surviving in a war-torn environment was laid aside for the time being.

* * *

Back in the Vumba, weeks after leaving the arid plains of Katerere, Sandra McCann wrote on 8 September from her mountain fastness, "A part of us is left behind there. We wonder just what will happen in that place – will the churches be overrun or will the power of God prevail? How we pray for an end to all the killing and hatred – the war has gone on for too long!" But she went on to share her joy at having moved to a "new and beautiful place, in a new school with all its many problems with a number of new faces and a whole list of new possibilities… what is going to happen? We feel excited about the future here."

Sandra mentioned the starting of a Sunday afternoon Bible study with a quarter of the students now attending, as well as the possibility of starting preaching points in the surrounding area and even in Umtali itself. Then she jotted, so poignantly in view of what was to come, "The latter glory may well be greater than the former.[2] Can we do it? Surely not – unless the Lord is with us every step of the way."

Handyman Roy Lynn, together with Joyce the school matron he had married, was trying to get clinics and church services going on a number of plantations and estates scattered across the peaks. They had successfully started five. Aware of Zimunya Tribal Trust Land 600 metres below them, they planned to initiate work there too. They lamented the physical distance that the location of the school placed between them and the local people, "It isn't quite the same as Katerere; being away from the Africans is difficult when you are trying to win friends."

Wendy Hamilton-White wrote to my parents in November in her warm, flowing style. Initially refusing to give up nursing in exchange for teaching when the school moved, she had eventually relented: "I praise God and thank him so much – frequently – for letting me be here. Do you remember that time, Brenda, when we prayed at 'my' house on the mission after we'd walked up the mountain that Sunday? It was quite a struggle to say, Yes, Lord, I am willing – but how glad I am that I did… One feels more and more burdened and part of this country as one gets closer to its people. I enjoy so much being part of the school."

Wendy added that the Scripture Union meetings on Saturdays were starting half an hour earlier, at 5.30 in the morning, so eager were the students to meet. So many wanted to tell others about their experience of God, their discoveries for themselves of the impact of His Word. She recalled an evening service at Katerere just the previous term when an opportunity to share was given and only one student had said anything. The dearth of spiritual life that had seemed to prevail at the time had changed. Perhaps the trauma of the landmine incident had brought new perspective into people's lives.

Small groups of students were spontaneously meeting to pray and sing together at different times during the day or into the evening. Many of the young people expressed their fear of going home for the school holidays. For some, hard physical labour awaited them, as they would join their families in the exhausting grind of subsistence farming. Others feared the pressure their faith would be placed under as they returned to non-Christian homes. Still others were heading back into areas seriously affected by conflict, facing threats and intimidation. Wendy knew of two more students who had made a profession of faith in that exciting September term of 1977. Yet she wrote home while invigilating a Bible Knowledge exam (Acts of the Apostles), "as I watch them scribbling away my heart is heavy for so many that, as student Douglas Gona said when he spoke at Assembly recently, 'may get 99 per cent in Bible Knowledge and still be turning away from Jesus.'"

Allaying her fears, during the early part of 1978, Wendy heard from a number of the school leavers who had gone on to other schools to study for their A Levels. Patson was one, a real rebel who had come to faith just before leaving and was going on with the Lord. He had joined a large government school and had got together with other former Emmanuel students and "members of the Family"! Samson, as a new believer of only five months, moved to a Mission school with more than 800 pupils but with no other Christians except for one member of staff. Boldly he asked the headmaster if he could start a Scripture Union group. From Goromonzi Secondary School Douglas Gona wrote to Wendy, "[former Emmanuel student] Killion Chipise is here too – we are praying to the Living God about many things. It makes me cry to the Holy Spirit when I see how many have no LIFE here at Goromonzi. Please, please pray for us every day – I mean it. I know a number of souls are going to be rescued here. I really feel the Lord brought Killion and me here for that purpose." Douglas went on to remind Wendy that his alma mater was not forgotten, "We are praying for Emmanuel that the Word of God may prosper. I feel it is the school (if not the only school) where truth is preached. To me it is the headquarters for ambassadors for Christ!"

After the trauma of losing classmates in the buses destroyed by landmines and the dislocation from the familiar lowlands of Katerere up into the unknown Eastern Highlands, there seemed to be academic as well as spiritual fruit with very good Cambridge O Level results for the Form 4 students.

Wendy also recorded her joy at being able to ride across the wild, rugged beauty of the stunning landscape that surrounded the school. The Ferrars, who lived at "Rippling Streams" close by, had loaned her a horse. Mrs Ferrar had been the nursing sister at the old Eagle School twenty-five years before. During the two years that the school stood empty "and the only sound was that of the birds", she had been praying that Christian people might be brought to occupy it. After the arrival of Emmanuel, Mrs Ferrar had wasted no time in working as an ambassador, assuring her widely scattered neighbours, white farmers, and business owners who were suspicious of these Pentecostal missionaries that the new arrivals were "all so normal". Not long after Emmanuel folk befriended them, Mrs Ferrar was baptized!

Even though Emmanuel Secondary School had been relocated to the Vumba, Mission Aviation Fellowship planes regularly flew members of the missionary team from Umtali back to Katerere. Roy Lynn's maintenance skills were frequently in demand. Wendy went as often as she could, joyful to be able to renew relationships and awed by the commitment of her black colleagues to serve there. Pious Munembe had wisely split the primary school into two and had moved half into the vacated secondary school buildings so that they could be seen as being well used by the local community. Uncomplainingly, Evelyn Munembe was running the hospital with a small team of Red Cross nursing assistants. Reliable Leonard Katerere continued behind his microscope in the laboratory. Wendy's conversation with Mai Chaka was all about Jesus and what He meant to them both "in these days of confusion".

Reversing the direction of travel, five of the African staff from Katerere came up to the Vumba over the Christmas break. An Elim Workers Conference was held and missionaries, local staff, and the colleagues from Katerere all ate together in the school dining room. Sue Evans wrote home to say how much she enjoyed taking on the challenge of planning the menus, catering, and cooking for thirty to forty people, using her experience gained years before while cooking in an all-night factory. Sue was also running the school office for Phil; what with caring for her children and her outreach activities, she worked from 6.00 a.m. to 11.00 p.m.! Cath Picken remarked to her friend Helen Carter in January 1978, "We had great fellowship with the Katerere folk and rejoiced together that God is blessing them in spite of their difficulties."

It wasn't only the Elim workers who shared those common meals. Some of the students in the school had stayed on in the holidays, afraid to go home or no longer having a home to go to. One thirteen-year-old student saw his father killed by guerrillas one month, and then his mother killed by the Rhodesian Security Forces four weeks later. Finding him a job at the school meant he could complete his education, as well as be provided with love in his devastated world.

He was not alone in his suffering. A girl had gone home in the holidays to her village only to find that the whole community was about to be uprooted into a so-called "protected village". But, along with others from her village, she had been told to take food to a meeting in the bush, for a guerrilla section there. The Rhodesian Security Forces had ambushed the meeting, killing more than forty people around her, then set her village on fire. Terrified, the young girl had fled deep into the hills, living wild for several days before finding her way back to the school.

In fact, there were a growing number of such students whose dreadful plight could not be ignored. Tim and Rachel Evans, home from boarding school for the holidays, found their family had grown! And so Christmas 1977 was celebrated with a huge common dinner where more than fifty people ate together. All enjoyed riotous games until clouds enveloped the mountains and a chilly rain began to fall.

Family-loving Sue Evans wrote to her mother after what for her was the strangest of family Christmases, "You know how I've always felt about putting the children first and not neglecting them. I can honestly say that when God called us to Rhodesia I was so against it because of the children, but felt I couldn't refuse God as I had offered myself to Him and so had Phil. I do praise God that even when I did not agree with His ways for me and Phil I still trusted Him enough to go when he sent me, and now at last He has brought me into an understanding of loving Him more than anyone or anything else. In these few weeks of accepting this new concept we have opened our hearts and home much more freely and shared with others, and the family has somehow become richer and happier for it."

Sue went on to say, "We are still very happy in Rhodesia. There are times when things feel rough here and we think about the difficulties, but they are far outweighed by the knowledge that God knows what He is about. I must admit that I don't always understand His intentions, but I have enough faith to believe that He is the best judge and the only one able to plot out our lives." With compassion and sorrow, Sue went on to recount the harrowing stories of some of the children that she and Phil were helping. She concluded, "We don't know even if all our schoolchildren will come back. People are suffering everywhere in the bush. It is sad but Christians are most needed in these situations, and it is these situations that really test the mettle of a Christian. It has been lovely to hear these African Christians praying… because as Christians we have to love and pray for everyone. This isn't easy as they have had family killed by Security Forces, family tortured and killed by guerrillas… many have been beaten and fired at themselves. That's what Christianity is all about, showing it in these situations and these circumstances."

Early in January 1978 Phil Evans mentioned to the Elim Mission Director in the UK that a number of students had come to faith at the end of 1977, "some notable conversions" as he had described them. Phil's mood was upbeat as he looked forward to the start of the new school term. Although a no-nonsense schoolmaster, Phil had a very easy teaching manner and rarely punished students in class, preferring to talk things through and build understanding. Many of the students found the Vumba to be very cold, so cold that they found it hard to concentrate. Phil would get the students out from behind their desks and lead them in a song, complete with vigorous actions, marching round the class until all were warm enough to carry on with the lesson!

But as the first term of the New Year got under way, it became clear that it wasn't just the cold that was provoking discontent. More than 250 teenagers were crammed into dormitories designed to hold just 120 small boys. Many had to go without beds, as they had been destroyed in one of the landmine disasters, and so were on mattresses on the floor, lying close together. In classrooms designed for sixteen pupils, nearly forty were being squeezed in. Bathroom facilities were inadequate. The steadying influence of a mature group of Form 4 students had been lost. Many students had spent their holidays in conflict zones, exposed to violence from Rhodesian Security Forces by day and radicalized by guerrilla *pungwes*, political rallies that ran all night.

As the students returned after the Christmas break, the teaching team were quick to realize that the mood had changed. There was an undercurrent of hostility and defiance. Phil Evans wrote home, "Young people in the now fast-emerging Zimbabwe need exceptional understanding and handling, as they are so open to many different influences and voices, and can so easily be stirred up."

Further serious challenges surfaced during the term. Food strikes took place. Students sat in the dining room, refusing to go to class and refusing to eat the food that was provided. Phil Evans set up an independent committee both to consider students complaints as well as to consider ways to challenge the growing defiance of the authority of the teaching staff.

Yet even this wise step was subverted, as Cath Picken outlined in a letter to a close friend. She mentioned an ambitious new local teacher who had joined the staff at the beginning of 1978. He had come with strong teaching credentials and his referees had spoken highly of his Christian faith. Quickly popular with many of the pupils, he rapidly built links with a group of senior students who were intent on disrupting authority in the school. He began to act as an alternative principal and, together with the committee ostensibly formed to investigate the root cause of the food grievances, had further undermined discipline within the school. Prefects and Christian students were openly mocked and threatened and were called "sell-outs" – a frightening description since those seen as collaborators with the government could die very terribly at the hands of the guerrillas. But dismissing the teacher might have provoked the guerrillas to close the entire school. Cath urged her friend to pray for the teacher and the group of agitators.

"It's like teaching in a completely different school," Mary Fisher noted, intensely shaken by what she was encountering day by day in the classroom. "Attitudes are so different and feelings of tension between the staff and also between staff and students run deep. The Christians are being persecuted (in our school!) You can see the change."

Then the boarding master caught a group of three boys stealing food from the school stores. He suspected they were hoarding food for guerrillas. Rather than displaying guilt, the boys brazenly invited the boarding master to join in. Refusing, he reported them to Phil Evans, who confronted the boys and disciplined them for stealing. A few nights later they disappeared with three friends, "over the border" into Mozambique just ten kilometres away across rugged terrain, in an attempt to join ZANLA. They had left a note as they fled to the effect that as the boarding master had punished them so they would get the guerrillas to punish him.[3] Within days a non-teaching African member of staff passed on a chilling message that ZANLA guerrillas were preparing to kill the boarding master, with the principal second on the list. It appeared that some among local guerrilla groups had been persuaded that the missionary team at Elim were non-cooperative.

Phil Evans attended a Principals' Conference during that difficult term and was somewhat relieved to discover he was not alone in the maelstrom of agitation. Other principals were experiencing similar waves of arrogant rebellion and mischief making, even where all the staff were black. Authority structures across the country were being turned on their heads in the incendiary atmosphere. The threat of violence in the war of independence was a tool wielded by many, not only as a means to gain control of the country but also for their own purposes. Young people taking against their elders, resentments directed at traditional rulers, old scores between neighbours, or a flare-up of family animosities all spelled new levels of danger.[4] If a teenage girl refused the advances of a young man, he would find ways to stir up trouble between her family and the guerrillas. Personal interest, greed, jealousy, and vindictiveness could find frightening new ways of expression, and the schools were no exception.

Wendy wrote of a sense of "being caught up in satanic onslaughts – almost drowning in the floods". It had been decided to end the first term of 1978 a few days early as the atmosphere was so poisonous. "The archenemy who is so cleverly using the political situation throughout this country for his own ends would love to see this school closed down, and it seems he has his supporters within these walls." By that time, Emmanuel was the only African secondary school in a radius of more than 160 kilometres that had not closed. Even though that first term of 1978 had been so difficult, so alarming, a few still professed faith for the first time.

Despite the immense pressure that he faced, Phil Evans bravely worked to keep the situation under control, discipline effective, and the school functioning as a school. But much hatred and vindictiveness had been directed at Phil himself as the senior authority figure in the school, and it had taken its toll on both him and his wife. Invited to coffee by Annette McCullough, a kindly friend, on a rare morning out in Umtali, Sue Evans broke down in tears on being asked how she was. Sympathetic, Annette simply sat with her while great racking cries shook Sue's body. The Evans family had only been in Rhodesia for just over two years. They had come straight into a very challenging situation that the other missionaries had had time to slowly adjust to. Sue felt very keenly the sorrow of sending Tim and Rachel, her two older children, away to boarding school. Their obedience to the call from God and their act of love and service towards the people of Rhodesia was being sorely tested.

The mountains were especially beautiful at that time of year. Wendy revelled in the beauty that she saw all around her, enthralled at the glory of the poinsettias as a blaze of crimson against the backdrop of the thick green jungle that crowded up to the edge of the campus. The rainy season was drawing to a close, and the dry, cool season brought clearer skies and stunning views. But Wendy too was drained and weary, overwhelmed by the emotionally testing time they had all been through. A sense of deep darkness and hopeless despair had enveloped her. Finally she called out loud, her voice echoing off the walls in her empty house, "Though you slay me, I will trust you, Lord!" "Suddenly," she wrote, "Jesus was there with me and my heart was warmed and lightened and full of praise." She asked her friends to pray that her heart would be filled not with fear but with love, for "perfect love casts out fear".[5]

Alarmed by the reports emanating from Rhodesia, during the April holidays the Elim International Missions Board sent my father back from the UK empowered to close the school down and withdraw all the missionaries if necessary. Spending time tramping round the site, my father chatted with people informally. He met each teacher individually, then met with the entire staff as a body.

Guided in the discussion by my father, the team began a process of identifying and clarifying the issues. Together they looked at all their options. My father let them know that they were empowered to close the school as they felt necessary, without further reference to the Elim headquarters in the UK. They discussed how the furniture and equipment would be moved into storage in hope that the school would be able to open again in future. The Form 4 students would meet in study groups with their teachers in Umtali, ensuring that they would be able to sit their crucial exams by the end of the year.

Wendy described what happened next. "The situation was such that it seemed the school would have to close down and only a miracle could reverse the situation. Many, especially former students, were praying, and we were driven to our knees. After much anguish and heart-searching plus intensive meetings and a literally flying visit from Peter Griffiths from the UK, the whole unhappy situation was quite suddenly defused." Openly talking and praying through all their fears and concerns and considering all the options, even what they saw as the worst-case scenario of closing Emmanuel Secondary School, brought a measure of calm and perspective to the situation. Courageously, the team decided unanimously against closing the school at that point. Despite the awful treatment many had experienced during the first term, they all wanted to try to keep the school open.

But for Mary Fisher, the hostility she had encountered in her classroom during that first dreadful term of 1978 had taken her beyond what she felt was bearable. Although she supported the school remaining open, she was still unable to sleep properly and was tormented by headaches. She was encouraged to go on an early furlough as soon as arrangements could be made. Mary planned to travel home via Ghana to visit her missionary sister there, but her visa was delayed. So Mary stayed on to teach for another month until her travel arrangements were complete.

The team agreed to set up a daily supply run to Umtali just fifteen kilometres away, and to stockpile nothing on site. If there was no food in the school stores then it couldn't be stolen for supply to the guerrillas. The committee set up to look at student grievances, which had become an alternative "authority", was dissolved and its replacement was to be chaired by the principal. The decisions seemed sensible. Only the start of the new term would show whether the problems had been solved.

Phil Evans drove my father to Salisbury to catch the plane back to England. Deeply concerned by the distressing school term Phil had just endured, my father commended Phil for his patient endurance in keeping the school open. But he could see what a toll it had taken on Phil. Despite being just weeks away from completing his degree programme, my father offered to return to Rhodesia immediately and relieve Phil of the immense responsibility with its unexpected complications that the younger man had shouldered in my father's absence.

Tempted by the offer, Phil considered it thoughtfully. But it was just four months more until the Griffiths family completed their furlough and returned to Rhodesia. Besides, Phil didn't want to deprive my father of the opportunity to get his Master's degree. Phil smiled at my father, "Peter, go home, complete your furlough, get your degree, come back, and then we'll be ready for a break ourselves!"

My father smiled back, the two men embraced warmly, then my father strode away. Phil stood watching him go, then turned and set his face towards the Vumba.

* * *

Far below the school but relatively close by in the lower-lying Burma Valley and Zimunya, the war raged on in heavily contested areas hard against the Mozambican border. Young teenager Patricia Maruza[6] was repeatedly called to all-night *pungwes* by one of the guerrilla groups in the Zimunya area. She had to prepare and carry food to the heavily armed men who ran the meetings. There was the terrifying process of "smelling out", of determining who were "witches and sell-outs" from among the hushed crowds. Dealing with the former brought legitimacy to the guerrillas as those who were prepared to confront evil in the community. The latter needed to be dealt with as a military and political necessity. The terrified accused were dragged out, lain on the ground, tortured by having burning plastic bags dripped on their bodies, and then some were beaten to death. Even though Patricia was so young, children were not spared from seeing all that went on. If any watchers cried or called out, they joined those being punished or killed. She could not forget the ruthless, frightening leader of the guerrilla group, with the *nom de guerre* of "Devil Hondo", or War Devil.

Rhodesian police officers visited Emmanuel Secondary School to warn the missionaries of growing insecurity. Frequently the officers came away dissatisfied, annoyed, and concerned at what they incorrectly perceived as foolish naivety and intransigence. But the relatively junior officers of the police were unaware of the high-level interactions that were going on between Elim Rhodesia Field Director Ron Chapman and senior officers in Umtali. Chapman had been discussing linking in to the Agric-Alert system with the police.

Those options were then relayed to the missionary team. Together they decided not to join the network. They feared that if there was a visit from the guerrillas and the Agric-Alert was used, it might bring an over-zealous Rhodesian military unit on to the premises. They had a legitimate concern that students would be killed in the crossfire. In the interests of the safety of the students, to avoid endangering their charges, there was a decision not to use the system.

In May, the school reopened for the second term of 1978. To the surprise of the staff, the angry rebelliousness and bitter disputes of the previous term seemed to have dissipated. Most were glad to embrace the new atmosphere, but Catherine Picken was not convinced all was well: "Maybe the little group that seemed out to make trouble have decided to keep quiet until a suitable time comes to act. I can't believe they have had a change of heart," she remarked. But Cath was thankful for the calm of the moment and went on, "Most are friendly and contented; it's just a small group that are discontented." Cath's wry and astute observations were balanced by her unruffled perseverance, her ability to draw others into practical, homely discussions of normal, everyday affairs, and so to reduce tension and calm fears.

Just after term began, a wave of illness swept through the school. Wendy's stamina and nursing training was tested to the limit. She found herself caring for up to fifty-five bedridden students at one time. Wendy's biology teaching was put to one side because Joyce Lynn, the school matron, who would normally have cared for ill students, was in hospital herself. She and Roy were expecting the arrival of their first child.

May slipped past. June brought the arrival of a new boarding master and his wife, much to the relief of the teaching staff who had shared dormitory duty on top of their heavy teaching loads. Another happy arrival was Pamela Grace Lynn, three weeks premature but otherwise healthy, a source of joy for Roy and Joyce, and a focus of interest and excitement for the rest of the team.

But hard on the heels of good news came the killing of Diane Thompson and Sharon Swindells, two young British teachers at The Salvation Army's Ussher Institute in central Rhodesia. On the night of 7 June 1978, they had been shot repeatedly in the back. Two other teachers had fallen, seriously wounded. Ron Chapman rang The Salvation Army commander to offer his condolences. The commander said, "Only a few hours before we were saying how wonderful it was that so far we had escaped altogether. Then this had to happen."

Ron responded sorrowfully, "Such a waste of young lives!"

There was a silence. Then a response slowly came, "Yes, I know what you mean. But is anything really wasted that is given to the Lord?"

Following an urgent call from Elim Mission headquarters in the UK, alarmed by the attack on The Salvation Army, the entire staff met. The missionaries did not want the school to close.

Intense debate ensued regarding a leadership proposal that white staff members should leave the school premises at nightfall, as attacks on other Mission premises had come at night. Shocked by closure of the Ussher Institute secondary school which had immediately deprived 300 students of their education, Phil Evans was willing to do whatever it took to keep the school open. Having white teachers less in evidence might reduce the chance of guerrillas closing the school. Sue and Sandra were positive about moving, as young Philip McCann was going to school daily in Umtali, and Joy McCann and Rebecca Evans had started playgroup. Peter McCann said little. However, when pressed he said he would prefer to stay at the school, but in support of his wife he was willing to move. Roy Lynn spoke for himself and Joyce in expressing his opposition to the move. Wendy was fiery, passionate in her repudiation of the idea, declaring that their calling as missionaries was to live among the people. This meant accepting the same risks faced by those they served, not going to live in the city.

Finally, though, it was decided that the white teachers would move, as this precaution gave the school the best chance of remaining open. They would live in Umtali and commute in to the school each morning. Elias Chikoshana had pluckily agreed to become vice principal and would be in charge once night fell. Phil Evans sought to reassure his team that all efforts were being directed towards continuing the school, safeguarding the spiritual work, ensuring the education of the students, and protecting the livelihoods of the staff. Together the staff knelt and poured out their hearts in prayer.

The date of 24 June 1978 was set for the white staff members to begin their move, to allow them time to find suitable accommodation in Umtali. News of the decision and the reasons underlying it was announced to the school.

A few days later, Phil wrote a letter to his mother. "There is some uneasiness here, Mum. I don't quite know if it will build up or evaporate. You can sense a feeling among the students that something is about to happen." Continuing to study the Shona language and culture as he was, Phil shared something that had struck a deep chord in him, "Most Shona people, especially those of marrying age and older have a *sahwira* – a special close friend who is a true friend through thick and thin, who will assume responsibility for the family in the event of death. A true type of Jesus." Phil Evans saw Jesus as his *sahwira*.

* * *

On Tuesday 20 June 1978, a letter was left for Phil, who showed it to Elias Chikoshana.[7] Crudely scratched on school paper, it was addressed not to Phil by name, but simply to "The Principal". A list of non-teaching staff names followed, and then the unnerving sentence, "Raise their salaries or you will be killed." It was signed by "Guerrilla S. Chimurenga", *chimurenga* being the Shona for "revolution", a generic name for a guerrilla. Phil asked what he should do, and Elias suggested discussing it with field leader Ron Chapman. Seeing that Phil had been shaken by the letter, after the day's work Elias went over to visit Phil just to sit with him. "I felt so grieved about this letter," Elias was to report later.

Before the letter arrived, a salary rise had already been agreed with Ron Chapman but had not yet been made public. Two days later, on his way to Katerere for the day, Phil passed the letter on to Chapman to be discussed with his police contact. The generator at Katerere had gone wrong and Phil enjoyed spending most of the day repairing it, delighted that it was working normally again before he finished.

At home in the Vumba, Sue was writing to Tim and Rachel, their older children at boarding school in Salisbury. To Tim she described the house they were about to move into in Umtali, "It is very nice but a bit smaller than this one. There is a huge workshop-garage with a pit. Daddy likes this as he can mend cars easily. Auntie Cath has the house just over the road from us. I was pleased your team won again – I'm looking forward to watching you play. I used to watch Daddy play when he was in sixth form! Take care of yourself and Rachel – be a good brother to her. God bless and keep you in His love. Love, Mummy, Daddy and Becky."

Early on the morning of 23 June 1978, Sandra McCann awoke and wandered quietly through her home while the rest of the family slept. She wanted to finish the sorting and packing, in preparation for their move down to Umtali. Wrapped in a blanket against the morning chill, she was distracted by the beauty of a false dawn at 5.30 a.m.

Picking up a pen, she began to scribble a letter. "We remain determined to keep the place functioning for as long as is humanly possible," she wrote. But the next time she would close her eyes that day would be in the sleep of death.

THE DEVIL'S KICK

They open wide their mouths at me, like a ravening and roaring lion... Thou dost lay me in the dust of death.

Psalm 22:13, 15b

I t was a deafening knock at the door. Levi Kombi, the school clerk tried to be quiet and chose not to answer, but the hammering went on. Voices spoke outside, "Why don't you answer? Are you not the clerk? We have your principal here. Open the door!"

Tremulously, Levi asked, "Who are you?"

The voices from the darkness responded, "*Magandanga*" ("vicious thugs").[1] Levi crept forward, opened the window, and tried to look out. From the darkness,[2] an open palm swung. The slap exploded against his face, sending his head thudding against the window frame. Stunned, he stood trembling as several other blows found their mark.

"You are refusing to open the door yet your principal obeyed. Come out with your keys to the office. We want money," hissed the voices. Levi turned back into the room and fumbled his way into his clothes. The moment he opened the door, cruel hands grabbed him and pulled him out. The unblinking eyes of gun barrels loomed out of the dark, and he was dimly aware of a large group of armed men around him.

He was led towards the school office. On the way, he saw a group of European people sitting together on the ground in the gloom near the sports field.[3] He was afraid to look too closely, but he glimpsed Phil Evans being pulled out of the group. Together Levi and Phil walked at gunpoint to the office. Phil whispered, "Levi, give them all they want. Don't refuse them."

At the office door the keys were snatched from Levi. Levi saw that Phil's arms were bound behind his back with electric cable. Phil could only stand there, helpless and humiliated, while rough hands were thrust into his pockets and emptied of the keys to the principal's office. The guerrillas ransacked the offices; as he watched, they opened the safe and cleaned it out. Levi and Phil were hustled back the way they came and sat together on the fringe of the larger group for a while.

The night sounds came thinly through the ear-buzzing terror that Levi felt. A harsh command came from one of the shadows standing guard, and the whole group stood up together. Levi and Phil walked together again into the unknown, but not for long. Levi was shoved out of the group to one side as the whites were led away from him into the shadows. His throat constricted with fear, he said nothing as he was forced back the way he had come, towards the office. To his surprise, there was a group of students standing there with a perimeter of armed men around them. After a short address, of which he remembered nothing, Levi was manhandled through the night once again, this time back to the door of his house. A face was thrust up against his, "Stay inside for the rest of the night. We are around, and if you get out of the house we will kill you."

In the exhaustion of his terror, Levi slumped on his bed. Before he knew it, the early morning sun flickered across his bruised face. Befuddled by sleep, the events of the previous night felt like a strange dream. A wailing sound carried through the cool dawn air, in through the window that was still open from the night before. He wrenched open the door to see a young woman reeling towards him, crying out in an agony of fear and grief.

Levi recognized her – she helped the McCann family with their children. Brokenly, she recounted to him how she had got up early that morning and gone over the McCanns' house to help with the children, as Sandra had asked her to. Surprised to see the door of the house already open, she walked in to find the lights burning. To her astonishment, supper was still on the table: a teaspoon sitting in an egg, a slice of toast with a half-moon bite mark perched on the plate's edge. There was a great silence instead of the noisy activity of a house with young children. She had called out repeatedly, but only the echo of her own voice had come back to her.

Turning, she had gone back out of the house and began to walk across to the school complex to see if the family had gone there. It was a misty morning, the clouds of *guti*, or fine drizzle, sweeping across the mountain ranges surrounding the school, and she shivered in the cold morning air. Passing the sports field, she glimpsed patches of colour against the green grass. Puzzled, she turned aside to see what was lying on the grass. Long moments passed as she stared, uncomprehending. Suddenly, a shudder of understanding shook her. Opening her mouth, she began to shriek with dread and then to run from what she had seen, a vision of death that no running would be able to leave behind.

* * *

Twelve hours earlier, on Friday 23 June 1978, the sun had set through clouds. The students in the school were engaged in their evening study. The teachers had returned to their homes and the evening routines had begun to unfold.

In the McCann household, Sandra supervised much-needed baths for Joy and Philip. Within minutes of getting into bed, the children were asleep. "Tomorrow is a big day for the school," wrote Peter McCann in a letter home. "They have joined a sports league, and tomorrow is the first fixture." Laying down his pen, he and Sandra McCann sat down to enjoy a light evening meal.

Close by, Sue Evans watched Rebecca splash in the water before dressing her in warm pyjamas. Washing up was the next item on the agenda for the Evans'.

Roy and Joyce Lynn were still establishing their routine with newly arrived Pamela, and each evening was a journey of discovery and delight. Joyce was busy preparing a bottle for baby Pamela.

Catherine Picken washed her hair and put her curlers in. She was planning to be in Umtali over the weekend and wanted to look her best. Picking up her Bible, she sat down at her table to read a passage before beginning her evening prayers.

Wendy and Mary had an early supper together. Mary laid out exam papers for marking in neat piles on the table, some of the last she would do before going away on furlough in the next few days. How she was looking forward to it!

Wendy was listening to music as she finished a letter home, "I've been so grieved at the decision that all Europeans should live in Umtali, travelling up and down each day. But *all* things work together for good… I know it!"

Sunset came by half-past five in winter. The moon would not rise for several hours yet. As the darkness grew thicker, armed men began to stir from positions of concealment, stealing forward through the secondary growth on the edges of the forest which surrounded the school and on to the campus. They knew where to go and what to do.

One by one, the raps on doors came. At the Evans house, as Phil opened the door, armed men quickly forced their way in. There was a brief struggle but the numbers of armed men were too many and they prevailed. One stepped over to the kitchen surface and, pulling his bayonet from its scabbard, cut the electrical flex from the toaster. Afraid of Phil's strength, the gunman quickly and roughly tied Phil's hands behind his back.

In each of the houses, the teachers were told to pack a few belongings as the armed men had come to escort them away, across the border into Mozambique more than fifteen kilometres away as the crow flies. The teachers were aware that abductions occurred, and the thought of heading out into the darkness to an unknown destination across broken mountainous terrain, pursued by the Rhodesian military while escorted by these cold-eyed, heavily armed men filled hearts and minds with terror.

Quickly, with trembling hands, Sue Evans assembled a few clothes and roused a sleepy and uncomprehending Rebecca from her warm bed. Phil stood helpless in the kitchen, his hands bound.

Her mother Joyce gently lifted tiny Pamela Grace Lynn from her cot and wrapped her as best she could against the freezing cold out on the mountains that June night. Roy, Pamela's father, gathered all he could think of that they would need to care for their newborn in the unknown days that lay ahead.

Following barked orders, Peter and Sandra put a blanket and a crocheted quilt around Philip and Joy's shoulders. Peter packed a few clothes into a small suitcase while Sandra knelt beside the children, holding them close, her heart beating wildly.

The knock came at the door of our house, which Wendy Hamilton-White and Mary Fisher were sharing while we were away. Having finished her letter, Wendy was reading her Bible and, as the interruption came, she placed her Bible open on the table in front of her and went to see who it was. She had been reading the apostle Peter's first letter:

*Humble yourselves therefore under the mighty hand of
God, that in due time he may exalt you. Cast all your
anxieties on him, for he cares about you. Be sober, be
watchful. Your adversary the devil prowls around like
a roaring lion, seeking some one to devour. Resist him,
firm in your faith, knowing that the same experience
of suffering is required of your brotherhood throughout
the world. And after you have suffered a little while, the
God of all grace, who has called you to his eternal glory
in Christ, will himself restore, establish, and strengthen
you. To him be the dominion forever and ever. Amen.[4]*

As commanded, together Mary and Wendy went out into the
night. The suffering that the apostle Peter had anticipated 2,000
years before was about to break over their heads.

* * *

It wasn't just the white teachers who were called together that
night. The evening homework period had started at 7.00 p.m.
as usual and had been quiet, the only sounds the scratching of
pens and the rustle of pages being turned.[5] Just as this ended,
an hour and a half later, vice principal Elias Chikoshana went to
the staff room. To his surprise, a stranger dressed in light green
battledress appeared at the doorway. Over his shoulder was
slung a long tube, a weapon that Elias did not recognize. Elias
greeted the man politely, but the man said nothing and stared
expressionlessly into the room. After a few moments the man
simply motioned with his hand, indicating that Elias was to leave
the room and head outside.

Student Elias Charamba, conscientiously working away even
though prep had finished, was surprised and frightened when
the door was flung open. Men carrying firearms ordered him out
of the classroom. Colin Kuhuni was called from his dormitory

along with all his fellow students. He was surprised to see others surging from all the other dormitories as well. The armed men gathered the students together outside at the reception area near the school entrance and ordered them to sit on the ground.[6] Colin noticed with a chill of anxiety that none of the white teachers was there. There was an air of tension and danger, an undercurrent of chaos. About ten heavily armed guerrillas were standing over more than 200 students, crouched or seated on the cold, damp grass.

One stepped to the front of the gathering and addressed the students. An AK-47 tipped with a bayonet was slung over his shoulder.[7] All that Colin clearly remembered of his rambling speech was that the school was to be closed with immediate effect.[8] Shattered by the news, he could focus on nothing else of what was said. Elias Charamba heard the guerrilla spokesman say, "You are being trained by Europeans. We have captured these Europeans... who were moving away. The school will be closed because the fees you pay are being given to the Rhodesian government who use the money to buy bullets."[9]

As they walked through the frigid darkness towards the fringe of the mass gathering, Oliver Manyemba and Thomas Muripira,[10] two Form 4 boys, could see into the brightly lit windows of Wendy and Mary's house. Inside, men were clearly visible, walking around freely. One bent over the table and then stood again, eating something from his hand. Another in a straw hat and wearing denims adjusted his AK-47, slinging it over his shoulder. There was no sign of either of the women.

The guerrillas said nothing about what they were doing with the entire school staff. Colin assumed a separate meeting was being held with the school authorities. Demanding the keys for the student-run school tuck-shop, the guerrillas took what they wanted and then let the students take what they pleased.

During the uproar occasioned by the looting of the tuck-shop, Colin held a risky whispered consultation with his friends standing close by. All shared his shock and dismay at having been told that their education would not continue. There was a sense of mourning. The address from the guerrillas had left a deep impression. It was abrupt, chilling, calloused in its casual disposal of the future of hundreds of students. Colin wrote later that it was "disrupting the very secure Christian nurture and environment we had so enjoyed for several years".[11]

Colin and his friends also discussed the whereabouts of the teachers. No one had seen them in the brief journey from their dormitories to the impromptu assembly area. None had appeared at the windows of their houses around the edge of the school complex, even though all the houses had their lights on. They appeared to have simply vanished.

Ordered back to their dorms by the armed men, the students were initially frightened into silence by the threats not to leave the buildings until dawn on pain of being killed. The students were told that more instructions would come the following day. But the events of the night were so stupendous and the news of the school closure so shocking that the noise levels grew and grew.

To Colin's surprise, not long after they had returned to their dormitory, the door opened and local teacher Ian McGarrick appeared and quietened the boys. None of the students in Colin's dormitory told Ian of the events involving the guerrillas, as they all assumed that he knew of the incursion. But seeing him appear in the dorms brought relief to Colin. In whispered consultation the students came to the conclusion that, like Ian, all the other staff must be back in their houses. Lying in the dark, his mind racing, Colin could not imagine what the future was going to look like. But then he remembered that the following day he would be joining other believing students for prayer and Bible study. Eventually, comforted by this thought, he fell asleep.

Many of the students chose to get up early every Saturday morning and gather to sing, to pray, and to read the Bible together at Scripture Union meetings. Wendy Hamilton-White came along too and usually led them in their devotions. Colin and his fellow worshippers started singing choruses while waiting for her to arrive. An hour passed and Wendy still had not turned up.

* * *

On the morning of 24 June 1978, British South Africa Police (BSAP) Section Officer Poole[12] rose very early. He had received a call the night before about stock theft at a farm in Umvumvumvu. As the senior police officer responsible for security at the Umtali Rural district,[13] he was going to the farm. He started up his armoured police Land Rover and had just rolled up to the security gate when his radio crackled into life. The woman police reservist managing the radio room said that she needed someone responsible for security to come and answer an urgent phone call.

Poole returned to the police station and picked up the phone. Someone who identified himself as Ian McGarrick said that he was a teacher at Emmanuel Secondary School. He had run up the hill to find a working phone at Speddings Farm about two kilometres from the Eagle School premises.

McGarrick sounded very tense. "I'm from Elim. I want to speak to someone older than you. You sound very young."

Poole responded tersely, "I'm in charge of security for the area so you'd better speak to me."

There was a pause, filled by the hiss and crackle of the line. Then McGarrick said, "All the whites have been killed here." Poole, startled and unsure of what he had heard, asked McGarrick to repeat himself. The stark words came down the line a second time: "All the whites have been killed."

"Right," Poole responded. "Wait where you are. I'm on my way."

Poole assembled his team of police constables. At the last minute a raw new recruit by the name of Ryker[14] came running up and begged to be allowed to join the team. Poole and his "stick" of heavily armed officers drove up into the Vumba to meet Ian McGarrick near the turn-off to Eagle School. Ian told Poole that he had heard a disturbance in the night and had got up to order his students back to bed. The following morning, on his way to the early morning meeting, he had seen something terrible lying in the grass and rushed to find a phone.

As Poole came down the long sweep of the road running around the side of the hill and into the school premises, he saw a lone body lying at the steps of the sports pavilion. He parked just off the road, his men spreading out, weapons at the ready. Poole looked down at the body of a man dressed in a mauve sweater and purple trousers. A *dhemo*[15] was still buried at the base of the man's neck. His face was severely battered, one cheekbone crushed and the eye ruptured. Poole noticed that his hands were tied behind his body with electrical cable.

While Poole was still examining the body, one of his men shouted. More bodies lay close by on a grassy embankment on the edge of the sports field. They had been separated into two groups. Four adults and three children died together in one group, four adults and a child in the other. Suitcases lay scattered about and ripped open.

Grimly, Poole professionally assessed the scene. He recalled that the moon had been almost full and had risen at 8:30 p.m. the night before. Beneath the cold silvery glare, the men had been made to stand close by as the guerrillas violated some of their wives and colleagues. Then the man with the bound hands had been killed first at the base of the slope in front of the women, cut down like a great tree with tremendous axe strokes.

Near him, a young man lay on his side, one knee drawn up, his head bludgeoned and bayonet wounds in his chest and neck.

A little distance up the slope lay a third man, face down with his arms beneath him. Massive blows had crushed the left side of his head. He had been beaten then bayonetted more than twenty times in both the front and back of his chest.

Below the scoreboard lay a woman, plastic curlers in the grass by her head, some rollers still caught in her bloodied hair. Broken, bloodied fragments of her glasses were stuck to the skin of her face, glinting like tears. Her chest had been run through multiple times with a bayonet. Protruding from the back of her head was a long wooden-handled axe.[16] Scattered around her were banana skins.

In the centre of the group lay a young woman in a torn blue jersey, her face a mass of welts. She had been stabbed three times, the wounds marching up her body in a disturbingly neat line. Six inches from her outstretched left hand lay a small baby in a pink flowered nightdress. Her eyes were closed. The left side of the infant's head was fractured, apparently by a single blow. Like her mother's, her tiny arm was outstretched upwards, fist tightly clenched in death.

Two more women lay just a pace from each other. Both had been killed by numerous stab wounds to the head, neck, chest, abdomen, and back. Close beside one woman were three children. A boot had crushed the skull of one child, the markings of the heel of the boot imprinted into the left side of the child's face. Another lay face down in red pyjamas, still clutching a brown blanket through which the child had been stabbed nine times. The third lay looking up into the distant sky, the centre of that little face distorted by a ghastly blow.

Twenty paces away from the others, beneath a small tree, lay a young woman in a denim dress, her long hair thick with congealed blood. The attack on her appeared to have been driven home with special ferocity, bayonetted repeatedly as she had been in the face, neck, chest, and thighs.

Logs of wood lay scattered around some of the bodies. All thirteen were very badly battered around the head or stabbed in the face, as if the killers had been trying to obliterate their identity, seeking to smash their individual humanity. As they slipped away into the dark forest after their deadly work, the killers must have been spattered and smeared with blood.

Ryker, the new recruit, retched and then vomited repeatedly next to Poole, his body's attempt to reject the horror lying there. Poole sent him to get blankets and sheets to cover the bodies.

Poole's team gathered all the students and the black teachers in the hall. One of his men, was told that the guerrillas were heading for the border with a hostage. Poole ordered his men to systematically search the school, in case the hostage was in hiding rather than having been taken.

With minutes, another officer, reported another dead body near the entrance to the school premises. Peering into thick undergrowth, Poole saw the outline of a woman. On all fours, he forced his way into the brush until he could reach her arm. To his surprise, he detected a weak pulse. He could see she had been bludgeoned about the head and her jaw was broken.

She was so deeply lodged under the bushes that it took some time to cut the vegetation back enough to extract her. She did not speak, nor show any awareness. Her injuries were so appalling that Poole was astounded that she was still alive. Gently lifted into a police vehicle and covered with blankets, she was driven down the winding road to Umtali General Hospital. Later that day she was transferred by air to more sophisticated facilities in Salisbury.

She had been among the main group of missionaries when the killing began. Surviving the assault, perhaps feigning death until the killers had gone, she had crawled away from the others, leaving a trail. Despite her grave wounds, she crept 150 metres from the killing ground.[17] Probably terrified that the killers would return, and blinded by the injuries she had suffered, she had used her reserves of strength to wedge herself into a hiding place.

Led by senior officer Detective Inspector Gerry McDade, a team from the Criminal Investigation Department arrived at the massacre scene and began their work.

* * *

We got up early on Saturday 24 June 1978 to travel together as a family to Surrey. My father was going to speak at the Elim Bible College graduation, in the Surrey village of Capel.

The sunlight came flickering through the trees as we drove through the green countryside of early summer. I leaned my head back against the car window, staring up into the vault of blue overhead. It was a summer's morning to fill the heart with a numinous joy.

As we drove up through the grounds, we expected to see the spreading lawns of the college splashed with colour; students, their families, and friends strolling on the grass anticipating a day of celebration. But the lawns were deserted. Pulling up close to the main entrance, we were curious and amazed to find that all was quiet. On graduation day we expected noise and movement and laughter. A student stepped out of the shadow of the doorway and quickly stepped forward. "I'm here to take you straight to the principal's office," he said, an unexpectedly solemn look on his face.

We followed him in a small family knot, increasingly bemused. Here and there we saw one or two people as we made our way through the building but they drew back or turned away as we passed. The door to the principal's office was opened and we saw Wesley Gilpin, the principal, standing behind his desk. My father advanced towards him, smiling, with his hand outstretched, and we followed him in.

Without preamble the principal said, "Pete, I've got some bad news for you."

My father's face changed and he said abruptly, "They've killed Phil."

Very gently the principal said, "I'm sorry, Pete. They've all been killed."

With those words, my father staggered as if he had been punched, falling down backwards with the shock. My mother stood, shaking all over as if she had a fever, saying, "Why are we still alive? Why have we got life and they're all dead?" I was traumatized both by hearing words which didn't make sense at first and then seeing the reaction of my tough, capable father who had coped with so much. The room rocked and swayed and a strange buzzing rang in my ears.

The summer light drained from it, the day passed in a colourless blur of faces coming into view and fading away again. Broken fragments of sentences. Joy Bath's face, normally so animated and full of fun, running with tears as she stood enfolded in my parents' arms. Treading carefully, unsure of feet and balance in the weightless atmosphere of shock, I was intensely aware of each movement and moment.

The Bible College graduation service went ahead. Although others offered to take his place as the speaker, my father felt he should do it. He had already planned to speak from Paul's letter to the church at Philippi: "It is my eager expectation and hope that I shall not be at all ashamed, but that with full courage now as always Christ will be honoured in my body, whether by life or by death. For to me to live is Christ, and to die is gain."[18]

Tears ran unchecked down my father's face as he recalled his friends and colleagues one by one and spoke of their determination to follow their Lord. A graduating student recalled, "I can see him now... his bloodshot eyes seemed to be alive with grief and hope. He paused for a long time, looked into our eyes again, and asked us if we would be faithful to the Lord Jesus whatever the cost. As we knelt to pray we were sobered but determined. His was one sermon I will never forget."[19]

We drove back to London. As we entered the city, at the door of newsagent after newsagent the headlines of the evening papers were prominently displayed, each like a slap in the face, a paroxysm of the heart: "Guerrillas massacre thirteen Britons".

As we walked through the front door, the phone was already ringing. In the days that followed, it seemed it would never stop.

* * *

Ten thousand kilometres away, other Rhodesian military units arrived at Eagle School and sealed off the hall with more than 200 students inside it. One by one each student was called into a room off the hall and interrogated. When the process was complete, the military ordered every student to go immediately to their room, pack their belongings, and be ready to leave within two hours.

So much pressure was exerted by the Rhodesian Security Forces to clear the premises that most students had no time to arrange funds for transport. Any money held by the school on their behalf had been stolen by the guerrillas the night before. Within an hour of the order being given, buses were already rolling onto the school campus. Students clambered into buses which were then driven past the killing ground, passing just thirty paces from the bodies which had not yet been moved. But all that could be seen were the camouflage uniforms of the military. The frightening events of the *pungwe* the night before, the announced closure of the school, the decision to move all the students so quickly, and the speed of developments was too much for many students, who filled the buses with the sound of weeping. Others sat mute, either shocked into silence or afraid to show their grief, suspecting that the guerrillas had been assisted in their assault by fellow students.

Bewildered, student Oliver Manyemba felt "like the earth

beneath our feet had vanished. All that had given us identity, hope, and direction was violently taken away." For many, there was a sense of complete unreality. Some lived in denial for days, unable to accept that their teachers who just hours before had been standing in front of them were dead. It was only when they saw photos of people they recognized, their dead bodies splashed across the newspapers or on the television, that they were finally able to begin to accept that the unthinkable had happened.

Poole and his police colleague[20] were appalled at being ordered not to bag and move the bodies. The missionary team were left where they were, lying in the soft rain for hours after being discovered. After the initial shock of the news, cold political calculation had begun to take over in the upper levels of the Rhodesian government. The propaganda potential of such an event was calculated to be very high. Members of the press corps were quickly contacted, flown by the Rhodesian Air Force to Grand Reef Joint Operations Command near Umtali, and finally driven by the army to the site. A phalanx of reporters, photographers, and cameramen arrived, asking questions, making notes. Flashes erupted and the whirr of cameras began to record every detail, in colour and close up, of the evidence of terrible human suffering that lay exposed on the rough grass.

Finally, the grisly process of clearing the massacre scene was allowed to begin. The body of a child was plucked awkwardly from the ground where it had been lying by its mother's side. It was not cradled in loving arms, lifted tenderly, and held close. Instead, its clothes tented from the police officer's hands as its body, already stiff with rigor mortis, remained rigid, parallel to the ground. Its head lolled back, blond hair trailing down. An adult-sized body bag was held open, gaping like a grotesque mouth, far too big for the tiny corpse.[21]

A flat-bed military truck was driven across the sports field as close to the killing ground as possible. Its sides were lowered to allow it to receive a growing row of bulging white body bags as each person, each human being, was piled in by the troops as if they were loading sacks of fruit from some grisly harvest.

The day was very heavily overcast. Poole wanted to bring in two tracker teams by air from the nearest air base,[22] but the helicopter pilots were not able to fly in through the low cloud shrouding the mountains. There was a delay in getting the teams who had to come by road instead.

Almost immediately after starting their work, the tracker teams discovered that the large group of killers had divided into two smaller groups. One set of tracks led towards the Mozambican border. Poole radioed this information through, and an army unit was hurried forward to the border to attempt to cut off that group's route into the relative safety of Mozambique. However, within hours, the tracker reported that the initial direction was a feint, as the tracks turned south, staying within Rhodesia.

The other set of tracks led down into the valley of Zimunya Tribal Trust Land and headed south. But the two groups of killers had picked the timing of their assault well. They were so far ahead of the pursuing troops[23] that the faint marks of their passing faded and the trails were lost.

* * *

The news of the killings at Eagle School fell abruptly into the lives of distant families and communities, shattering them irrevocably.

Tim and Rachel, the two older Evans children, were away at boarding school in Salisbury, asleep in the safety of the capital city while the attack was happening 300 kilometres away. It was a sunny Saturday morning and Tim had been writing a letter home when his room had unexpectedly filled with adults.

After he had been told, Tim returned to his room and his letter. Picking up a pencil he scribbled the simple, shattering sentence, "Mummy and Daddy and Becky are killed."[24] Did the act of writing the worst news a child can ever hear make it more real? The unfinished letter was found later by his grandmother, tucked away among his belongings.

Most of the tiny Elim church in Huddersfield, the McCanns' home church, had gone on a church outing to Scarborough that Saturday. When the news came through, fifty-two people huddled close in a shelter on the seafront, singing and praying together. No one had the heart to continue their day away, so quietly, sombrely, people made their way home again.

Wendy Hamilton-White's niece was dedicated in St Carthage Cathedral in Lismore on the Sunday after Wendy was killed. Her niece was named Victoria Judith Wendy White.[25]

That Saturday morning, Anne and Tom Pickering, Joyce's parents, were delighted to receive a letter from Joyce in the first post. "We have not been threatened in any way. I don't feel fear like we did at Katerere, but the church headquarters decided we should move before we were threatened into it." Just one hour after Joyce's parents enjoyed reading her letter together, a grim-faced delegation knocked at the door. Their daughter, their son-in-law, and their granddaughter had died together. The Pickerings had not even seen a picture of their grandchild. Anne Pickering said, "We have prayed for the forgiveness of our enemies. We can do no more."[26]

Elim's International Missions Board met in emergency session early on Sunday 25 June, with my father present. The Elim leaders recognized that, although Emmanuel Secondary School had to close following the murder of most of the staff, Elim's work would continue through the Katerere hospital, clinics, schools, and churches that were now completely in black Christian hands. The board decided that the funerals would take place in Rhodesia, "the land loved by those who died". Plans were made for memorial services in the United Kingdom as well as for care for relatives, especially for Tim and Rachel Evans, left as orphans.

An offer of forgiveness had begun to emerge within hours of the news being broken to relatives, arising in many grieving hearts as a supernatural response to the horror of the event. Elim Pentecostal Church issued a press release. Its final sentences brought the bereaved and the murderers together in startling juxtaposition: "We join in prayer for those who lost loved ones and for those who carried out such a cowardly and useless act. It is the churches' desire that they all should find with us the love of God as manifest in Jesus Christ, this world's only Saviour."

* * *

The following day at the government mortuary in Umtali, police surgeon Anthony David Owen worked alone to carry out the post-mortems as quickly as possible. He stood for several hours by the autopsy table from early morning until the sun was low on the horizon.

One by one, the bodies were brought through to him and the bags peeled away. A police officer stepped forward to identify the body the surgeon was about to examine. Four times identification was a formality as he looked down at his own patients, his toil rendered sorely personal. The most poignant moment was seeing the tiny body of Pamela Grace Lynn, whom he had delivered by Caesarean section three weeks before her murder.

All too familiar with the types of injuries caused by the multiplicity of weapons of war, Dr Owen identified stabbing consistent with two different types of bayonet from the SKS and AK-47 assault rifles. But other implements were used too: the evidence was accumulated, the wounds located and listed and described in formal medical language, the causes of death recorded.

There were moments when his professional reserve slipped. An exclamation mark, a capitalized word or a heavy underscoring on the reports betrayed the emotion churning underneath the multi-syllabic medical jargon. A police docket was opened for the twelve dead. The police intended to treat each death as a criminal murder.

* * *

By the night of 25 June, my father was on a plane to Salisbury with John Smyth. A senior executive with South Africa Airways who attended an Elim church had arranged tickets at short notice, placing both men in first class, a kind touch that my father deeply appreciated. Despite the comfort, both men spent a disturbed night, grieving the tragedy that lay behind them and dreading the tasks that lay before them.

Flying in to Rhodesia, they arrived at Eagle School on the afternoon of Monday 26 June to be confronted with desolation amid the beauty of the setting, the school echoing and silent, the homes empty and still. Three Christian friends laboured at the immense task of sorting and closing up the households of the dead, trying to bring a measure of order to chaos. My father experienced an overwhelming sense of hopelessness and despair.

He visited Mary Fisher in Intensive Care in Salisbury. Her body swathed in dressings, she remained unresponsive and comatose, and the mechanical hiss and whirr of her ventilator dominated the room. Mary's mother Anne and sister Ruth were to fly out, along with seventeen relatives of the others.

Among the many funeral details clamouring for my father's attention, arrangements needed to be made for accommodating the family members of the dead. For most of the relatives this would be their first flight. Only two of the nineteen relatives had passports – the others made the trip using emergency travel documents quickly issued by the Foreign Office. Their first opportunity to visit the country where their loved ones served would be to see them buried in its soil.

There had been emotional scenes at Heathrow Airport as my mother went with Paul and me to see the group off. As we stood together and prayed, a phalanx of television cameras surrounded us. Pioneering missionaries Cecil and Mary Brien stood slightly apart from the rest, formidable in the depth of their sorrow. White-haired, his tall figure bowed, deep lines of grief were scored into Cecil Brien's weathered face. They too were travelling to say goodbye.

* * *

Despite the orders to disperse, many Emmanuel School students did not. When my father arrived in Umtali on that Monday he managed to contact a number of students directly. He asked if they would tell as many others as possible to meet with him the following day. On Tuesday morning 27 June, the majority of the student body had gathered. That meeting was deeply emotional for all involved.

My father began to speak in an entirely unexpected way. He called on the students to genuinely forgive those who had killed their teachers, had endangered their education, and had threatened their future. Daringly, he went further, urging the students not only to forgive but also pray that the killers would come to know Jesus Christ as their Saviour and Lord.

Confused, bewildered, angry, anxious, afraid as they were, these first words that my father said provoked a rumble of angry dismissal. Hearing this, my father, weeping, stood before the young people, opened his Bible, and read from Acts 7, challenging the students to follow the example of Stephen who, while being murdered, prayed for the forgiveness of those who were stoning him to death.

Oliver Manyemba, listening to my father plead with the student body to forgive, was tempted to reject his words. But then an image flashed into his mind. It was Peter McCann, his science teacher. Every Saturday, Peter McCann joined the Christian students, taking them through the book of Romans. What came into Oliver's mind was the last session that Peter had ever led, on the Saturday before he died. Peter had spoken thoughtfully and clearly on Romans 8:

> *What then shall we say to this? If God is for us, who is against us? He who did not spare his own Son but gave him up for us all, will he not also give us all things with him? … Who shall separate us from the love of Christ? Shall tribulation, or distress, or persecution, or famine, or nakedness, or peril, or sword? As it is written, "For thy sake we are being killed all the day long; we are regarded as sheep to be slaughtered."*
>
> *No, in all these things we are more than conquerors through him who loved us. For I am sure that neither death, nor life, nor angels, nor principalities, nor things present, nor things to come, nor powers, nor height, nor depth, nor anything else in all creation, will be able to separate us from the love of God in Christ Jesus our Lord.*[27]

Peter McCann was laid on the killing ground. A sword had pierced his body repeatedly. He had been slaughtered like a sheep, his body butchered like an animal. His warm lifeblood had run from his body, had cooled in the night air of the Vumba mountains and had soaked into the soil of his adopted country. He was dead. And yet the words that Peter McCann had spoken were full of life, echoing in Oliver's mind.

Oliver could see that my father's face was marked with grief and pain, but he too was speaking words full of extraordinary power. And so Oliver was enabled to start a journey towards overcoming his own hatred, anger, and fear.

* * *

Nearly one week after the killings, hundreds gathered for the thanksgiving service for those who had died. It was held in Umtali's Queens Hall, as there was no church big enough to accommodate the numbers that came. Eleven flower-decked coffins were arrayed across the front of the hall, white for the children, mahogany for the adults. Newborn and newly dead, tiny Pamela Grace shared a casket with her mother, clasped in her arms.

Captured by a press photograph, my father was among the first of the platform party to enter the hall. He was looking down at the ground, placing his feet carefully as he walked, half-twisting his body awkwardly away from the lengthy row of pallets where his colleagues lay.

Her parents and young sister taken without a word of goodbye, Rachel Evans stepped forward during the service to place Rebecca's favourite fluffy toy on the wood above her sister. Rachel wept quietly for much of the service. Impassive in his shock, Tim Evans remained, as if in a trance, on the other side of his grandmother Florence who had travelled out to be with them.

My father stood before the hall which was packed with people. Clutched in his hand was a soiled, crumpled scrap of paper on which he had scribbled a few thoughts in pencil. His voice trembling and breaking, he spoke of his friends. He began with the McCanns, alluding to the child they had lost years before, buried in the soil of Katerere. At the time Peter McCann had said to my father while looking at the coffin holding his dead son, "I know Paul isn't there but with the Lord." "Now," said my father, "they are all together." He added that when Paul McCann had died, he could weep with them. Now he had to weep alone. He spoke of Roy, Joyce, and Pamela Grace Lynn, that "everybody loved them". In turning to the Evans, to Phil, Sue, and Rebecca, he said, "Phil was like a son to me, so much love with one great concern – to know the Lord." For the previous eighteen years he had worked with Cath Picken. Always faithful to her word. Always loyal to her colleagues. Now she had been faithful unto death to her Lord. Wendy Hamilton-White had inspired my parents with her close walk with God, with her prayerfulness. As they had parted, not realizing it would be for the last time, it was with warm embrace and expressions of love.

"It was my privilege to work with them. I was not worthy to lead them," my father said before he went on to recall the story of the stoning of Stephen, who said as he was being crushed,[28] "'Lord Jesus, receive my spirit.' And he knelt down and cried with a loud voice, 'Lord do not hold this against them.'"

My father cried out over the dead bodies of his friends, "We long that those who did this will come to know and love the Lord and share heaven with those they killed, as Paul shares heaven with Stephen."

Elim Field Director for Rhodesia, Ron Chapman, still deeply distressed from the task of identifying his colleagues at the scene seven days before, looked down at those lying before him and then out at the congregation. "We are not praying for our victims. Rather we pray that God will be merciful to those who perpetrated this act of shame, that they might know grief and repentance and God's mercy."

In contrast, Umtali's mayor Douglas Reed commented to reporters,[29] "There have been prayers for the inhuman savages who did this. While I take no issue with those that preach this gospel I would be less than honest if I did not state that the Old Testament teachings have more appeal for me than turning the other cheek." He added, "It is my earnest hope that the perpetrators of this ghastly deed be speedily brought to justice," referring to the biblical text of "an eye for an eye".

* * *

Hearses had to be driven in, hurriedly borrowed from other cities to transport such a large number of coffins simultaneously. The funeral cortege wound through the luxuriant green bush like a march of great black beetles, hiding the coffins within their shiny carapaces.

At the service of committal, before a hushed crowd, the words of Hebrews 11 and 12 carried through the dusty winter air:

> *For time would fail me to tell of [those] who through faith conquered kingdoms, enforced justice, received promises, stopped the mouths of lions, quenched raging fire, escaped the edge of the sword, won strength out of weakness... Some were tortured, refusing to accept release, that they might rise again to a better life... They were stoned, they were sawn in two, they were killed with the sword... destitute, afflicted, mistreated – of whom the world was not worthy...*
>
> *Therefore... let us run with perseverance the race that is set before us, looking to Jesus the pioneer and perfecter of our faith, who for the joy that was set before him endured the cross, despising the shame, and is seated at the right hand of the throne of God.*
>
> *Consider him who endured from sinners such hostility against himself, so that you may not grow weary or fainthearted.*[30]

In the graveyard, five graves had been cut into the earth to receive twelve bodies. Wendy and Cath were buried in their own graves, but three had been dug especially deep as the Evans, McCann, and Lynn families would be buried together. Many found the stacked coffins of the family groups disturbing, and they seemed to take an age to sink out of sight.[31] As their remains were committed to the ground, the gathered crowd sang a cappella:

> *Yea, though I walk in death's dark vale,*
> *Yet will I fear no ill;*
> *For Thou art with me, and Thy rod*
> *And staff me comfort still.*

At the graveside, as the strains of the song faded away, my father turned to John Smyth. "John, we will never be the same again".[32]

Frank Taylor, a friend of Wendy Hamilton-White's family, had written a letter: "To be a Christian is a wonderful thing and yet at the same time terrible, for, if they all had not been Christians they would not have been there. It was not their bravery but their faith that kept them there."

On the back of Frank's letter, my father scribbled, "I'm a broken man..." The writing trailed off but resumed, "...broken for the Lord to rebuild in His way. Broken I hope for the Lord to be seen."

* * *

Mary Fisher died the day after the funeral of her colleagues. She had never regained consciousness. Although there were signs of healing as her slender body strived to recover from her welter of injuries, they were too many, too grievous. Her heart and lungs had failed, a complication of the severe head trauma she had endured.

Her service of thanksgiving was held, a much smaller, quieter, meditative event with little media attention. Mary lived selflessly and was mourned in a simple solo ceremony. A sixth grave was dug, and Mary was buried beside Wendy.

For my father there was the exhaustion of sustained grief.

Years later I came across some crumbling old papers and realized they were scribbled notes he had made just after Mary Fisher died. He had sat with a colleague, David Ayling, and they pondered "if only" over and over again. Typically, my father jotted their thoughts down as they wrestled with the issues. If only they had pulled out when the two young Salvation Army women had been shot dead at a Mission in the south of Rhodesia just two weeks before. If only the missionary team had not left Katerere and Emmanuel School had closed instead of moving. If only the school had never been opened back in 1964. If only Cecil and Mary Brien had never gone to Katerere in the first place. The "if only" road grew longer.

But as they talked and argued and thought and wept together, a key thought took hold of my father. Perhaps a Christian perspective would turn the words around. It was not "if only" but "only if". Only if the Briens had gone to Katerere would the people there have heard the good news of Jesus. Only if Elim had opened schools would former students Pious Munembe be the Manjanja Primary School principal, Evelyn Munembe be the Elim Hospital matron, Ephraim Satuku be the pastor, and Paul Makanyanga be the missionary working in Botswana, as just a small taster of what had been achieved.

Only if the missionaries had gone to the Vumba and stayed there would… my father paused to ponder what the second part of his sentence might be. There was no good answer that he could see at that moment. Then the words of Jesus from the Gospel of John came into his mind and he wrote, "Well, what will happen? Unless a corn of wheat falls into the earth and dies, it remains alone; but if it dies, it bears much fruit.[33] Thirteen corns of wheat have fallen and died. God is still writing this chapter."

IN HIGH PLACES

Justice is conscience, not a personal conscience but the conscience of the whole of humanity. Those who clearly recognize the voice of their own conscience usually recognize also the voice of justice.

Aleksandr Solzhenitsyn[1]

Mid-morning in central London on Thursday 29 June 1978, the Labour Cabinet gathered at 10 Downing Street in London, England. The main business of the meeting was the terrible events that had taken place nearly a week before.[2] The appalling news with widespread, detailed media coverage of the brutal murder of unarmed men, women, and children had provoked outrage and revulsion across the United Kingdom.

Just the day before, the Foreign Secretary, David Owen, had come under severe pressure in Parliament. In response to a strongly worded request to identify who was responsible for the killing, David Owen stated to the House that he would support a United Nations-led inquiry into the assault, adding, "I do not believe that we should have an unresolved issue of such severity as this."[3]

There was one question that Cabinet members had wanted the Foreign Secretary to answer that morning: "Who had carried out the killings in the mountains of eastern Rhodesia?" But the massacre of Elim missionaries had caused consternation in the British Foreign & Commonwealth Office (FCO) for broader reasons than the killing of British civilians alone. There were major concerns about the ongoing negotiation process which was seeking to bring an end to the war in Rhodesia[4] and which had been threatened by the Elim massacre.

David Owen, a young, gifted Foreign Secretary, had only been in his post since February 1977, having suddenly been elevated to the position following the death in office of his predecessor. Whereas the British government had a policy of refusal to negotiate with the Irish Republican Army, Owen made a point of talking to all sides in the Rhodesian conflict, regardless of the reported actions of their respective armed wings. In the week following the massacre, Owen's political opponents heavily criticized his approach for what they saw as government inconsistency.

Owen believed that neither side could win the Rhodesian war outright and that it was within the grasp of the British and American governments to settle the "Rhodesia question", the transfer of power from a white supremacist government to majority rule. Just four days before the massacre, the Rhodesia Desk of the FCO had prepared a detailed assessment of the military situation in Rhodesia. They believed that the prosecution of the Rhodesian war by nationalist guerrilla movements was largely ineffective in military terms. However, the armed struggle was placing the white Rhodesian government under strain. It did not have a long-term political strategy underpinning its military ability, so it would never be in a position to defeat the insurgency. Each side might jockey for position by military means, but negotiations managed by the major powers would eventually decide the outcome, that "the decisive battle in this war will be fought well away from Rhodesia (in Washington and London)".[5]

But the massacre was a potential game changer, and put much of David Owen's personal political credibility at stake. The British Foreign Secretary had worked closely with American Secretary of State Cyrus Vance and the United States Ambassador to the United Nations Andrew Young on the broad strokes of a plan which would involve the United Nations in the transition to majority rule for Rhodesia. In September 1977, representatives from front-line nations Angola, Botswana, Mozambique, Tanzania, and Zambia gave formal support to Owen's Anglo-American plan to bring majority rule to Rhodesia.[6] This support was considered a major triumph for both Owen and Young as these countries provided havens for guerrilla groups (mainly the Patriotic Front), and some also provided weapons and training. It was expected that the leaders of the front-line states would convince Rhodesian guerrilla groups to accept the plan.

Meanwhile, South African pressure on the Rhodesian government to accept the plan was brought to bear. This was pressure which the Rhodesians could not ignore, as South Africa controlled both access to the sea and fuel supplies for Rhodesia.

Robert Mugabe, as head of ZANU with its military wing ZANLA, and Joshua Nkomo, leading the Zimbabwe African People's Union (ZAPU) with the corresponding ZIPRA, had temporarily united to form the Patriotic Front. Ironically, Mugabe, Nkomo, and Rhodesian Prime Minister Ian Smith had all rejected the plan's ideas for the creation of a new army using elements from both the guerrilla forces and the government security forces. All considered the other side's forces untrustworthy. But the overall plan was still in play, and David Owen and Cyrus Vance were concerned that the plan should not founder.

News of such a bloody mass killing at this time was thus most unwelcome for a number of reasons. Immediately after the massacre, encrypted cables were being sent several times a day from the FCO to their commissions, embassies, and agents, trying to discover who did what.[7] One encrypted, restricted cable was sent by Dr Owen himself to Salisbury and Pretoria, in which he wrote, "grateful for any hard evidence as to who was responsible for the massacre, as soon as possible".[8]

The influential New York Times stated on 27 June that they believed the Elim massacre was carried out by the Patriotic Front for the explicit purpose of damaging white morale and provoking an exodus that would lead to collapse of the Rhodesian ability to maintain a military response and so bring about a fighting victory. The paper went on to say, "A moral claim to power is all that sustains their [Patriotic Front] movement in the eyes of the world. Terrible acts like last Friday's killings will poison opinion against the Patriotic Front and make insupportable any thought of Western assistance to a future Zimbabwe that it might lead."[9]

This 27 June editorial from the New York Times was telegraphed urgently from New York by American-based Foreign Office representatives and distributed immediately to no less than twenty-five departments and individuals within the FCO in London. The strong, clear statement from an influential member of the American press regarding responsibility for the killings and the impact on relationships with leaders whose men had carried out such crimes rang alarm bells in the British FCO.

The editorial apparently hardened a developing FCO position that to seek clear evidence regarding culpability was far too risky given the likely consequences for ongoing negotiations involving the Patriotic Front. Despite an early commitment to identify the perpetrators of such a heinous crime, this resolve melted swiftly away as the potential political implications of officially accepting who was responsible came forcefully home.

The cable traffic seeking to "obtain concrete evidence" abruptly stopped by 28 June.[10] On 28 June, David Owen informed his representative in Salisbury that there would be an official "expression of our concern over the killings", but that the British Foreign Secretary considered an independent inquiry to determine blame unwise.

The next day, the very day the missionaries were buried, David Owen briefed the Cabinet on what he knew about culpability, which he claimed was very little. He mentioned that within hours of the news breaking, Robert Mugabe had personally taken the unusual step of directly issuing an official statement explicitly denying any involvement of ZANLA guerrillas. Mugabe claimed that he had received eyewitness reports of the attack on Elim seven hours after its occurrence. These witnesses had fled into the bush and contacted genuine ZANLA guerrillas, stating that the killings were carried out by Rhodesian Special Forces as a "bloody diversionary tactic" to switch attention away from cross-border raids into Mozambique.[11]

Eddison Zvogbo, ZANU Secretary for Information and Publicity, described the ZANLA targeting process to a British diplomat on 28 June. Zvogbo stated there was centralized control of ZANLA guerrillas by their operational headquarters in Chimoio, Mozambique, from which they received targeting orders and to which they provided written reports after operations. The guerrillas were strictly controlled. "The missionaries were certainly not on the target list," Zvogbo claimed, mentioning the meeting with ZANLA guerrillas that my father had been ordered to attend less than a year before the killings as evidence of good relationships with the missionary team.[12] Tellingly, the diplomat added at the end of his cable, "For the moment, the defence rests."

In addition to ZANU's strenuous denials of any responsibility for the massacre, Owen told the Cabinet that the Patriotic Front were increasing the pressure on him. If the Anglo-American agreement collapsed, their demands would rise: the Rhodesian police to be dissolved rather than realigned, Dr Owen to provide them with a "guaranteed election win", and the dismissal of the entire Rhodesian Civil Service. These demands would be completely unacceptable to the Rhodesian government and would ensure that the war would continue.

In summing up the Cabinet discussion, the British Prime Minister said that indiscriminate killing was deplorable, but "such incidents should not divert us from our efforts to achieve a settlement". Although it was not stated, he implied that negotiations should continue with all parties, regardless of who had blood on their hands. David Owen was given the unanimous support of the entire Cabinet in continuing his approach through the Anglo-American plan.

An internal FCO report on a 26 June meeting between Elim representatives and the Foreign Secretary was quickly circulated. The Elim leaders had surprised Dr Owen by offering to pray for the Foreign Secretary in the challenges and pressures he was facing right there in his office. However, the report highlighted that the "Elim leader did not know who had carried out the massacre and he was determined not to become involved in political controversy". Dr Owen had told the Elim delegation that he thought this was wise.[13] No doubt it was also a relief to David Owen that there would be little or no pressure from the Elim leadership for answers regarding culpability.

So the effort to determine who carried out the killings was stepped down within days. Dr Owen's early suggestion to Parliament that he would seek a United Nations-sponsored inquiry, made while faced by angry MPs baying for answers, was quietly downgraded. The option of an investigation led by the World Council of Churches was then dismissed because the Elim Pentecostal Church movement was not a member of the WCC. Even the proposal of paying for the services of a forensic expert and legal counsel to obtain and review evidence was finally reduced to simply paying for a Rhodesian-based lawyer from the legal firm Coghlan, Welsh and Guest to attend the Rhodesian government inquest on behalf of the Elim Pentecostal Church.

The content of further communications evolved from seeking the facts to discussion around political management of the fallout. FCO communications focused on claims that it would be seen as racist and one-sided to push for clarity on the killings that had taken place at Elim Mission but ignore other incidents that had taken place, such as a night-time *pungwe* led by ZANLA guerrillas in Gutu a month before which had been ambushed by Rhodesian Security Forces, leading to the killings of between fifty-two and ninety-four black civilians who had been caught in the crossfire.

The US State Department was equally concerned by the massacre's potential impact on the Anglo-American plan. The US Embassy in Pretoria was put to work by the US State Department and the US Mission to the United Nations. By 18 July, the US Embassy in Pretoria quoted their contact, a journalist who had been in the region for just two months, who claimed to have accompanied the first unit to arrive at the scene of the massacre. The journalist stated that it was his view that the massacre had been carried out either by ZIPRA, by Nkomo's forces, or by the Rhodesian government in an effort to smear Mugabe's ZANLA. His somewhat counter-intuitive reasons were that students at the school had told him that the attackers had self-identified as ZANLA, something he found automatically suspect. He had also been told that they spoke Manyika, a Shona dialect that he believed was less common among ZANLA guerrillas. On this rather tenuous evidence, the US State Department held the position that the massacre had not been carried out by ZANLA.

However, a much more detailed report was circulated in the State Department ten days later, compiled by a second journalist who had been in Zambia and Rhodesia for many months. He started from the position that the Rhodesian Security Forces had killed the missionaries. He set out to prove it, knowing that finding proof and breaking the story would be a major journalistic coup. However, the more investigation he undertook, the less credible he found his original position, and he finally reported to the US Embassy in Pretoria that the evidence pointed to ZANLA guerrillas having carried out the attack.

Within a week, a second cable marked "Secret" rather than merely "Confidential" was sent from Secretary of State Cyrus Vance to United Nations Ambassador Andrew Young. The cable contained a clandestine report provided by the Bureau of Intelligence and Research (INR), a unit within the State Department itself, its role to "harness intelligence to serve US diplomacy". A source close to Mugabe had said that "a ZANLA field commander had carried out the massacre on his own initiative and ZANU was considering how best to take disciplinary action". Despite these two reports indicating culpability, Secretary of State Cyrus Vance's secret cable ended, "It seems doubtful that we will ever know who was really responsible."

US Ambassador to the United Nations Andrew Young met with ZANU's Deputy Publicity Secretary Eddison Zvobgo on 2 August 1978. Zvobgo discussed the Elim massacre with Ambassador Young, telling him how grateful he was that British Foreign Secretary David Owen had made statements casting doubt on who had perpetrated the massacre. Among ZANU leaders there seemed to be anxiety about evidence surfacing that might link ZANLA, their armed wing, to the killings, and so undermine their relationship with power brokers in Washington and London.

But ZANU need not have worried. It would seem that the US State Department moved from a position of believing that the responsibility did not lie with ZANLA and being willing to publicly state this to holding information pointing towards ZANLA but not declaring it. Their silence on the issue would protect their part of the Anglo-American talks on a Rhodesian settlement. Like the British political team, the US did not want to either upset Mugabe as ZANU's leader or to be seen to be doing deals with people that they knew had carried out such an act. The way forward was to join in the obfuscation of the identity of the perpetrators and claim that, owing to the fog of war, responsibility would never be known.

* * *

My father's first meeting with Patrick Laver, Head of the Rhodesia Desk, took place in Whitehall on 2 August 1978. My father told Patrick Laver that he wanted to outline his views on who had committed the massacre in the interests of truth. My father believed that those who carried out the killings were part of ZANLA, ultimately under the command of Robert Mugabe, and he gave his reasons. The killers had claimed to students and staff that they were ZANLA guerrillas. A number of the armed group appeared to be aged sixteen to eighteen years old, too young to be members of the Rhodesian Security Forces. They used the Zezuru dialect of Shona, which was spoken in northern Zimbabwe, whereas the Rhodesian Security Forces recruited mainly from the Karanga-speaking south of the country. The guerrillas took blankets from their victims, implying that they were living rough in the bush. My father had met with the Superintendent of Police in Umtali and had asked him point-blank whether Rhodesian Special Forces had been operational in the area at the time of the killings and whether they could have been involved. The policeman had told him that they were not, that he had repeatedly requested the deployment of Selous Scouts in his area of control and had been refused because there were not enough. In addition, my father had managed a clandestine communication with a ZANLA commander whom he had met a year before. The commander had indicated how unhappy he was about the killings. He had not confirmed that ZANLA cadres had carried them out, but he did not indicate that anyone else was responsible.

Laver asked my father about the mood in Rhodesia regarding the Internal Settlement and white morale. Faced by significant gains made by guerrilla forces internally, together with mounting international pressure, Ian Smith, as leader of the white minority Rhodesian government, had attempted to form a racially mixed government acceptable to the international community, culminating in the March 1978 Internal Settlement. An interim government was in place, with elections to follow as three black candidates vied for power, including former Methodist Bishop Abel Muzorewa. Ordinary people were wearied and frightened by the war and saw the Internal Settlement, although greatly flawed, as an opportunity to return to a peaceful, normal life.

My father told Laver that although he believed there had been some popular support for the Internal Settlement, particularly among African women who thought Muzorewa could bring peace, it seemed he could not stop the war, and his support was seriously eroded. White morale had plummeted between April and July 1978, sensing that the Rhodesian Security Forces might not contain the war. Many would leave the country before the end of the year. Despite his stark assessment, my father planned to return to Rhodesia in December 1978, six months after the killings.

Laver summarized the meeting and wrote a brief assessment of my father: "Peter Griffiths struck me as an intelligent man of complete integrity." Laver's summary was circulated as a confidential memo to key figures in the FCO as well as the Prime Minister's Office and was sent to Rhodesia to the FCO representative there. Foreign Secretary David Owen read it and commented, "I think this is a fair assessment," before signing it on 4 August 1978.

But my father had wasted his breath. There were apparently

no changes to the FCO stance regarding responsibility for the Elim killings. But just a few days after this debriefing, there was another turn of events, one which was not so easy to ignore.

* * *

On 10 August 1978, nearly seven weeks after the killings, Section Officer Poole was patrolling the far south of the area under his responsibility. He and his men had crossed through Zimunya Township, overshadowed by the Vumba mountains, and driven thirty kilometres south. Rearing up out of the open flat plain before them was the remote Himalaya mountain range. Beside a sign to nearby Bushman paintings, Poole's section left their vehicle and moved towards a nearby village. Poole suspected that the village had been providing guerrillas with food. When questioned, the villagers admitted that they had prepared a meal for the ZANLA section and indicated that they were still close by, under cover in a dry riverbed not far from the village.

Poole split his six-man team into two groups. One was to wait in ambush as a "stop group". The other he led into the dusty ravine, hoping to flush out the guerrillas. His group advanced cautiously down the dry riverbed, the brilliant, sharp-edged sunlight creating deep pockets of dark shadow along the banks from where an attack might come. Edging their way round a bend, they confronted about a dozen guerrillas sprawled across the sand, eating a midday meal. Poole and his men opened fire. Seizing their weapons and springing to their feet, the guerrillas immediately "bomb-shelled", running in several different directions. Some ran straight into the ambushing stop group, which also opened fire. The crackle of automatic weapons echoed and boomed across the dry hot plain for less than ten minutes.

Warily, the police searched the area, looking for tracks, evidence of wounds, or equipment dropped or abandoned. The search found the bodies of two guerrillas, killed during that short, sharp firefight. Poole had radioed for air support, and helicopter gunships arrived overhead shortly afterwards, but no further encounters took place.

Poole and one of his colleagues searched the bodies of the two dead guerrillas. Their weapons were still hot, indicating they had been fired during the brief battle.[14] Neither of the guerrillas was carrying bayonets.[15] One was wearing a good-quality watch, which Poole suspected had been taken as a spoil of war. He removed the watch from the dead man's wrist, and on turning it over he found the back to be engraved.

Continuing his search of the corpses, he came upon a diary on one of the bodies which was written in English, describing the attack at Elim.[16] Poole thought that his patrol had encountered members of one of the guerrilla sections that had been at Elim on the fateful night. Poole and his men picked up the tracks of other members of the guerrilla section, which they followed until darkness overtook them.

Following standard procedure, the following day, 11 August, the bodies were loaded on to helicopters returning to Grand Reef Forward Air Field just outside Umtali. Special Branch officer Inspector Bryan Rogers dealt with captured or dead guerrillas and their equipment. The helicopters disgorged the two dead bodies of the guerrillas killed around midday the day before, along with recovered firearms, kit, and equipment, and Rogers began his work. The air activity drew the attention of a British Parliamentary Delegation, two visiting Tory MPs, John Stokes and Ivor Stanbrook, who happened to be visiting the base that day and wanted to focus their attention on the Special Branch team. Covering the story was BBC reporter Ian Smith as well as David Caute, a *Guardian* journalist.[17]

Ian Smith's dramatic report was broadcast on the night of 11 August. On hearing the headline, my father surprised us by promptly rising from his chair, walking over to the television, squatting down in front of it, and staring intently at the screen, not wanting to miss a word of what was said. The camera panned across dry, brown grass on to two men lying on stretchers in the winter sunlight as if they were taking a rest. One looked young and fresh-faced while the other was mature, tall, and heavily bearded with deep lines etched into his grim face. Both were clad in brown outfits, their forearms crowded with dozens of bracelets, treated with *mushonga*, traditional medicine to protect them in combat. Above their heads had been placed the weapons they had been carrying when killed: two AKs with a jumble of black steel, and rust-coloured bakelite magazines next to them, plus a wooden-handled Chinese stick grenade.

A search of the bodies and their kit and equipment by Inspector Rogers revealed notebooks carried by the guerrillas. One was a diary belonging to one of the dead men. Caute spelled the guerrilla's name as "Luke Madjuimbo" rather than "Madzvimbo", because the Shona name contained a sibilant often mispronounced by those not familiar with the language. It was the custom of guerrillas to methodically record their activities, usually on a daily basis. Extracts from these reports would then be passed back to ZANLA headquarters in Mozambique. Madzvimbo's diary recounted a number of attacks carried out by the guerrilla section. There was an ambush on a civilian vehicle on 21 July 1978 in the Burma Valley, a low-lying area located close to the Vumba mountains. On 1 August 1978 an attack on a road camp was carried out by the guerrilla group. Both attacks were acknowledged by the Rhodesian authorities as having taken place.

In that same notebook, an entry had been made regarding Elim Mission. Inspector Rogers read aloud from the diary to the BBC camera:

*Friday 23rd June is the day and date we reached at
Yugo Mission Vumba near Matondo camp in Zimunya
district. Time of operation: from 6.30 to 9 pm. Total
number of comrades who were there, 21. Things
captured from the enemy: radios 1, tape recorders,
table cloths 4, cameras 5, portable radios 4, portable
machines 1, cassettes 7, bedsheets 2, bathing towels
1, pillow cases 1, kitchen towels 1, screwdrivers 5.
Money: British pounds 57, South African rand 2,
Rhodesian dollars 413,81½ cents. Weapons used: axes
and knobkerries. Aim: to destroy the enemies. We
killed 12 whites including four babies, as remembrance
of Nyadzonya, Chimoio, Tembwe, and in Zimbabwe
massacres.*

Added below was, "pairs of stockings 28, table watches 4, wristwatches 4, trousers, towels, bags, shoes".

Closing his report, journalist Ian Smith raised the question of responsibility for the massacre and outlined accusations by ZANU that Rhodesian Special Forces had committed the crime to discredit the nationalist forces. But he found the evidence compelling that the two guerrillas had been involved in the killing of the missionaries. Asking who, then, the men were answerable to, he concluded, "It now seems quite clear that these men were under the command of Robert Mugabe... When I last talked to Robert Mugabe in February he told me categorically it was not the policy of his army to kill innocent civilians. He must now repudiate the action of his men. If he does not it is going to make it extremely difficult for any white Rhodesian to accept all-party talks with Robert Mugabe."

But no repudiation was forthcoming.

Other sources surfaced to link ZANLA guerrillas killed in combat with the Elim massacre. *Zimbabwe News* was the official publication of the political party ZANU. Issues featured "Operations in Zimbabwe", a regular article giving details of guerrilla assaults throughout the country. In the July–August 1978 edition of *Zimbabwe News*, a report was included of an attack on a road camp on 1 August 1978.[18] It stated a very specific number of vehicles destroyed in the attack, together with their type: "five 7-ton trucks of the racist road department and a D.C.7 caterpillar were set ablaze". This report in ZANU's official publication matched the account of a road camp attack recorded in the dead guerrilla's diary as reported by the *Rhodesia Herald* on 12 August 1978, complete with matching numbers and types of vehicles destroyed.

Regardless of the number of vehicles actually destroyed, or Rhodesian troops killed during the attack on the road camp, a report from a ZANLA guerrilla's diary had ended up in an official ZANU publication, where ZANU explicitly claimed responsibility for that attack. The road camp attack was recorded in the same diary as the assault on Elim Mission. One attack was reported in ZANU's official publication *Zimbabwe News* and one attack was not. ZANU claimed responsibility for one but concealed responsibility for the other.

Years after the war, "The Fallen Heroes of Zimbabwe",[19] the official list of ZANLA war dead, was published. Accessed through the US Library of Congress, there were only two guerrillas reported as having been killed on the tenth day of any month in 1978 in the Zimunya area. The month was July rather than August, possibly in error as only one other name separates these two guerrillas from all those killed in August. The two men were said to have been killed in a surprise attack. One was Luke Madzvimbo, listed by ZANLA as killed on the day of the battle described by Poole in the area that he mentioned. It was Madzvimbo's diary that had been recovered with his body and read out by Special Branch officer Bryan Rogers and recorded by

BBC reporter Ian Smith. *Guardian* journalist Caute's report also included Madzvimbo's name.

Luke Madzvimbo, self-confessed participant and diarist of the killings of Elim missionaries, was officially claimed by ZANLA as a member of their forces and listed on the Roll of Honour as one of their official war dead.

* * *

An inquest into the deaths of the missionaries and their children was held in Umtali by the Rhodesian authorities on 21 August 1978. Detective Inspector McDade of the Criminal Investigation Department gave evidence, as the massacre was considered to be a crime rather than an act of war. Beginning with the causes of death, the grim geography of mass murder was mapped out, distances measured, positions indicated, and the slain represented by letters, which required half the alphabet.

McDade went into technical details regarding wounds, some consistent with the use of pointed spike or "pig-sticker" bayonets as well as conventional knife-blade-type bayonets. Other wounds pointed to the use of axes and logs of wood. For some, a sequence could be established, where a weapon had been used first on one individual then on another. The face of a child showed the clear print of the sole of a "SuperPro tackie", a tennis shoe much favoured by the guerrillas, consistent with someone stamping heavily on the child's head.

Those killed "died in the position they were found", said the officer. There were no attempts to cover or conceal the bodies, and they were left as they lay, in a macabre display of power. No watches were found on the missionaries; their bodies appeared to have been searched and looted. The killings must have been the final act by the guerrillas before they slipped away into the night, as they were likely to have been liberally splattered with blood.

A sheaf of post-mortem reports carried out by Dr Owen at

Umtali General Hospital Mortuary was admitted into the inquest evidence, together with graphic photographic evidence showing the sufferings of those who had died. Appended to each of the post-mortem reports was the doctor's official finding on the cause of death, each one a variation on a theme of horror.

How the events of that evening had unfolded was then explored. Teachers Mr Chikoshana and Mr Tinonesana, the boarding master, Levi Kombi, the school clerk and a number of pupils who had been present that night spoke of their harrowing experiences, responding to questioning by the magistrates and the lawyers present. Levi Kombi had gone to bed by 7:30 p.m. that night and had fallen asleep, before being violently woken at some point after that and marched alongside Phil Evans to the school offices, centrally located in the complex. Apart from their killers, Kombi was apparently the last person to see the missionaries alive, gathered together on the school grounds, close to the killing ground, shortly before their execution.

The *pungwes*, or clandestine political meetings, held first with the boys and then with the entire student body, took place more than 200 metres from where the bodies were found. There was a heavily wooded ridge between the point where the students were gathered and the killing ground, carefully chosen so the terrible sounds of mass murder would not carry to the students and provoke the possibility of an attempted rescue.

The inquest also reviewed the entry for 23 June 1978 from the diary found on the body of Luke Madzvimbo, the political commissar killed in battle on 10 August. It described the Elim massacre, the numbers killed, and the weapons used. It included the names and ranks of eight of the guerrillas who took part. McDade stated that further details on the killings that were contained in the diary would be known only to the perpetrators.

A watch recovered from the body of one of the guerrillas killed in combat ten days before was produced in evidence. It was handed to survivor Ian McGarrick in court. Recalling the day that Roy Lynn had shown him his watch, McGarrick was able to identify the watch as Roy's and mentioned the joy Roy had taken in his fine possession. On playing one of the cassette tapes retrieved from the kitbag of a dead guerrilla, Mary Fisher's fine voice soared hauntingly from the machine, her song of worship momentarily filling the room: "For me to live is Christ, and to die is gain."[20]

The inquest then focused on the vulnerability of the unarmed group of missionaries. Their willingness to stay on and serve despite the security situation had infuriated many white Rhodesians. However, Inspector McDade admitted under questioning that building a security fence around the sprawling property would have been impractical, and in any case only would have provided "a small deterrent".

Ron Chapman, Elim's director in Rhodesia, was asked about the decision by the missionaries not to be linked in to the Agric-Alert radio system, which connected Rhodesian commercial farmers to one another and directly to the Police Anti-Terrorist Unit, which would react to a call for assistance. He explained that his colleagues feared that if there was a visit from the guerrillas and the Agric-Alert was used, it might bring a potentially over-zealous Rhodesian military unit on to the premises. The missionaries had a legitimate concern that students would be killed in the ensuing crossfire. To avoid endangering their students, the missionary team had decided together that they would not use the system.

Ron also emphasized the frequent security reviews with the missionary team. Advice from the police had not been ignored, but carefully considered within the larger picture of enabling the school, clinic, and nascent church work to continue. Following the killings of two Salvation Army women on Friday 9 June, the Elim team decided that white staff would move into Umtali, although "some were very, very reluctant to do it because they felt they were here to serve the Africans and they felt their influence would diminish if they did it from a distance". Ron had worked with Phil Evans to find housing in Umtali for everyone within days. But the killers had intervened before the move could take place.

There was no individual verdict on each person, but the inquest had a single common finding: "Death due to multiple injuries received when the deceaseds [sic] were attacked with bayonets, an axe and pieces of wood by members of a terrorist gang belonging to ZNLA forces."

* * *

My father went to see Foreign Office Rhodesia Desk head Patrick Laver again, before returning to Rhodesia in early 1979.[21] At this second meeting, Laver told my father that Robert Mugabe had "unofficially" apologized for the Elim massacre, acknowledging that it was men owing him allegiance who had carried it out, and that the platoon commander responsible had refused to return for discipline.[22] Would Laver have informed the Foreign Secretary[23] of this apology?

Who ordered the ZANLA sections to carry out this mass murder? Was it was a personal decision of the commander on the ground, as Mugabe privately claimed? Was it ordered from a higher level? Zvogbo had made a bold avowal regarding ZANLA targeting and discipline, yet innocent lives were unjustly taken at Elim by two ZANLA sections. Despite being aware that it was his men, Robert Mugabe, as President of ZANU, had added to the injustice, first through a public denial of ZANLA culpability and then by stating that he had been brought eyewitness evidence that the killers were Rhodesian Special Forces.

Although apparently willing to admit secretly that the killers were ZANLA, Mugabe's assertion that the commanders responsible would be recalled for discipline seemed to have been simply a sop to the British Foreign Office. No disciplinary action was carried out. To the contrary, one of the guerrilla sections was involved in a further operation which was reported approvingly in an official ZANU publication.

Seeking the truth through an inquiry following the massacre was never seriously pursued by the British authorities. On the same day as the mass funeral, even as the dead were being buried, the British Prime Minister wrote off the bloody slaughter of his own citizens as a "deplorable incident". The Cabinet gave the Foreign Secretary their unanimous backing to continue all-party negotiations, apparently without pause for reflection or policy review, without even a suggestion of serious questioning regarding responsibility or possible sanction if proof should be forthcoming. Evidence of culpability that began to surface within weeks was noted but neither made public nor acted on in private.

Truth was sacrificed by the British government for what was seen as the greater good at the time: keeping talks going, which included Robert Mugabe's ZANU as part of the Patriotic Front. The failure of the British and American governments to hold ZANU to account communicated a lesson: illegal and unrestrained violence in the service of power could be overlooked. That lesson was learned far too well.

BURNING ON, BURNING BRIGHT

For like a shaft, clear and cold, the thought pierced him that in the end the Shadow was only a small and passing thing: there was light and high beauty for ever beyond its reach.

The Lord of the Rings[1]

Once a world unto itself hidden in the misty mountains, it was no longer a gentle peace but a deathly silence that enfolded Emmanuel Secondary School. The clapper of the bell that formerly marked the passing of the lessons hung undisturbed, powerless now to unleash a sudden cacophony of chairs squealing on floors, slamming desk lids, and an impatient hubbub of young voices. Stagnant, oily air slowly eddied in the deserted halls, and classes no longer quickened and stirred with the ready laughter, eager discussion, and rapt attention of hundreds of young men and women. The fiery, clattering ranges of the kitchens fell back into shadowed, chilly gloom. Only the sudden ghostly scurry of fleshy, pale geckos drew the eye with their sudden darting movements.

Beneath the curtains of rain drawn across the brooding peaks, a handful of people crept across the giant empty stage that the estate had become. They had the mournful task of sorting through and packing away six homes that were no longer lived in. Entering house after house, they were confronted with the signs of lives suddenly paused, as if each person had simply stepped out fleetingly and was about to breezily meander back in to reclaim their interrupted task. The page of the Bible lay ready for turning. A red pen lay atop the next essay about to be marked. Two mugs faced each other across a table, an inch or so of coffee in the bottom of each. A plate for drying was laid just for a moment on the counter, the tea towel perched next to it ready for use.

As my father entered Phil and Sue Evans' home, his eye was caught by a poster tacked to the wall. It showed a pair of bound hands. Beneath them was the legend, "If you were arrested for being a Christian, would there be enough evidence to convict you?" Tied behind his back, Phil Evans' hands had figured prominently in press photographs. My father carefully untacked the poster and folded it to keep as a challenging reminder.

Dark and dismal though that time was, my father's burdens were lightened and his heart warmed by friends who came alongside, willing to turn their hands to do whatever was needed. Close friend Audrey Greenshields, the capable young headmistress of the top girls' school in the country, worked alongside Annette McCullough to pack up the contents of the houses. Intending to move into Umtali, some of the missionary families had already started to sort and pack their homes. Despite this, the job remained immense.

In her role of helping to lead Umtali Teachers College alongside her husband Gerald, Annette had warmly welcomed many black students into their home. As a result, she had known loneliness, having been ostracized by the polite white community in Umtali, who were scandalized by the McCulloughs' fraternizing across the race line. The arrival of the Elim missionaries, similar in their attitudes, had led to new friendships for her. Painful though Annette found it to pack up the homes of her friends, she was glad to serve them one last time.

The McCulloughs had had a guest staying with them when the massacre took place – a senior civil servant within the government's Department of Social Services. Able to access the monies necessary to send Emmanuel students to homes scattered across war-torn Rhodesia following the massacre, he worked with Gerald to provide each student with cash. Annette saw the timing of his visit as no coincidence, remarking, "Our God is careful to plan every detail of our lives in advance." That remained true even in disaster.

After the funerals, my father spent a further three weeks in Rhodesia. He arranged for the transfer of Emmanuel students to other schools. So many schools had closed because of war and spaces were at a premium. However, the principals of schools that still remained open were very sympathetic, and nearly all the students found a place.

Despite the kindness and sympathy of many, it was a bleak time. The school was closed and emptied, the majority of the teaching staff murdered, the students scattered across the country, while the war in Rhodesia raged on.

Reflecting during that time of utter darkness and despair, my father jotted down, "Through a series of events, God began to show us that He had been in control all the time and that those that died were counted among the number of the martyrs He had decided on before the world began." He was meditating on a passage in Revelation where John, the author, is given a vision of the martyrs who cry out for God to bring justice on the earth and avenge their blood. They are told to have patience, "until the number of their fellow servants and their brethren should be complete, who were to be killed as they themselves had been".[2] Often seen as a sub-Christian prayer in contrast to the prayers of Jesus and Stephen for forgiveness for their murderers, my father understood the prayer of the martyrs recorded in Revelation as a balance, as a reminder of God's justice. At issue was God's own character, His justice and righteousness, His ability to keep His promises to do good to those He loved. If the unjust death of His servants and the escape of their murderers was the end of the story, either the goodness of God or the sovereignty of God was at stake. Either the death of my father's friends was an unnecessary waste, a tragic mistake, a triumph of evil, or it still lay within the will of God but the story was not yet at an end.

In those three weeks my father buried his friends, cleared their houses, wound up their affairs, found places for his students, and did what he could to investigate and understand the killings. But the widely publicized issue of the offer of forgiveness and the call to repentance to the killers by the relatives of those who had died in the Vumba caused a backlash in Rhodesia. Forgiveness had become a controversial topic. Many white Rhodesians had objected to anyone offering forgiveness to "savages, bloodthirsty psychopathic killers".

He was desperate to get back to us in England, exhausted and drained by his ordeal in Rhodesia, yet my father agreed to extend his stay in order to speak at a women's meeting in an elite white suburb of Salisbury on this contentious issue: Forgiveness.

Numbed emotionally after the trauma of the previous weeks, my father spoke calmly and inexpressively. He pointed out that whatever was thought about the idea of forgiveness for the murderers at Elim, Jesus prayed for the forgiveness of those who murdered Him. "Although we may not be murderers, we are all sinners," he added, "and we all need the forgiveness of God found only at the cross, when we repent and call out to Jesus to forgive and save us."

At the end of his talk, anyone who wanted to know more about God's forgiveness was invited to write down their name and address in a notebook. As he was due to fly out of Rhodesia the next day, it was only much later that my father discovered that six women had done so. Accordingly, each had been visited and counselled and each had made a profession of faith. Just three weeks before, six women had been murdered for their faith in the Vumba mountains. My father felt God was saying to him, "Now in the very first meeting you offer forgiveness and salvation in My name, how many women have I brought into My Kingdom on earth to continue the work?" The answer was six. My father saw something more significant, encouraging, and comforting than a simple coincidence of numbers.

The morning before his rescheduled flight back to London, my father had time on his hands. Audrey Greenshields was running a course for principals at the Domboshawa Training Centre outside Salisbury. On the spur of the moment my father went with her. Unaware that anyone knew he was there, my father was surprised to be called to the office for a telephone call. He picked up the receiver, and a voice said, "Peter, this is David Witt. You don't know me but I am a government official with the Ministry of Education. I have been authorized to offer you the job of developing the religious education curriculum and writing teaching materials to be used in schools throughout Rhodesia. When are you returning to England?"

My father responded, "I have to be at the airport at 6.30 this evening, but I'm planning to return to Rhodesia in January 1979."

Witt said, "In that case I'll need your answer by 5.30 tonight!"

Shocked by this sudden and unexpected turn of events, my father sat meditatively for some time. Suddenly he realized that he had been unwittingly preparing for this change in direction. His meticulous summaries of dozens of books and hundreds of articles reflected his close interest in curriculum development.

His dissertation had focused on preparing a religious education syllabus for Rhodesian students, an approach he had taken purely because he had wanted to strengthen the teaching of religious education at Emmanuel Secondary School. Had all this been preparation for something else?

Before the storm had even begun to subside, while still deeply grieving, and feeling confused and overwhelmed, my father felt the quiet whisper of the voice of God piercing the wild, strident, raging of emotion that shrouded him, pointing out the way forward. At 5.30 that same evening, my father rang Witt to tell him that subject to Elim leadership's approval, he would take up the position on his return to Rhodesia. The path ahead seemed suddenly clear.

* * *

Any horrified pause in the rhythm of the war following the massacre did not last. The March 1978 Internal Settlement, ostensibly to transfer power to moderate black nationalists, was failing. Smith had not stepped down, nor had belief in white superiority been abandoned. The new political arrangement left control of the judiciary, public service, army, and police in white hands, so popular support rapidly waned. International recognition was not forthcoming. Amnesties and calls for a cessation in hostilities fell on deaf ears. ZIPRA and ZANLA guerrillas increased the fight against what they saw as a "sell-out" arrangement.

Rhodesian cross-border raiding into Mozambique, Zambia, and even Angola continued and intensified. Civilian convoys were ambushed, and attacks were creeping closer and closer to the cities. Train tracks were sabotaged and trains fired on, leading to the cancellation of overnight trains across the country.

On 3 September, civilian flight RH825 from Kariba to Salisbury was hit in the starboard wing by a Strela-2 surface-to-air missile. The pilot skilfully guided the stricken aircraft into a cotton field but hit an unseen ditch. The Vickers Viscount cartwheeled and broke up, killing the crew and most of the passengers. Dazed, wounded survivors were rounded up and murdered on the ground by the ZIPRA section that had fired the missile. Retaliatory cross-border raids by the Rhodesian Air Force, ostensibly against ZIPRA guerrilla camps, killed hundreds of young refugees. On 28 September 1978, Rhodesian Armed Forces commander Lieutenant-General Peter Walls declared, "The war is building up to a climax. There is no single day of the year when we are not operating beyond our borders."

My father knew the writing was on the wall for the minority white government. He could see that it was likely that either ZAPU or ZANU would be the next government. One party was aligned with the Soviet bloc and the other with the Chinese. Both movements employed Communist rhetoric. How long would a religious education syllabus be tolerated in a country run by a government linked to two aggressively atheist regimes? It seemed that even if my father took the job he had been offered there would be little future in it. But he had a deep conviction that God had spoken, and he needed to respond in obedience despite the sombre prospects of success.

Amid the terrible trauma of the year, the University of London awarded my father his MA with distinction. Despite the increasingly chaotic charnel house that Rhodesia was becoming, as a family we began to prepare for our return. Yet after that single phone call from David Witt, nothing further came from the Rhodesian Ministry of Education. In October 1978, my father decided to write anyway to inform them that he had successfully completed his degree and had bought a quantity of materials in London to help in the writing of the curriculum which he understood they expected him to prepare.

He posted his letter. The very next day, after three months of absolute silence, a letter dropped on the mat of our flat in London. The contents of the envelope were explosive. Key decisions taken in the Ministry of Education meant they had withdrawn their job offer. There was no department of Religious Education in the Curriculum Development Unit to return to after all. What was happening? What was God doing? What about the sense of guidance that my father had received? My parents were bewildered and dismayed.

If my father had received that letter just twenty-four hours earlier, he would not have written to the Ministry of Education, but his letter was already on the way to Rhodesia. Little did he know it at the time, but my father's letter caused consternation in the ministry. The decision to set up a Religious Education team in the Curriculum Development Unit had been balancing on a knife edge. The arrival of his letter, innocently communicating his plans to return, tipped the balance the other way. His acceptance of a job offer had been made in good faith. The Permanent Secretary was reminded by his colleagues that he had an ethical responsibility to keep the post open, given that my father had accepted a post offered at their initiative, had booked to return, and had already bought materials. They would be creating a Religious Education team after all, the job would exist, and the offer would be honoured.

In December 1978, just days before our return, guerrillas perched on a railway line 170 metres from their target and fired several rockets into giant fuel storage tanks within the boundaries of Salisbury. Eleven tanks ignited, causing an inferno that sent a plume of black oily smoke towering 200 metres into the air, visible for twenty kilometres. A third of the facility was destroyed and the fires took days to control. Exhausted firemen ran out of firefighting chemicals, and further supplies were hastily sought from South Africa. Years later I discovered that members of the guerrilla task force that carried out the fuel depot attack had also been involved in the Elim massacre.

Fuel had been in short supply for years following United Nations sanctions with rationing of petrol; management of fuel coupons had become a daily reality for motorists. So the loss of millions of gallons of fuel and the reduction of storage capacity was an economic and propaganda coup for nationalist forces. Within weeks, trains, planes, and cities, spaces previously secure for white civilians, were shown to be within reach of guerrilla forces, landing another blow to white morale.

Following this major attack, the UK-based Elim Missions Director expressed concern about our return, but my father was determined. Two concessions were extracted: that my parents would never travel together out of Salisbury, to reduce the likelihood that they would be killed together, and that if the Missions Board wished them to withdraw they would comply. They also had the option of withdrawing without reference to the Board if they saw fit.[3]

Just months after the killing of their friends, in faith and obedience, my parents took us back to their adopted country, war-torn as it was. Living in town after many years in the bush required some adjustment. Nearly everyone was armed. When having supper at a friend's house, it was hard to tear my eyes away from six or seven automatic weapons stacked in the middle of the lounge floor as each arriving guest added their arms to the pile. The windows of department stores were taped to limit injuries from flying glass in a bomb blast. And the bomb blasts came as the threat of urban warfare became a reality.

At school we practised drills designed to protect us from mortar or rocket fire. A teacher blew a whistle, which would be followed by the sound of thirty-five pupils throwing themselves headlong under their desks. Rhodesian Security Forces suddenly sealed off streets in the central business district, driving trucks across both ends, requiring everyone to produce identity documents. I saw those unable to satisfy the Security Forces being led into the middle of the street and forced down on the road with a rifle pointed at them as the search continued. Until then, the war had been largely invisible in the cities while all too apparent to those living in the rural areas. Now, no one could ignore the war.

The next twelve months were marked by ever increasing violence and fear. Six weeks after our return, a second civilian Viscount flight RH827 was shot down shortly after take-off from Kariba, killing all passengers and crew. Rhodesian Security Forces fought off attacks within the precincts of major towns. Guerrillas launched multiple strikes on Umtali, and mortar bombs, rockets, and light artillery rounds landed in the city from the surrounding mountains. Daily, civilians were shot dead in crossfire, executed as collaborators or killed by landmines. Commodities and fuel were scarce, mining and manufacturing operating at very low levels. White commercial farmers were killed and agricultural production was falling. Basic medical, agricultural, transport, and maintenance services were no longer provided across much of the country as civil administration ground to a halt. Schools continued to close, with more than 400,000 children unable to continue their education. Political collapse and a full military victory by guerrilla forces seemed just a matter of time.

* * *

Within days of our return in January 1979, my father flew to Katerere. He had heard that a landmine had been found on the military airstrip close to the Mission. On the shaky premise that local people must have known of the landmine and yet did not report it, the Rhodesian Security Forces had retaliated by burning the homes of those living close to the airstrip. This had left local people, many church members among them, destitute and without food stocks to tide them over to the next harvest.[4] The MAF pilot skilfully landed his Cessna loaded with medicines, clothes, food, and my father on the limited space of the Emmanuel Secondary School football pitch!

Such visits to Katerere were both sobering and encouraging. The churches across the area were battered by the war. There was no transport, and meetings drew unwelcome attention from both sides. In addition, anti-Christian rhetoric and action by some guerrillas meant some turned away from Christianity to worship ancestral spirits. The only church still openly meeting was on the Mission complex.

In fact, more was going on than met the eye. The "cell" system which had been put in place by Ephraim had been prescient. He had warned his people it might be needed in days to come and had prepared them well. Now the days of fear were upon them, people were meeting in homes. The church had vanished underground, but it had not died.

In stark contrast to Mission stations looted and destroyed by local communities, my father found the buildings on the Elim Mission complex were well cared for despite the war still raging in the area. He discovered that eighteen months previously, Ephraim Satuku had called a meeting of village heads, the chief, and influential people in the villages surrounding the Mission. A goat had been killed, food prepared, and all ate together. Pious Munembe took up the story, "We told them that we did not think the war would last forever and that peace was just around the corner. We said it would be nice to gain independence with all these buildings still standing because we would use them to continue the secondary school. Then we took them around the whole Mission – the buildings and what we wanted them to look after, and we all agreed that this was the best thing to do." Ephraim and Pious had wisely made the community the guardians of the Mission.

In addition, Pious and Ephraim had quietly tried to build relationships with those guerrillas in the area whom they saw as sympathetic and reasonable. ZANLA platoon commander and political commissar Comrade Ranga was one such man, the son of an Anglican headmaster and who described himself as a Christian. Pious knew him as someone who wanted to save as many lives as possible and saw Ranga act, sometimes heroically, to that end. Although many guerrilla commanders were menacing towards Christianity, relationships of trust with men such as Comrade Ranga were crucial to the survival of the Mission.

The withdrawal of the missionaries in 1977 from the Katerere area spelled the end of the missionary-led church but marked a new beginning of a truly indigenous work, led by black Christians with great courage, wisdom, and integrity. Seeing this, my father wrote to Elim HQ in the UK urging them to sequester Emmanuel Secondary School funds and not to use them for other purposes, however well intentioned. With the eye of faith shared with Ephraim and Pious, my father foresaw the reopening of Emmanuel in "a few years' time", even in the violent chaos of those bitter days.

At the end of the first rainy season after the funerals, a headstone was placed on the mass grave in Umtali. The Elim Missions Director wrote from the UK to ask whether a graveside service of remembrance would take place marking the first anniversary. But in Shona culture, a year after someone had died, a *kurova guva* ceremony would be held at the graveside to accept and welcome the dead relative's wandering spirit, or *mudzimu*, back to the family. For this reason, my father felt that a graveside service should be avoided because it might be misunderstood. In a touching aside, he added that neither he nor my mother could cope emotionally with a graveside commemoration.

Instead, a dedication service at Central Baptist Church in Salisbury was held, as a call to renew a personal commitment to live for God as part of remembering those who had died. Former Emmanuel Secondary School students spoke and my father preached. Apprehensive before the service, my parents were moved by the numbers who came, and found the tribute to be unexpectedly healing.

As he walked out to his car with my mother, my father was approached by a journalist who asked him, "Could you tell me in one sentence what God has taught you as a result of the death of your colleagues and friends?"

My father paused for a few seconds, and two verses of Paul's second letter to the young church in Corinth came to his mind, and he quoted, "For this slight momentary affliction is preparing for us an eternal weight of glory beyond all comparison, because we do not look to the things that are seen but to the things that are unseen; for the things that are seen are transient, but the things that are unseen are eternal."[5] To this he added, "I am beginning to learn to stand where God stands and to take an eternal view of what happens in this brief span of time."

* * *

The Commonwealth Heads of Government met in August 1979 in Lusaka, Zambia. Britain was put under diplomatic and economic pressure by Nigeria, her biggest trading partner in Africa: all British investments in Nigeria would be blocked until the Rhodesian crisis was resolved. Host countries for nationalist forces, Zambia and Mozambique were desperate to end the war that had cost them dearly in lost lives, damaged infrastructure, and economic devastation.

For the Rhodesian government, the economy was under severe stress, white morale was falling, and emigration was rising sharply. Nationalist forces were severely strained with shortages of munitions, clothing, medicines, and food as thousands of high school and university students crossed into recruitment camps in Botswana, Zambia, Tanzania, and Mozambique. Guerrilla training of these new recruits was increasingly meagre.

Commanders ordered ill-disciplined, poorly trained recruits into Rhodesia in a "final push", who were then killed in large numbers. This was mirrored in the Rhodesian Security Forces, who deployed so-called "Security Force Auxiliaries", poorly trained militias who were often little more than bandits.

Caught between multiple forces, the rural people's intense suffering was worsened further by drought and crop failure. All these pressures led to the 1979 Lancaster House Conference, chaired by Lord Carrington, the newly appointed British Foreign Secretary, and including delegates from all sides in the complex, fragmented conflict, most grown weary of fighting.

Just as the Lancaster House Conference got under way, my father's first book with the Religious Education team in the Ministry of Education had been completed and was being trialled in forty schools. Told initially that their focus would only be on primary religious education, my father was delighted and daunted when he was asked to develop materials for secondary school students.

The first convention in the newly acquired Umtali Memorial Church, named in memory of Elim's martyrs, was held over the weekend of 10–11 August 1979, with 150 attending, equally divided between men and women.[6] In a touching show of support, Ephraim and Pious came from Katerere, cycling the first ninety kilometres since ZANLA guerrillas would not allow them to use motorbikes and the public transport system remained paralysed.

Despite peace talks, Elim leaders in Katerere continued to walk a tightrope. Rhodesian Security Forces had accused some of the staff of "feeding terrorists", which my father hotly refuted. But they had threatened violence against the mission staff, on one occasion beating nurses in the hospital. Conversely, ZANLA guerrillas threatened to close Manjanja Primary School on the Mission complex, leaving hundreds of children without education and staff without jobs. Pious Munembe, as principal, was under great strain, steering between the two forces. If he were to have to leave to find work to support the family, Evelyn would not be able to stay on alone, and Elim Hospital would have to close too. The only centre providing medical and educational services in an area of 25,000 square kilometres would be left empty. Despite the relationships with the community, abandoning the complex altogether could leave it easy prey for vandals and thieves who had stripped windows, door frames, and roofing material from abandoned mission properties across the country.

My father wrote to the Elim Missions Director in the UK, asking for a call to prayer for Pious and Ephraim to be issued across the hundreds of Elim Churches in the UK. He closed his letter with great emotion: "When I meet some of the men and women up there [at Katerere] I think of the letter of Jerusalem, 'Our beloved Barnabas and Paul, men who have risked their lives for the sake of our Lord Jesus Christ."[7]

Famine in Katerere meant great hardship for the people, so my father was flying in supplementary food. But he discovered the people were not only trying to feed themselves in a time of drought, but they were also coping with demands to be fed by ever-increasing numbers of guerrillas. The difficult decision was taken to supply food for immediate use on the Mission only, to avoid stockpiling food that might be demanded by guerrillas.

On 30 October 1979, armed men went to Ephraim's house at night. They forced him to open the office and stole the radio-telephone and generator, despite his protests. Ephraim was warned that if he reported this to the military, the guerrillas would return to kill him, and only him. Ephraim did not report to the military locally, but he told my father, who made sure that the Rhodesian Army Chaplain General knew. A kindly man, the Chaplain General ensured that Ephraim would not have draconian Rhodesian legislation used against him.

By mid-November, in response to the call for prayer, there

had been definite improvement in the Katerere situation. The threat of closure of the primary school had receded, and clarity regarding the feeding programme and a courageous visit by Pious to the military camp to complain about the beatings had led to better behaviour from the Security Forces. And while there was no return of the stolen radio-telephone, other guerrilla groups in the area had let it be known they were unhappy with the theft, reinforcing the protection of the Mission.

"We often met for prayers and to thank God for protecting us from the Security Forces and the comrades themselves, because our fellow Africans were dying, being accused of sell-outs and so on. And we thanked God for the food being supplied by the Mission Aviation Fellowship and so on." Pious Munembe described the situation to a visitor from the UK just as some kind of end to the exhausting, frightening years of war looked as if it was in sight.

* * *

At Lancaster House, with support from the leaders of the frontline states, Lord Carrington skilfully brokered a peace agreement between the warring factions in Rhodesia. Signed on 21 December 1979, it ended a seven-year war that had cost more than 20,000 lives. Economic sanctions imposed on Rhodesia were lifted in late 1979, and British rule resumed under a transitional arrangement. Commonwealth Monitoring Group troops numbering 1,200 started deployment across Rhodesia in preparation for the ceasefire a week later. Rhodesian Security Forces were confined to barracks, while Commonwealth troops manned sixteen hastily created Assembly Points to house guerrillas and initiate a demobilizing exercise.

My father was angered on hearing the plan to put Assembly Point Echo at Elim Mission in Katerere. Without checking, Lancaster House planners had assumed that the Mission was empty and derelict like so many others around the country. Mission buildings would potentially be damaged by the influx of hundreds of armed men. He petitioned for Assembly Point Echo to be moved off the Mission, anxious that the hard work to protect the Mission by Ephraim and Pious in the hope of rapid expansion at the end of the war would not all be undone at the last.

My father flew to Katerere with British Army officers to meet urgently with the Security Forces.[8] After tense negotiations, they agreed to move the Assembly Point to Bhande Primary School, using the classrooms there as the core of the Assembly Point. Australian troops would be based at the District Commissioner's Camp one kilometre away from Elim Mission and near the foot of the escarpment which led up to the Rhodesian Security Forces base. A Commonwealth Monitoring Force Officer and four men would headquarter in our old house on the Mission to ensure the protection of the premises. Back in London, ZANU delegates agreed to the change and my father received a call to confirm the new arrangement.

The Commonwealth Monitoring Group military planners took a huge gamble. Their peacekeeping mission was based on consensus rather than coercion and relied on moral persuasion rather than troop strength. No one knew what would happen. Would the ceasefire hold? Would the Assembly Points fill? What if hostilities broke out again? A few lightly armed peacekeepers would be no match for either side.

To the astonishment of the Monitoring Group, slowly at first, and then in large numbers, heavily armed guerrillas began to emerge from the bush. A tenuous and tense ceasefire ensued. At one point the Australian contingent at Assembly Point Echo was surrounded by belligerent ZANLA guerrillas with mortars, machine guns, and rocket-propelled grenades, but they negotiated their way through the stand-off without shots being fired. Once again, Elim Mission in Katerere had been spared.

By 7 January 1980, nearly 20,000 guerrillas were in assembly points. In less than three months, the combatants were disengaged and integration of three armies had begun. Such actions had created the conditions necessary for elections to take place and for a new state to emerge. Impossible though it seemed, the war did come to an end, and Southern Rhodesia became independent Zimbabwe in April 1980. "We have peace," commented my father, "although we're not sure yet at what price." But the recurrent vivid dream I had as a child during the war years in Katerere – fleeing in terror from men of violence into the night – gradually faded into nothing.

* * *

In the new nation, my parents continued to work for the Elim Pentecostal Church of Zimbabwe, under the leadership team to which they had handed over control four years before.

Elim Hospital was already full as travel became possible, and Ken Jenkins, a young Zimbabwean doctor, went to help Evelyn Munembe expand the medical work. By October 1980 the primary school had 200 children, more than ever. The rapid expansion of the church work in the Katerere area was heartening, but resulted in Ephraim being overworked and in need of help.

Remarkably, eleven ZANLA guerrillas, combatants in the Katerere area during the war, were now openly attending services in the main Mission church.[9] Some had been Christians before the war. Others had come to faith during those turbulent times, won over by the living faith of men and women like Ephraim and Winnie Satuku, and Pious and Evelyn Munembe.

Asked to plan for the reopening of Emmanuel Secondary School, my father searched for funding. Generously, the American government provided £20,000.[10] Hundreds of textbooks were bought and tonnes of books and equipment trucked in on newly opened roads. The boarding school was fully re-equipped and science laboratories were restored to functionality. Just sixteen, I was between school and college at the time, I learned the elements of bookkeeping to track the purchasing of equipment, and I processed the backlog of applications. More than a thousand students applied for just eighty Form 1 places at Emmanuel Secondary School.

Emmanuel Secondary School reopened in Katerere on 20 January 1981 with eighty-two Form 1 students and four teachers, two and a half years after it had been closed so abruptly and brutally in the Vumba.

My father's insistence on sequestering Emmanuel Secondary School funds for future use and his urgent intervention during the ceasefire had gone hand in hand with Pious and Ephraim's courageous and shrewd wartime management of the facilities under their responsibility. Jointly, even in the darkest times, they had trusted that God had not abandoned them, that He was Emmanuel, "God with us", and that one day the school of His promise would reopen. Their faith had been vindicated.

* * *

In addition to working alongside his Elim colleagues during the death throes of war, walking the tightrope of the ceasefire, and through the transition to a representative government, my father had continued to throw himself into his full-time day job as an Education Officer in the Zimbabwean Ministry of Education! Independence meant a policy change was mooted to remove Christianity from religious education and replace it with traditional religion. My father constantly attended meetings to defend and justify his team and their approach.

Despite much opposition, by November 1981 his third teacher's book had been published and distributed. The first two books, covering the early school years, were already in their second edition. With the third book, more than a million children in Zimbabwe were being taught religious education, with a focus on the Christian faith, using my father's team materials.

During 1982, my father oversaw a project to place twenty Bibles in each of Zimbabwe's 4,500 schools. In addition, two million children were given a personal copy of Luke and Acts. His team completed books for Years 4 and 5. It was an extraordinary time of opportunity and productivity which my father seized with both hands.

My father's educational books were being published by the Zimbabwean branch of the British company Longman. The general manager David McKenzie had taken it upon himself to check the proofs of some of my father's books. Unknown to my father, David's family were caught up in a very stormy period. It looked as if the fabric of family life and relationships was about to crumble and collapse. David took up the story: "One evening, as I was in the garden worrying about a situation which simply could not be resolved in human terms, a phrase from one of Peter's books came to mind. The Spirit of the Lord came upon me and in that instant I became a Christian. The Lord in His goodness and mercy and loving kindness, through no voluntary act on my part, had intervened, and through the months that followed gave me the faith and hope and trust to sort out our difficulties and to start again in newness of life."[11] David and his family became lifelong friends, and joined the church we attended in the newly named Harare (previously Salisbury).

My brother Paul chose to be baptized by my father that year along with three former Emmanuel students who were studying at the University of Zimbabwe, very close to our home in Harare. In December 1982 my mother wrote, "Almost everywhere we go, Emmanuel students come up to greet us and we are continually being reminded that all those years teaching out in the bush were not wasted, but rather as we see some of them and their commitment to the Lord we know that through them there is hope for Zimbabwe."

Soon after our return, through former students of Emmanuel, my father began to receive invitations from various schools to speak at their Christian Union meetings. So many students contacted my parents through letters, telephone calls, or visits, expressing their warmth and love.

One such student, Colin Kuhuni, had become a Christian at Emmanuel Secondary School on a Sunday evening when my father had preached. Finding a place at St Augustine's Mission to continue his third year of high school, he arrived there still grieving and despondent. Shocked to find the student body largely indifferent to the Christian faith and a tiny Christian group on the brink of expiring, Colin suddenly understood that he had miraculously found a place in his new school not just to complete his education. Witnessing to a former guerrilla and staunch Marxist Leninist student, Colin infuriated the student, who bullied him mercilessly. Eventually, Colin sought a hidden spot among rocks distant from the school. Engaged in fervent, audible prayer, Colin mentioned his tormentor by name, asking for God's intervention and grace on him. Unknown to Colin, the bully was nearby and heard Colin's prayers. The following day he approached Colin as a changed man and asked his forgiveness, and he became a staunch member of the Christian group within the school. Colin saw the body of Christian students grow in numbers and in depth of commitment.

At Marist Brothers School, Patrick Mandisodza reflected on what had taken place, and wrote to my parents, "The Lord's intervention on 23 June resulted in a total dispersion of all the pupils. It was the Lord's decision that could not be altered by any human being in the world." The Lord's intervention? It seemed a shocking way to describe what had happened – that God had intervened, that events at Elim were under His control, and that God had remained good while acting in a sovereign way.

But Patrick went on, "For this reason they were like sheep

being led to the slaughter. It was not their decision but Christ's. The Lord revealed to them His glory and they sealed their testimonies with their blood... They departed in peace, though in the sight of the world it was a disaster. This has given all Christians hope in the Lord. Many things have happened since their departure, some have fallen away and some have become strong and faithful to the Lord. Really it is... Christ's selection or pruning and appointing His Workers. Now I believe it is my duty to spread the gospel. Christ Jesus led me to Marist Brothers in Inyanga and He really used Oliver and me. It was a wonderful experience to all of us. I am at this place being used by God during Saturday and Sunday services."

Oliver Manyemba summed it up vividly in conversation with me: "The devil saw the fire of the gospel burning brightly at Emmanuel Secondary School. So he ran up and gave the fire a big kick and thought he had put it out. But all he did was spread sparks across the country, starting new fires all over."

Greatly moved by the increasing number of such stories, my father wrote of Emmanuel students: "They left the scene of martyrdom with hearts burning to make Christ known wherever they went."

Yet others besides the students could not forget this martyrdom.

WHISPERS AND RUMOURS

I move from place to place in an attempt to escape my memories of the war. One day I hope to leave them behind. But ghosts follow me wherever I go. I don't want to think about the war. I want to forget it but I can't. Terrible memories get in the way of everything I do.

Alexander Kanengoni[1]

Dust motes dancing in shafts of light, the winter sun poured in through the glass panels surrounding the front door. Colin Kuhuni, a lawyer and former student from Emmanuel School, had dropped in to say hello. We sat in the sitting room in easy chairs, catching up with each other's news. The front door opened and I looked up, shading my eyes to see my father silhouetted against the bright afternoon sunshine. His face was shadowed, his expression invisible. Unusually, he said nothing, and turned to his left. We heard his quick, confident step in the corridor. Moments later the door to his study banged closed, and silence ensued for the next half hour.

As Colin and I talked on, I heard the study door reopen and my father's footsteps returned slowly along the corridor. He turned into the sitting room. He looked ashen and his hands were trembling. In alarm, both Colin and I half-started to our feet, but my father motioned us to stay seated. He said, "I have just had the most remarkable meeting of my life." Struggling with his emotions, he paused. I was astonished to see my normally capable father acting so strangely, and my mind was racing. What could have affected him so?

Taking a deep breath, he went on, "I have just met one of the men who murdered my friends."

Colin's legal instincts prompted him to say, "Tell me what the man you just met looks like."

My father outlined his appearance: a very tall, angular man with an expressive, vivacious face.

Thoughtfully, Colin said, "That's the man who addressed us that night with his rifle slung over his shoulder. He was the one that told us that Emmanuel School was to be closed immediately."

My father sat down with Colin and me to tell us what had happened. He mentioned that over a period of months he had heard of rumours beginning to circulate that some of the armed men responsible for the murders at Emmanuel had come to faith. Unsurprisingly, my father was reluctant to investigate these reports as he had no wish to meet anyone claiming to be responsible for the murder of his friends and colleagues, "even if he was in Bible College". But he also did not want to allow false stories to gain circulation or credence in such a serious matter. If such a story were to be widely told and then exposed as a fabrication, it would be deeply painful for the families of those who had died. In discussion with Elim Headquarters in the UK, my father was urged to seek the veracity of a story being reported in Canada. Elim Headquarters had already made contact with the agency linked to the story, pleading with them not to publish.[2]

Then a second rumour had surfaced close to home that a guerrilla involved in the attack at Elim had come to faith in Christ and was in a Bible College in Harare training to be a preacher.[3] My father knew the director of the Bible College that had been mentioned, so he rang him about the tale. The principal suggested that my father accept an invitation to visit the college and speak to the students at their devotional session. This would give him a natural opportunity to be at the Bible College. My father could then meet the man concerned and make up his own mind about him.

Very apprehensive, at about 11.00 a.m. on 10 June 1983, my father was ushered into the principal's office and introduced to a young man who called himself Garikai. Immediately the principal withdrew and the two men were left on their own. Garikai seemed reticent at first. My father heard why later – someone had tried to interview Garikai with a hidden tape recorder, something Garikai had thought dangerous as well as lacking in integrity. Garikai was unsure whether my father could be trusted.

More significantly, having been told of my father's connection with the Elim missionaries and now as a Christian himself, Garikai suddenly felt overwhelmed with the enormity of what he was about to recount. A deep fear of saying anything overshadowed him, and yet at the same time he wanted to unburden himself. As the two men continued to talk, some of the strained nature of the atmosphere began to dissolve. Garikai seemed to sense that my father held no bitterness in his heart, no deep reservoirs of anger. And so Garikai began to recount something of his remarkable story.

During the war, guerrillas hid their identities behind *zita rechimurenga*, or "names of the revolution". For many guerrillas, the process of choosing a war name went beyond simply concealing identity. As young men and women joined one of the armed wings of the nationalist movements, choosing a war name was the first step towards a new identity. Garikai had chosen the war name of Devil Hondo, or "War Devil", a name that was deliberately disturbing, demonstrating a conclusive break with his upbringing. As he recounted his story, Garikai referred to himself throughout as Devil Hondo, using his war name almost as if he was telling the story about someone else.

* * *

It was a long, hot Sunday afternoon, towards the end of November 1980. The war of independence had ended, the guns had fallen silent, and Rhodesia had become Zimbabwe just seven months before. In the south of the country, ZANLA guerrilla Devil Hondo was sitting in a military camp, idly leafing through an issue of *The Chronicle* newspaper.[4]

His eye was caught by an article, which began in bold type: "Dear Comrade". In the format of an open letter, a Peruvian, Rafael de la Torre, recounted his story as a Marxist guerrilla fighting a revolutionary war. Haunted by his involvement in terrible acts of violence, Rafael had found peace through the love and forgiveness offered through faith in Jesus Christ.

Increasingly angry, Devil Hondo began to read the article out loud to members of his guerrilla section sitting close by. He realized that the article was a paid advertisement. Below Rafael's story was an invitation for any comrades who wanted to know more to write to a Margaret Lloyd through a post box number.

Incensed by what they had heard, the men discussed the matter and agreed that Devil Hondo should write to Margaret and invite her to meet with them, ostensibly to answer their questions. But they intended to kill her for posting an advertisement that they found deeply offensive. Together with the members of his section, Devil Hondo composed a letter. Placing the letter in an envelope, he sealed and addressed it, sliding it into the thigh pocket of his fatigues. My father recalled the subconscious movement of Garikai's hand along the front of his thigh as he recounted what he had done with the letter.

Climbing into a military Land Rover, Devil Hondo drove to the mailing area in the camp, slid his hand into the same pocket to retrieve the letter, only to find that the letter was not there. Turning out all his pockets had the same result. The letter was nowhere to be found! So Devil Hondo picked up a pen and scribbled a second version of the letter. The story of Rafael had affected him more than he had cared to admit to his comrades. The strange disappearance of the first joint letter gave him an opportunity to write a letter from his heart this time.

A civilian administrator working for the British South Africa Police, Margaret Lloyd had placed the advertisement. Her practice was to prayerfully consider all the responses she received from the advertisements she placed. To those who provided a return address she would then write a personal letter, often enclosing portions of the Bible.

Margaret received many replies to the story of Rafael de la Torre. Some wanted to know more. Others contained vile threats, promises to find out where she lived and kill her. But one response[5] which she received on 3 December 1980 stood out:

> *Say Sister,*
>
> *I saw your advertisement in the local newspaper about Comrade Raf especially Jesus Christ! Yes I would like to accept Jesus as my personal serviour. I am Comrade Devil Hondo. I am now staying with parents. Please just help me, that is if you care. Please please sister I am so corrupt. My life is scattered, horrible one. Someone please help me. I am a nowhere man. Living in a nowhere land. Make up my nowhere plans. A nobody. I want*

a complete change. Oh no I don't even understand
myself. Since 1974 I was in the bundu. But I am
alive. God knows what. I wish Jesus, Jesus, Jesus
could hear my plea. I will write and make my
confession if you'll reply me. I was once a Christian.
That is long back. I drink, smoke fag and drugs
even going for whores but instead of being happy I
become so guilt conscious. I become scarred. I am
a young man of twenty-two. Help build my life. My
hand is short to reach out and touch the Lord.
       Yours in dismay,
       Comrade Devil Hondo

Following her usual practice, Margaret prayerfully considered the letter and then responded, enclosing a Gospel of John. She posted it off with a prayer for the unknown Devil Hondo, little guessing what her courageous act would lead to.

Born on 4 April 1958 in Que-Que, Garikai grew up in a small town built around several goldmines on the central watershed of Rhodesia. He was one of eleven children, whose father was a Christian pastor. Garikai started his secondary schooling at Goromonzi Secondary School on the outskirts of the capital of Rhodesia. Goromonzi was an elite government secondary school which became a hotbed of nationalist politics. He was just sixteen when he was persuaded to drop out of school and join one of the armed wings of the nationalist movements. His dangerous clandestine journey across the Rhodesian border into Zambia marked the beginning of a second journey into something much darker than Garikai ever dreamed of.

Conditions in the ZANLA camps at the time of Garikai's arrival were chaotic.[6] The number of ZANLA guerrillas had increased from 200 in 1972 to more than 3,000 in 1974[7] but with little planning to match the growth in recruit numbers. By 1979,

160,000 people, a mixture of recruits and refugees, had found their way into Mozambique. Food was frequently in desperately short supply. There were so few plates that recruits sometimes had to receive what food there was on leaves or in their bare hands. Young people undergoing a demanding physical training regime were literally starving. Limited supplies of clothing came in bags marked "United Nations Refugee Aid", but there were no uniforms. There was a serious shortage of blankets in the face of cold winter nights when temperatures could drop to freezing. Many of the recruits became ill.[8]

There were not only the physical challenges of survival. The camps could be frightening places for other reasons. Despite the nominal adherence to Marxist ideology opposed to religion, there was a resurgence of traditional religious practice. Guerrillas sought to access and control spiritual forces, believing that ancestral spirits would protect them as they struggled to return the land to rightful ownership. "Nightly spirit possessions by the ancestors, their arrival heralded by an eerie whooping sound were a familiar feature of every camp in the liberation struggle," wrote former ZANLA member Fay Chung.[9]

Many of the sexual mores of traditional Shona society dissolved. Female recruits were nicknamed "warm blankets", because their sexual abuse by men was so rampant. Perpetrators ranged from the lowest ranks to the highest leadership.[10] Women feared the night-time arrival of vehicles in the camps, as this usually indicated that leaders of rank were arriving. Fay Chung would hear screaming and crying in the darkness as officers forced themselves on the young women of their choice. In the absence of normal social structures, those with power took whatever or whomever they wanted. Not only was abuse widespread, but victims could not seek justice. Rudo, a female guerrilla, recounted the experience of many: "When there is a rape or somebody has been raped, there was no mother to tell that somebody had abused you. There was no law, there was no justice where you could report to – there was no court of law. If you fell pregnant no one assisted you."[11]

Thousands of young people were continuing to pour into the training camps, some illiterate and some from university backgrounds, a volatile and diverse group. Although training camps were physically separated from refugee camps, the latter were used as recruitment points for the war effort.[12] Many were below military age, but little attempt was made to differentiate between refugees and recruits. Control was enforced through public corporal punishment.

Shoes and boots were in very short supply. There was little in the way of guns and materials of war. Training could take place with sticks in place of guns, and sometimes guerrillas were only provided with a weapon on crossing into Rhodesia. Fighters with little or no training were deployed, leading to a very high casualty rate when guerrilla groups encountered Rhodesian Security Forces.[13]

This combination of factors led to rapid disillusionment for many recruits and guerrillas. The camps divided into factions, the better-educated, younger Marxists against traditional religious leaders and older colleagues of peasant stock, and the simmering disagreements between them sometimes exploded into violence. An attempted rebellion against the ZANLA High Command took place in 1974, led by young officer Thomas Nhari. It was summarily put down, with some of the leaders being publicly executed. In the aftermath of the Nhari rebellion[14] a split in the nationalist forces led to a faction leaving Zambia and travelling overland to Mozambique, which was on the brink of gaining independence from Portugal, to open bases there.

The misery in the camps was worsened by a turn of events completely unanticipated by the camp authorities. In the early morning of 9 August 1976, a column of armoured cars and trucks, some mounted with aircraft cannon, entered Nyazonia camp, thirty-five kilometres inside Mozambique. The vehicles were painted with Mozambican army colours, and the troops on board were dressed in Mozambican army kit so were waved through the camp gate by the guards. But on board were eighty-four commandos from the Rhodesian Selous Scouts – a Special Forces unit.

The vehicles drew up in the centre of the camp. Up to 5,000 men, women, and children gathered around the vehicles, enthusiastically cheering a welcome to those they believed were allies. A barked command, and the commandos opened up with the heavy weapons mounted on their vehicles, pouring a devastating indiscriminate barrage at close range into the crowds that were dancing and ululating before them. Within seconds, the parade ground was transformed into a charnel house, the celebratory atmosphere replaced with the thunderous chatter of the guns and the screams of the wounded or dying. Hundreds were killed, among them women and children. Many of the survivors were deeply traumatized by the horribly disfigured bodies of the slain, torn apart by the weaponry used. They swore to take their revenge – indeed, this massacre at Nyazonia by Rhodesian Selous Scouts was cited as motivation for the killing of the Elim missionaries in the diary of Luke Madzvimbo, the guerrilla killed by Poole and his men.

So intense and pervasive did the internal struggles become, and so common and bloody the cross-border attacks by Rhodesian troops, that at times many in the camps lived in great fear of both internecine skirmishes within nationalist groups and Rhodesian cross-border attacks.

ZANLA commander Josiah Tongogara might have had little education, but he was a militarily gifted leader, charismatic and full of energy. He was wary both of politicians, whom he saw as untrustworthy and corrupt, and of younger, ideologically driven guerrilla commanders (although he was quick to identify and promote those with military skills).[15] He was also heavily criticized by traditional religious leaders for failing to prevent the widespread abuse of women. Looking for a power base, the followers who obeyed his every command without question were the uneducated older guerrillas, a devoted group of women guerrillas, and the child soldiers. They gave him their "total and unquestioning loyalty",[16] becoming the devotees with whom Tongogara surrounded himself. Very tall, a natural leader with an energetic manner and expressive, vivacious face, sixteen-year-old Garikai, now going by his war name of Devil Hondo, became one of these child soldiers.[17]

Despite the left-wing rhetoric of the time, very few senior military commanders actually embraced Marxism as a guiding ideology. Those who did take Marxist thinking seriously, the so-called *Vashandi*, were sidelined and imprisoned in northern Mozambique. The socialist jargon so freely used by the senior echelons of ZANLA came less from conviction and more from the need to win supplies – guns, training, and food – from the Eastern bloc. It was also useful in radicalizing young recruits.

One of Devil Hondo's older contemporaries wrote, "Reading Lenin disturbed me: his emphasis on the use of violence and crime in order to achieve highly laudable goals upset my Catholic value system. I found it difficult to accept the idea that bank robbery and murder in the name of revolution were perfectly acceptable options. Nevertheless I understood intellectually that Lenin was offering a practical way of making Marx's ideas a reality."[18] Violence was seen as a tool, an acceptable form of political discourse that could be deployed against anyone, civilian or military, who was seen to be in the way of the fight for independence.

Anxious to make his mark, Devil Hondo endured great danger and physical hardship, absorbing military training eagerly, keen to master his new vocation. As a child soldier, a young, impressionable teenager, he had also been exposed to severe corporal punishment, was aware of the slaughter in the camps, had seen leaders engage with impunity in the sexual exploitation of women, and had been taught that even extreme violence was fully acceptable in the pursuit of the war aims of his movement.

Following his training, Devil Hondo was appointed political commissar and platoon commander of a section of seventeen guerrillas, a number of whom, like him, were under the age of eighteen. Many ZANLA guerrillas, inspired by the Maoist concept of a people's war, were focused on winning the hearts and minds of the people. They spent most of their time engaged in creating political awareness and support among rural people in Rhodesia. In many areas that support was freely offered, where black Rhodesians sought to be free from the injustice of being ruled by an increasingly oppressive white minority.

But where that support was not freely offered, there was no compunction about the use of terrible acts of violence by guerrillas against unarmed civilians. Devil Hondo's section was no exception: "It was no longer war but common banditry. I wanted to show the enemy that terror, brutality and cold-blooded murder were our monopoly. That was a communist privilege."[19]

When the war ended in December 1979, Devil Hondo was just twenty-one years old, but was a veteran with five years of war behind him.

Then his eye had been caught by the "Dear Comrade" advertisement in the newspaper. With very little to do, Devil Hondo then began to read what Margaret Lloyd had sent him. He began to visit churches in the Bulawayo area, searching for answers, searching for God. Discussing with his men his struggles and what he was reading and learning, he found that seven of them were also wrestling with the past. They were finding that the quiet days in camp gave them time and space into which were flooding unwanted images and memories. Confronted with fear, shame, and guilt, the young men were searching for peace, looking for ways of coming to terms with the traumatic, blood-soaked days and nights they had endured and created.

There came a night in the military camp that Devil Hondo was never to forget. Together with other members of his section, they were talking over some of their exploits during the war when suddenly and simultaneously they saw a vision of a cross. Devil Hondo saw what he interpreted as the hand of God coming through the vision as if to crush him in judgment. Among the cries of consternation and fear from the others in his section, Devil Hondo heard himself shouting out to God for mercy, for deliverance from what he saw as a just judgment for his sin. And so Devil Hondo came to believe in Jesus Christ. Following his conversion experience he returned to using his pre-war name of Garikai once again.

* * *

After coming to faith, Garikai had decided to request demobilization and make a new life for himself outside the military. Many companies in independent Zimbabwe remained white owned, and were reluctant to employ former guerrillas. Combatants had often had their education interrupted and so were disadvantaged in the labour market.[20] Disabled veterans simply could not compete where unemployment levels for the able-bodied remained high. Many more may have escaped physical disability but struggled with mental illness and alcoholism, creating perceptions that they were difficult and would cause trouble.

Invited to join a travelling evangelistic team, Garikai was given opportunities to speak in churches, to pray, and to lead groups of young people in Bible study. He was delighted to discover that people responded warmly when he preached. When a young man came to faith in his youth group, Garikai was filled with excitement.

Yet there were many moments in his new life that Garikai found very difficult. He endured mockery from neighbours, who jeered at his poverty. He heard a minister say that those that killed others during the war could not be forgiven, which plunged him into despair. Margaret wrote to him, citing Scripture and declaring that God had declared him forgiven, whatever a man might say to him. Garikai found great comfort in her words, and he persevered, while recognizing that he needed depth in his understanding of his new-found faith. Just over a year after his conversion, Garikai began attending Bible College in Harare. His decision eventually led to the encounter with my father.

At that first meeting, tremendously hard though they both found it, Garikai gave some of the reasoning that had lain behind the killing of Elim's missionaries. Guerrilla commanders wanted to be able to get into the country more freely and to open up more crossing points.[21] By mid-1978, sometimes up to 150 guerrillas a night were crossing through dense bush south of Eagle School. But they had to make contact with local groups to escort them through more dangerous areas. ZANLA commanders wanted to expand possible crossing points northwards into an area that was still well populated. Killing the missionaries and closing the school would frighten people out of the area, expanding the range of crossing sites.

Garikai told my father that the guerrillas wanted to cause a wide impact, battering white morale not just locally but also across the country, and so undermine the tottering Rhodesia Front government. The missionaries didn't have weapons so they were an easy target for a major atrocity, which was deliberately gruesome and racially targeted.

The sections that carried out the massacre were largely composed of new recruits, freshly arrived from Mozambican training camps and bent on revenge attacks for Rhodesian cross-border raiding. Elim was a convenient soft target where the novices could be "blooded",[22] where the innate profound psychological aversion towards killing another human being could be broken down.

Finally, it was a punishment for the missionaries for not responding to orders to move off the premises. Garikai claimed that three written messages had been sent to the Elim missionaries to leave. When they hadn't responded after three days, two guerrilla sections had joined forces and went on campus to kill them.

After his men had gone in that night to seize and bind Phil Evans, Garikai had confronted Phil in his kitchen, ordering him to leave the country. Phil responded to say that he could only leave if Jesus Christ told him to do so. Garikai responded mockingly, questioning the existence of Christ. "What shoe size did Jesus take?" Garikai had taunted. "About how tall would he have been?"

Phil's quiet response to Garikai's derision was to offer to prepare a meal for Garikai and his armed group.

His offer rejected, Phil was marched roughly into the night to the school office. Once the looting of the office was complete, the missionaries were herded on to the sports field. With his men standing menacingly around them, Garikai spoke to Phil again. Cruelly, Garikai told Phil to close his eyes and pray because he was about to be skinned alive. Phil pleaded for the lives of his family and his colleagues, begging Garikai to spare them even if he was to be killed, asking for his life to be taken in exchange for theirs. Garikai accepted the exchange, telling Phil that he was about to die although the others would be spared.

But Garikai had no intention of keeping his promise. Forced to his knees, Phil closed his eyes and turned to God in the fearsome darkness. As Phil called out in prayer, so Garikai gave the signal, and across the killing ground, the assaults began. Hearing the screams and cries of his family and colleagues,[23] it became obvious that no exchange had been contemplated and they were all to die. Phil struggled to free his hands, remonstrating with the gunmen, pointing out they all had guns and like cowards were killing defenceless people. With that Wendy called out, "Don't worry Phil! They cannot kill the soul!" In the face of an impending, terrible death, Wendy was recalling the words of Jesus to his followers: "So have no fear of them, for nothing is covered that will not be revealed, or hidden that will not be known. And do not fear those who kill the body but cannot kill the soul."[24] Angered, the murderers pressed home their attack on Wendy with savage ferocity.

Realizing that they were all to die together, the team of friends cried out to God repeatedly. Garikai had been unable to forget their voices, and their words rang in his memory. What they prayed had not made sense to him at the time. They reminded God that they were there in obedience to Him and not because they chose to be. And even as the cruel work of the executioners began to make ever more savage inroads on their bodies, as they endured despoliation and battering, they cried to God continually to forgive and save those who were hurting them so dreadfully.

Garikai picked up a piece of paper and wrote down the actions of his group, adding that his men had acted "as if we were demoniac possessed". He gave further details of the suffering the missionaries endured, over which a veil of silence will remain. Underneath his account, Garikai wrote a simple, short, powerful sentence: "They were innocent, I tell you."

Unwittingly, Garikai echoed the comment of a Roman centurion in charge of an execution detail 2,000 years before.[25]

In his study, recording an outline of the meeting just moments after he arrived home, and despite all that he had just heard, my father also wrote a remarkable sentence: "We prayed together and had the witness that we were now one in Christ."

Garikai had taken so much from my father. Yet my father

dared to call Garikai his brother in their shared faith in Christ.

Shaken to the core, and far beyond tears at that point, my father had been given the gift of knowing that, in their final moments, his brothers and sisters had followed in the footsteps of their suffering Master. They had remained obedient to God at the cost of their own lives. Their innocence was recognized even by their killers. My father realized that the dying prayers of his friends for their murderers to find God's forgiveness had been answered right before his eyes.

But that was not all that would emerge.

* * *

Captain Dick Paget of the Rhodesian Army Medical Corps was responsible for founding Tsanga Lodge, an innovative rehabilitation centre for badly wounded Rhodesian servicemen, based in the mountains of the Eastern Highlands. As the ceasefire took effect, the integration of three different armies began. In early 1980, Captain Paget knew there would shortly be an influx of wounded ZIPRA and ZANLA guerrillas to the Rhodesian Army's rehabilitation centre. He addressed his staff on the eve of the arrival of the first guerrillas at Tsanga: "What we have to remember here at Tsanga Lodge is that each individual in this war fought for what he or she genuinely believed in. The job we have here at Tsanga Lodge, staff and patients alike, is to help our fellow humans who have been injured in this war."[26]

Despite Captain Paget's upbeat and inclusive approach, there was apprehension among patients and staff alike. How would the guerrillas, former enemies, now members of the party ruling the country, act now they had gained the upper hand?

One of those staff members listening to Captain Paget was Isobel Staunton.[27] Her uncle had been tragically murdered on his farm by former guerrillas soon after independence. At that time she described herself as "a Christian in my head only". The minister who led her uncle's funeral said something that gripped Isobel. He said, "This man has died for a reason." Groping in the dark, overwhelmed by fear and anger, Isobel found herself grasping this statement. She prayed to a God she didn't know that her uncle's death would serve some purpose in her life.

As Isobel arrived back in Inyanga to restart work after the funeral, Dick told her that former guerrillas would be arriving in the near future. So close to her bereavement, the news left Isobel angry and frightened. The medical team were in the Tsanga Lodge pub when it was announced that the first small group of guerrilla patients had been driven in through the gate of Tsanga Lodge. Isobel hadn't known what her reaction would be, but she immediately broke down and sobbed.

Two of the other women in the pub took her outside. One was a paraplegic woman whom Isobel had been sharing what little she knew of God with. She pointedly said something that challenged Isobel to the core: "Izzy, if I can see that you can forgive and love these guys I will believe in your God." Isobel knew that on her own she was incapable of offering any kind of forgiveness and love. And so she cried out to God to change her life.

Guerrillas arrived in ones or twos and made little difference initially to the cohesion and atmosphere. Severely injured as they were, the fighters' main focus was usually on their own healing and rehabilitation. They had their own apprehensions about how they would be treated by Dick Paget and his staff, considering that the team had managed so many Rhodesian soldiers severely injured by guerrillas.

One of the guerrillas Paget described as a "really splendid guy, a first rate medic and a delightful character. I would have loved to have him on the Tsanga staff… We had many interesting discussions and I was sorry to see him leave."

But among that first group of ZANLA guerrillas was a "nasty piece of work" by the name of Chenjerai Mupedzisi, who was admitted to the Lodge having been rendered paraplegic in a road traffic accident at the war's end in 1980.[28] Bitter and full of rage, Chenjerai was disruptive and violent.

Struggling with her grief and confronted with her inability to care for her erstwhile enemies, now her patients, Isobel took a break and went to Harare. To her surprise, the same minister who had taken her uncle's funeral, who had spoken the words that were still echoing in her head, was holding a service at a nearby Country Club. Isobel made a beeline for the meeting, knowing that she had to see him and ask him what he had meant at the funeral. Gently and clearly the minister pointed Isobel to the Lord. She recalled, "I was born again and filled with the Spirit."

Isobel returned to Tsanga and found that inexplicably she was able to love and care for the new arrivals, including the tough and demanding Chenjerai: "It was Christ in me that did." Isobel took opportunities to share her new-found faith with Chenjerai when she could. He seemed to listen to what Isobel had to say, despite his surly, offensive manner.

Captain Paget's courageous attempt to make Tsanga a place of healing for all former combatants, whatever their previous allegiance, was not to last. A visiting officer of the new Zimbabwe National Army and former ZANLA combatant made remarks to which Captain Paget took exception. The altercation led to punches being thrown, but the heated debate was eventually calmed and peace was restored. The two officers apologized to each other and the whole issue was forgotten. But Paget believed Chenjerai forced the issue with the authorities, even though his colleague was willing to let it be. As a result, Paget was forced to relinquish the leadership and leave Tsanga Lodge.

Just before Paget's departure, Clifford Kapofu,[29] an African pastor working for a group called Intercessors for Zimbabwe, was invited to speak at Tsanga Lodge. While Kapofu was preaching, Chenjerai began to scream and cry out for mercy from his wheelchair. Chenjerai was taken to another room as his anguished shouts and weeping were profoundly disturbing for the other patients in the room. Clifford Kapofu went out and listened to what he had to say.

Chenjerai poured out a confession. He claimed to have been a member of the second of the two ZANLA sections that had joined forces in the Eagle School attack. He had been haunted over the years by his involvement in the killing of the missionaries in the Vumba, among other atrocities he had committed. Despite approaching spirit mediums for help, Chenjerai had found no relief from his torment. Overwhelmed by guilt and shame, he was longing for absolution and peace. Clifford Kapofu told him that help would only come if he asked Jesus to forgive and save him. Chenjerai prayed earnestly, longingly for the mercy of the risen Christ, and it was granted to him.

Much to Paget's surprise, Chenjerai seemed to lose his vindictive rage and surliness. The young ZANLA guerrilla asked to see the Pagets at their farewell party and thanked them for their work. Uncharitably, Paget dismissed the behavioural change that Chenjerai had undergone as "typical of the befuddled thinking pattern of those that followed Mugabe"![30] But the change in Chenjerai was much more than Paget understood. An Assemblies of God minister began to visit Chenjerai regularly, and witnessed him begin to grow and mature in his faith and to share his story with others.

The seed that had been planted in a welter of blood and sorrow five years before had borne strange and beautiful fruit again.

* * *

Garikai arranged to see my father a month after their first meeting. My father was astonished to hear him say that seven other members of his guerrilla section had come to faith, apparently through Garikai's own witness within a month of his conversion. All seven had participated in the killings at Elim.

But Garikai was not aware of Chenjerai's story, members as they were of two different sections that had combined forces for the killings at Elim and then gone their separate ways. My father was struck by the fact that nine of his colleagues had prayed for the forgiveness of those who were killing them. Eight missionaries had died together that night and one had died a week later. Eight guerrillas found faith from one section and one from another section. Nine had died; nine had found new life.

My father and Garikai decided together that although Garikai was free to share his story verbally, a written account would be too dangerous. Both my father and Garikai believed that they could be in trouble with the authorities.[31] Ironically, both the man who had committed atrocity and was seeking to confess and the man who had experienced atrocity and was wanting to forgive found themselves threatened by the potential reaction of the authorities.

The unlikely relationship between Garikai and my father continued after he left Bible College. For a number of years, Garikai worked as an itinerant evangelist in neighbouring countries, visiting Botswana, Swaziland, Zambia, and Malawi. In early 1986, in his typically exuberant style, Garikai let my father know[32] that, while working as part of a team running evangelistic campaigns in Malawi, he had met and fallen in love with a Malawian Christian girl. Garikai was about to get married, a prospect that filled him with joy. He mentioned that he felt the need for a season of stability and accountability, formally attached to a church rather than freelancing. He signed off, "I wish I could visit your people's headquarters, in your company, that is. I wouldn't want to meet them without you being there!! This I promise, and I hope they are not angry of my past. I would do with their forgiveness and reconciliation. Does this make any sense to you also?"

A few weeks later he contacted my father as a trusted friend. Garikai was responsible for the wedding dress. He had chosen the dress, as he and his bride had agreed to hire rather than buy a dress. When he went to collect the dress from the hire company, Garikai happily talked about his wedding to those working behind the counter. On hearing that the ceremony was to take place in Malawi and not Zimbabwe, to Garikai's dismay the firm refused to rent him the dress. On hearing of Garikai's predicament, my father enlisted help from members of the church where he was an elder, Northside Community Church in Harare, and Garikai was dispatched to the airport, considerably relieved and with a beautiful wedding dress just the right size.

Touching down in Malawi, Garikai excitedly found his way through the border control formalities as he anticipated the moment of reunion. Collecting his luggage and clutching the precious wedding dress, he walked out through Arrivals and into a waking nightmare.

His fiancée had been on her way to the airport to meet him. Her brother was driving, but he had lost control of the car. He had been injured, but in the crash Garikai's young fiancée was killed, moments before their reunion and days before their wedding.

Garikai was devastated. He returned to Harare alone and in mourning instead of married and jubilant. He needed time to lament his loss, to grieve for what might have been. Months of silence followed his personal tragedy.[33]

Recalling Garikai's desire for a season of stability and accountability, just over a year after his shattering heartbreak my father proposed a six-month trial period for him as a deacon at Northside Community Church. But my father wanted nothing to be hidden from the leadership team there. Gathering the leadership together, my father outlined Garikai's story, holding them all to confidentiality. My father's publisher, David McKenzie, by now on the leadership team, found it difficult to accept the proposal. He was not alone. Many on the diaconate struggled. Some had served in the Rhodesian Security Forces, and Garikai represented the very people they had been fighting against.[34]

My father listened carefully to the objections and concerns and then, looking at one of the main protestors, he said pointedly, "When you came to faith in Jesus Christ we did not ask you what you had done during the war. We did not want to know how many people you had killed. Instead we remembered the words of Paul: 'Therefore, if any one is in Christ, he is a new creation; the old has gone, the new has come.'"[35]

David realized that my father, the person most affected, had forgiven Garikai. In advocating for Garikai's joining the Northside team my father was demonstrating a new depth of spiritual leadership. His proposal was accepted. But David still wondered how it was possible that my father could forgive the leader of a murderous gang that had killed some of his closest friends and colleagues. Over time, as he reflected on what my father had expressed in the meeting, David came to understand the power of forgiveness which enabled that kind of reconciliation, only achieved through the cross of Christ.[36]

And so, five years after first meeting my father, Garikai started work at Northside Community Church, having moved to live nearby. The wider church family knew that a new staff member had started work but did not know of Garikai's past. They did not even know that his coming to Northside was because of his connection with my father. The matter was kept at a strikingly low key: there was no trumpeting of forgiveness. The personal cost of daily forgiveness was a cost largely hidden inside my father's heart.

Together with my father, Garikai took the lead in speaking at lunchtime meetings in the Central Business District of Harare, seeking to engage with young professional people. He had become a gentle man, smiling and softly spoken, but my father realized that he had an ability to preach dynamically. Garikai shared his life with a new congregation that Northside Church were establishing in the suburb of Hatcliffe. He helped to run midweek house group meetings there, as well as leading and preaching at the Sunday services. Lameck and Rose Zulu, mature Christians and also heavily involved in Hatcliffe, befriended and cared for Garikai.

Years later, Lameck wrote, "For the period that we worked with him, [Garikai] was a very committed and mature Christian. Life had changed to the point where his war background was not visible. He did not talk about his involvement but just to say he was an ex-combatant. He had a friend, Baureni, that he came with to Hatcliffe who was also a mature Christian, and an ex-combatant. So, the Hatcliffe congregation knew that these two were war people, but their Christian faith was sound enough to remove all fears, and instead people appreciated them".[37]

But despite his growing maturity and effective ministry to the Zulus, Garikai appeared to be increasingly uncertain of his future. The reintegration of former combatants either into the new Zimbabwe National Army or into civilian life had been patchy in quality.[38] For many guerrillas it failed altogether. Like many others, Garikai's involvement in the war of independence had seriously affected his teenage and early adult years. Although an intelligent and capable man, he had missed out on a thorough secondary education. Despite his time at Bible College, he yearned to continue to make good the deficit.

Garikai could also sense tremors rumbling deep underground, threatening to topple the fragile new life he was building. He remained unsure of his acceptance within the Christian community if his full war history were ever to emerge. Garikai's concerns were grounded in reality. Out to dinner one night with my parents, I overheard my father in conversation with a white former member of the Rhodesian Army who also attended Northside Church. Without revealing Garikai's identity, my father told the story of how he had come to faith.

Lines of disgust etched into his face, the former soldier asked, "Peter, do you believe this fellow will be in heaven?"

My father simply replied, "Yes, I do."

There was a short, tense silence. Then the former soldier said, "Then I don't want to be there. I'm not interested in sharing heaven with the likes of him."

A look of deep sadness crossed my father's face. Quietly but devastatingly he responded, "Then you don't yet fully understand either the depth of your own sin or what Jesus achieved through his death on the cross."

Furthermore, Garikai's desire to repent and to seek forgiveness and reconciliation could have been interpreted as betrayal of the nationalist cause, as becoming a "sell-out". He remembered his own angry desire to kill the person who had placed the story of Rafael de la Torre, the Peruvian Marxist turned Christian, in the newspaper. He knew there might be other former guerrillas without his experience of faith who would react in a similar way to his story if it were to become more widely known.

At the time of the Elim killings, the question of responsibility had been highly contentious. Who had carried out the killings remained controversial after independence, as the government would react strongly to being implicated in the Elim massacre, something they had always denied. If someone were to reveal publicly that Garikai, a former cadre of the armed wing of the ruling party, had confessed to the murders, life could become very dangerous for him.

Under the circumstances, Zimbabwe was not the safest place for Garikai. He was offered an opportunity to move to another country and he wanted to go. My father was concerned. After Garikai had faced all the insecurity and fearsome experiences of the war, followed by years of roving ministry, my father was not sure that a move overseas would be right. He wanted Garikai to stay in one place, to put down roots, to be part of a loving pastoral church family over some years. But David McKenzie talked my father into seeing that an opportunity abroad might enable Garikai to live without the fear of discovery, to find a fresh start.

In early 1990, Garikai received a proposal from the people at Hatcliffe Church. They wanted him to lead them, to be their full-time pastor, a measure of the esteem they held him in. With sadness, Garikai declined. His plans to leave Zimbabwe had come to fruition. As they said goodbye, little did my father know that he would never see Garikai again.

MORE ALIVE
THAN EVER

In te, Domine, speravi: non confundar in æternum.
(O Lord, in thee have I trusted: let me never be put to
shame.)

From the "Te Deum"

t was November 1992 in an apparently peaceful and increasingly prosperous Zimbabwe. I had taken my father to see a doctor after he had briefly struggled to speak clearly when preaching the night before. As I drove out of the consulting room car park, I paused, looking to the right at the oncoming traffic. I asked my father a question but heard no answer, just a peculiar thumping sound. I looked to the left. My father's neck and body had arched like a bow, his face half-turned and thrust up hard against the glass of the car window. There was a low grunting as the air was forced out of him by the powerful spasms that were rippling through his torso. His right arm quivered and jerked, his thumb driven between his index and middle fingers, his hand tightly clenched into a fist. His heels drummed on the floor.

Overcome by the sight of my father in the grip of a convulsion, I was unable to stop the cries of sorrow and agony which poured uncontrollably from me. Mind racing, I rammed the truck into reverse. Wheels spinning and engine roaring, we jounced and crashed backwards across the car park, across the kerb, and right up to the consulting room door.

Wrenching open the driver's door, I spilled headlong from the truck. I burst into the doctor's waiting room, screaming for help. Blurs of colour in the cool gloom, startled faces turned towards my shrieking entry as their mouths formed noiseless Ohs of surprise. Turning and racing back to the truck, I saw that my father had toppled over on the truck's bench seat. Lying there, his body was still hideously convulsing. I pulled myself back into the truck and dragged his upper body into my lap, wrapping my arms around him, pleading with my father not to die.

The physician came running out and together we pulled my father from the truck and somehow into the waiting room. Hands trembling, the physician broke open a glass vial to draw up a drug. The needle punched into a distended vein and the horrible jerking slowed and came to a stop. The snorting, animal noises quietened to regular breathing again. There was a stunned silence from the clients in the waiting room, an unwilling audience to an unexpected drama. The distant sound of an ambulance dee-dawing its way through the traffic grew stronger.

My father remained fully conscious throughout his convulsions, fully aware of all that was happening around him, including my cries of fear and sorrow. The first thing he croaked was, "I thought I was going home then. I was ready to go…" and then typically he added, "I don't think much of your bedside manner!" I laughed through my tears.

Exuding an air of quiet confidence, the ambulance crew strode in to our frightened confusion and took over. The twin doors of the emergency vehicle slammed shut on my father's familiar form, strapped helplessly to a stretcher like a prisoner of war taken captive in a new kind of conflict. As the brightly marked vehicle pulled away, I followed in my truck, and we wove our way through the traffic towards the hospital.

In the grip of the convulsions and unable to control the powerful spasms of his own body, my father had not been afraid, despite believing himself on the brink of death, "I had yielded myself to the Lord thinking that He was taking me home to heaven."[1]

Over the next few appalling months there were to be many times when I relived these moments only to wonder if my father would have preferred to die during that first massive convulsion. Mercifully hidden from me as I steered through the traffic, there was much more to endure in that stage of my father's race to the finish line.

However, I did know that as a family we had crossed a great boundary. Whatever lay ahead in this life, my father would never be the same again physically. Once again, the course of our lives had changed suddenly, irreversibly, and dramatically.

* * *

Headed by my father, the Religious Education team within the Curriculum Development Unit of Zimbabwe's Ministry of Education were nearing the end of their commission. They had been tasked to design syllabuses and write the teachers' and pupils' books for each of the thirteen years that a Zimbabwean child would be at school. The Zimbabwean Ministry of Education had mandated that each child should receive at least three lessons of religious education each week throughout their schooling career. Together the team had produced more than fifty teachers' and pupils' books from the first year of school through to A Level. My father travelled the country, running training courses for teachers, testing the materials, and teaching a class regularly so that he remained in touch with the "chalkface".

Continuing to work as a member of the Executive of the Elim Pentecostal Church of Zimbabwe, my father wrote to Elim's international Missions Director, "We had our executive meeting on Friday – a deep sense of love in addition to the realization that the work in Katerere is making substantial progress in numbers and depth. On Saturday we had our annual conference in the Memorial Church in Mutare. There is a strong desire to see growth, expansion, and evangelism. I might add that I have rarely known such unity and sense of purpose with our expatriate workers. There is a total absence of dissension. Katerere seems to be a story of consolidation and expansion. Mutare is making little progress but at least there is oneness and a desire for growth. It needs leadership which will be provided when Pious Munembe goes there."[2]

My father preached weekly at Northside Community Church in Harare. My parents had seen the church grow from 120 to more than 700 attending on a Sunday morning. There were strong links with Elim Katerere through a project supporting children who had lost one or both parents through AIDS, as well as engagement with mission work in neighbouring Mozambique.

The days had become a whirlwind of activity. How far things had come since those desolate days of 1978!

In 1990, I was preparing to serve in northern Mozambique with the Leprosy Mission but was still employed as a young doctor for the Ministry of Health in Zimbabwe. Working in anaesthetics, I was on call at one of the teaching hospitals in Harare. It had been a busy morning, preparing a number of children who had been wounded in a shooting incident for surgery later that day. I rushed home for some lunch before the busy afternoon. As I ate, the door burst open, and into our dining room tumbled three lively young women, dusty from a seven-hour bus journey into Harare from Katerere.

Extrovert that he was, my father was delighted with the

unexpected company. Linda had come out from the United Kingdom to be a teacher at Emmanuel Secondary School and had stayed with my parents while doing her Shona language study. Two friends had come to visit her for a holiday in Zimbabwe. Becky was a bishop's daughter who had been nursing at Addenbrookes Hospital in Cambridge. The third, a long-haired young woman with an infectious laugh, was Anna, a zoologist turned theologian heading to Thailand to work with a mission agency. Finding out that Anna played the flute, my father said, "I hear flute players make great kissers. Anna, is that true?" She laughed and blushed, hiding her face in her long, dark hair.

My father was both charming and charmed by the company, but I needed to get back to the hospital. Unusually, he tore himself away from the lively conversation and followed me out to my car, asking abruptly, "Which one of those women are you going to marry?"

Taken aback by the unexpected nature of the question, I protested laughingly, but he pressed me for an answer. Forgetting her name, I said, "If you insist – the one with the long hair."

He looked at me, suddenly serious, and said, "She's the right one," and turned on his heel back to his lunch. Half-laughing, half-annoyed, I stared curiously at his retreating back, then shrugged and climbed into my car.

Just eight months later, I stood in front of Northside Community Church in Harare on my wedding day. Forgetting that his microphone was already on, my father leaned forward and hissed at me, "My son, take your hand out of your pocket!" General merriment ensued as his last-minute advice intended only for me boomed through the church. I turned to face that long-haired young woman, radiant and smiling with joy on the arm of her father.

Anna and I were married on 1 January 1991. My father conducted the wedding service. Pious Munembe laid his hands on us and prayed for our life together. The reading we had chosen was Isaiah 12: "Behold, God is my salvation; I will trust, and will not be afraid; for the Lord God is my strength and my song, and he has become my salvation."

Life at that moment for my father seemed rich and full and rewarding. In October 1992 he wrote to his old friend Bill Sheehan in Wales, telling him that Anna and I were studying Portuguese in the university town of Coimbra, Portugal, and preparing to work in Mozambique. He added news of extraordinary happenings at Emmanuel Secondary School. Many students had been filled with the Holy Spirit and about 100 had professed faith in Christ for the first time, in a way that was similar to the "rushing winds" of conviction and conversion that had blown through the school in October 1974. My father had just returned from the Elim Annual General Meeting in Mutare, and was delighted to see Pious Munembe re-elected as Chairman of the Elim Pentecostal Church of Zimbabwe. The meetings had been characterized by a sense of harmony and fellowship. He added poignantly, "I hope the trauma of past years never returns."

* * *

Nurse Joy Bath had been attending Elim Bible College when her friends and colleagues were killed in the Vumba. Together we had lived through that terrible day when the news was broken of the death of their colleagues. My mother, my father, and Joy were the three survivors of the missionary team that had worked in Katerere during the 1970s. Bound together in their common faith, through friendship, and by the fellowship of suffering, they had kept in touch over the years.

Graduating from Elim Bible College, Joy had gone on to work as a missionary nurse in India before being denied a visa. Her dream had been to return to work in Zimbabwe, and that dream came true. In the late 1980s Joy arrived back in Katerere to work at Elim Hospital and to rejoin the medical team as a nurse midwife. Feisty and as full of fun as ever, Joy enlivened our home in Zimbabwe with her frequent visits.

In February 1992, Joy was assisting in the operating theatre. A man had mangled his hand in a grinding machine and the surgeon was repairing his fingers. It was a long and delicate procedure and Joy started to feel hungry and dizzy. Suddenly gripped with agonizing abdominal pain, Joy put her head down on the operating table next to the patient's head, keeping him asleep by shooting the anaesthetic into his vein every time he moved while sending for the relief surgical assistant, Debbie Brown. By the time Debbie arrived on the scene, Joy was crumpled over on the floor, still managing to keep the patient asleep!

A dose of painkillers and a long sleep helped, and Joy was back at work the following day. But she remained chronically unwell over the next month, with recurrent fevers and malaise, although she struggled on with her nursing work. She asked if some of the church leaders would come and pray for her, which was a great comfort. At the end of that unsettling month, the hospital truck needed repairs in Harare, so Joy accompanied Debbie Brown on the journey.

They set off early to miss the heat of the day, but the two nurses hadn't gone very far when the truck had a puncture on a lonely stretch of the dirt track. Debbie had real difficulty getting the jack to work, and struggled for more than an hour. Joy was so weak she could only watch from the shade by the roadside. With true grit Debbie managed to jack the truck up, and then a huge rural bus roared around the bend and pulled up in a choking cloud of dust. Passengers spilled from the bus to help, and in no time the wheel was changed and they were on their way again. Joy was dropped off at our home, fit only for a drink and then bed.

On hearing that Joy was struggling with a dry, troublesome cough and chest pain, a doctor in Harare admitted her straight to hospital. Concerned, my father drove her there and then went home to find some of my mother's nightclothes for her to wear. Not expecting to stay more than one night in town, she had come ill-prepared for the days of investigations that were to follow. Her breathing was so distressed and noisy that Joy was given a room to herself so she didn't disturb others. The days went by and still the doctors remained uncertain of the underlying cause of Joy's mystery illness.

Weakened by her illness, Joy needed a nurse to bath her. Looking down at her own wasted body as she lay helpless in the bath, Joy casually mentioned to the nurse that she looked like the AIDS patients she had been caring for at the Mission hospital. The nurse made no comment, but the very next day Joy was asked if she was willing to be tested for HIV. Joy felt it wasn't necessary – she couldn't remember any time when she could have become infected. But the test was done.

A cold, clear, highveld winter's day dawned, the brilliant sunshine carving sharp edges into cold pockets of shadow. The early morning light streamed across Joy's bed as her doctor stepped softly into the room. Joy smiled broadly on seeing him, confident that her result would be negative.

Quietly and gently he broke the devastating news to Joy that her blood test was positive and that she had AIDS. Joy's initial reaction was disbelief. Surely it was a mistake, and retesting would prove it. But suddenly the kaleidoscope shifted in her mind, and all the odd pieces suddenly fitted into a pattern. Bizarre rashes, chronic fevers, and the slow strangling weakness she had felt for months all pointed to this diagnosis.

Just moments later my father arrived on a visit, a cheery grin on his face. Joy simply blurted out, "I've been tested positive." His face instantly clouded, and he sank down on to the end of her hospital bed. Together they gave way to emotion.

Joy's doctor found them weeping together as he returned a

few minutes later to say, "For you, Joy, the fact that you are HIV positive is not a matter for shame, but for pride. You have the virus only through your calling and dedication to service." Joy had known that working in a rural hospital was a risky business as up to a third of the pregnant women she looked after were HIV positive.

The same day, my father travelled to the Mission to let Joy's friends and colleagues know. A group left for Harare immediately. By then Joy knew she would be flying home. She could not shake the sense that she might not see her Mission colleagues again. Very little was said. Emotions were running riot. No words of comfort seemed adequate.

Still in the early days of the HIV pandemic, there were great difficulties with the airlines refusing to fly Joy back to the UK. Finally, after discussion with an airline doctor in London, permission was granted. My father and Joy's close friend Debbie accompanied her in the ambulance to the waiting plane, praying that Joy would survive the thirteen-hour journey by air and road to a specialist unit. Joy slept through the journey, while her medical escort had an anxious night!

Week by week, the reality of Joy's illness sank in. Even though she had attended AIDS training courses and nursed AIDS patients for the previous four years, it hadn't dawned on her that she might become ill too. She mentally upbraided herself for her thoughtlessness. Medical staff caring for Joy in the UK were competent and considerate, but some made it clear that they did not believe that she had contracted AIDS as a result of her nursing.

If some doubted her story, others questioned her faith, "You have worked abroad for God for eighteen years, giving Him so much, and yet you are sick with AIDS. Aren't you angry at God? God protected you during the war; why hasn't He protected you this time?"

Struggling to respond to their disdain, anger, and cynicism, Joy was wrestling with her own questions. Where was God in the tremendous jolt of the diagnosis, the bleak and comfortless sorrow of leaving Zimbabwe, the formidable weakness and pain that she was enduring?

For weeks Joy lay in hospital, so ill and so overwhelmed that she felt unable to read, write, reason, or pray. Yet in that shadowed valley, something profound began to happen. When she became a little stronger, Joy wrote to my parents of those days. When it seemed she could do little but suffer, "God brought me so close to Him. I had a tremendous feeling of privilege. God has entrusted this disease to me. Reminded of Mary the mother of Jesus, I could identify with her. She was called highly favoured. She was privileged to be chosen to bear the shame of pregnancy, facing what people would say about this 'immoral woman'. They continued to point a finger at her even when Jesus was grown up. Challenged by this thought, I asked myself, 'Even if I am misunderstood, can I bear this responsibility and privilege? How shall I go through all this so as to be a blessing to others?'"

In line with her Pentecostal beliefs, Joy pleaded with God right from the start for healing. But as time went on, she questioned her approach to healing. "If God heals me, then what?" She mused, "I must have been given this disease for a purpose. I can't go back to what I was doing before as if nothing happened. No, it has to be a step further on from that."

Joy's deep experience of the presence of God and her growing realization that her illness was not meaningless ran parallel with continuing distress. The drugs she was taking to try to control the virus caused her hair to fall out. One evening she wept on seeing tangled knots of hair on the porcelain as she washed her hair over the sink. Her brother Keith came in and, seeing how distressed she was, simply put his arms around her and held her tight. Joy knew too many AIDS sufferers, her patients, who had been abandoned by relatives and friends. She wrote warmly to my parents of her appreciation of being part of a loving family, especially in the face of a life-threatening illness that attracted such stigma.

* * *

It was November 1992, just months after Joy had returned to the UK. Having completed our Portuguese studies, Anna and I were unable to travel into Mozambique as quickly as we had hoped. The war there meant we could only travel in by air. Mission Aviation Fellowship had delayed our departure because of a temporary shortage of aviation fuel, so we were staying with my parents as we waited. One Sunday afternoon we played tennis in the sprawling, beautiful gardens of a family friend, old against young, parents against children. Anna and I fought hard for game after game, just managing to stay ahead. My father couldn't accept the result. Panting and red-faced but determined, he cajoled and coaxed us into trying to extend our lead while intending to have his revenge.

The inevitable happened and he triumphed. Only then could the match end! Drinks followed in the living room, but as we were all rehydrating, my father lay sprawled back in his chair. As children do, we teased him about his age catching up with him. Looking drawn and exhausted, he did his best to muster a smile. Although curious to see him so exhausted after a match, we knew he had worked so hard to win. No shadow fell across us on that beautiful summer's evening as we laughed and talked, revelling in each other's company.

A sunny Tuesday evening two days after his marathon tennis match victory, my father went straight from work to the church. Teaching a class on preaching, he began by reading aloud from the Old Testament. He was embarrassed to stumble over some of the words, but attributed his mistakes to tiredness and the tricky

Hebrew names he had read aloud. But when he finally got home, my mother was startled to see that one side of his face seemed to be drooping a little. Anna and I got in late that night and the house was already dark, but my mother got up and padded into our room to mention her worries.

Early the following day, my mother came in to ask me to look at my father's face. I cracked some light-hearted remark but obediently followed her up the corridor, clacking my way over loose wooden tiles and into their room. One glance was enough: the asymmetry of his face was subtle but frighteningly obvious. Our family doctor referred him urgently to a consultant physician who asked me to set up a CAT scan for my father the next day.

We waited in the imaging centre while the films were processed and read. To my surprise, the radiologist suddenly appeared in the waiting room and stared intently at my father. I realized that the specialist was having trouble reconciling what he had seen on the scan with my father's apparently normal appearance. We returned to the physician's consulting rooms with the films, and he was quick to tell me to drive my father directly to the hospital. He had phoned ahead and they were already expecting him. As I drove him out, his body was suddenly gripped by the convulsion which I found so frightening.

Calling Anna at home, I asked her very calmly to go and get my mother from the school where she was teaching. Immediately alarmed when I described the events, Anna thought to herself that my father might be dead by the time she arrived at the hospital. She drove over to Chisipite Girls School, picked up my mother, and together they raced to the hospital, so worried about what they would find when they got there. Anna and my mother ran through the hospital, up to the ward, and into my father's room. Newly and unusually volatile in his emotions, one moment my father would talk about being ready to die, the next he was joking again about my bedside manner.

Returning home briefly to snatch some lunch, Anna, my mother, and I sat together round the kitchen table, holding on to one another. We were reeling, overwhelmed and dazed with the impact of what had happened that morning. My emotions spilled out of me, taking me by surprise with their unexpected force as I literally howled with grief and pain. We could not think, could not pray. Brokenly we could only repeat the name of Jesus.

I called my brother Paul, who was working in London. Within three hours of my call, Paul was on an Air Zimbabwe flight to Harare. A poor sleeper on planes at the best of times, it was a nightmare journey for Paul, disturbed both by the news and by the deep emotion I had shown on the phone. He knew how serious things might be and did not know what he would find on the morrow.

Initially, the doctors believed my father had suffered a stroke. The valves of his heart were still damaged following his myocarditis as a child. I wondered whether turbulent blood flow around one valve had caused a clot of blood to form which had broken free and been pumped up into his brain, causing an area of brain death. Over the next few days, his weakness began to improve. From his bed he corrected the last manuscript for his series of pupils' books. We began to look forward to welcoming him home again.

Ten days after his first admission and a day or so before he was due for discharge, the phone rang in our darkened house. It was around 3.00 a.m., and a nurse was calling from my father's bedside. She put him on and in a weak voice he asked me to come in and see him. In the cool of the early morning, I found him afraid, half-sitting, half-standing next to his bed. I could see straight away that his facial paralysis had worsened again. He visibly relaxed as I came into the room, and he handed me a piece of paper.

In the early hours of the morning, he had awoken, filled

with foreboding. Pulling paper towards him, he had begun to write down his thoughts. At the top of the page his handwriting was clear and precisely placed, but then it ballooned raggedly, slanting across the page. I realized I was looking at the moment a second bleed had taken place in his head, swelling and putting pressure on certain areas of his brain and causing weakness of his hand.

Looking closely I deciphered what he had written. It was an outline of his funeral. Pious Munembe and Ephraim Satuku were to speak at the service. He had jotted, "They are very close to me and risked their lives for me during the war here." He wanted Dr Ken Jenkins, a fellow elder and close friend, to preach. And he chose two simple hymns to sing, scrawling, "'Amazing Grace' – for I have become more amazed than ever that God should treat me, and indeed the whole world, with grace, in a way which we do not deserve. And '*Ungatora Hako Pasi*' – which is a Shona hymn that Brenda and I had at our wedding. It loosely translates, 'You can take the world and all its joys/We for our part will take Jesus and all He offers/His grace is overwhelming and sufficient for all.'"

An urgent brain biopsy revealed not a stroke in my father's brain but a highly malignant, relatively fast-growing tumour of brain tissue. Two days later the surgeon removed a tumour larger than a golf ball. My father's rapid deterioration had been caused by the tumour bleeding into itself, rapidly swelling and pressing on motor areas of the brain, causing the paralysis.

Initially, my father recovered very well from the surgery, and quickly regained most of the use of his arm and leg, but some facial weakness remained. He could still think clearly but he remained emotionally volatile. We couldn't tell what was because of the trauma of the operation, the impact of his diagnosis, or damage to the frontal lobe of his brain by the tumour.

We knew the prognosis was poor. Median survival for high-grade astrocytoma was only two years. On the Sunday after my father's admission, I took his place in the pulpit to speak from 1 Thessalonians 5: "Rejoice always, pray constantly, give thanks in all circumstances" – the passage he was supposed to speak on that Sunday. I needed to hear those words myself.

Joy, struggling with her own difficult diagnosis, wrote to my father. "When I first heard you had been diagnosed as having a malignant brain tumour I was absolutely devastated. I felt like shaking my fist at God, 'Why Lord? What are you doing? First me and now Peter. The work of Elim in Zimbabwe has suffered many blows and now another one is being struck.'" But then Joy went on to ponder further. Perhaps she had been too proud, believing that God relied on his human servants so much that His work would be damaged if two of His servants were no longer able to serve in the way they thought best. And of course that was not the case. God's work could and would continue without them.

My father responded to say that he was finding it painfully hard to discuss his chances of recovery. He had come to the realization that percentage cures and survival times were not the most important thing. He wrote, "What is essential is the daily giving of ourselves to God and so fulfilling His purpose in our lives, no matter how long or short we have. Long ago I came to the conclusion that becoming a Christian is no insurance policy against disaster and tragedy. The difference between a non-Christian and a Christian in times of tragedy is that the believer can be assured that Jesus is with him through it all, and that he can take an eternal perspective on all that happens in life. I recalled how Dr Brien used to pray in our mission prayer meetings, 'Lord, help us to live in the light of eternity.' How we all need to do that."

Joy continued to ponder the past, thinking how easily she could have been one of those who died in the massacre. "God saw fit to save me from death at that time. I remember you musing on this too and you said that maybe you were not worthy to be among them… God spared you and me from death then. But now we are both confronted with the possibility of death from an incurable disease. I have AIDS. Sometimes it still comes over me in waves. Life is too short so I want to do as much as I can that is normal. Being afraid to do things in case it makes me ill is no longer my policy. If I feel well enough to do something then I do it even if I feel shattered afterwards. I have the joy of knowing I'm living life to the full as best I can. My confidence is in the fact that God holds the key of all unknown and I am glad. Yours together in the suffering of the cross."

An old friend, a consultant at the Royal Marsden, a specialist cancer treatment hospital in London, phoned from the UK to offer his help. The Elim International Missions Director made sure the air tickets were covered. The radiotherapy treatment at the Royal Marsden Hospital ran its course. But despite the finest of treatment, investigation at the end of the treatment showed that the cancer was still growing. There was little more to be done. My father returned home to Zimbabwe to die.

Our house filled with all the paraphernalia of serious illness. Pills, capsules, elixirs, vials, syringes, needles, gloves, walkers, commode, bedpans, catheters, salves, and powders littered the place. Although medically speaking there was little she could do, his doctor Debbie Murphree came to see my father and sit with him every day. Her sister Nyasha posted us a card daily with a Bible quote, beautifully written. Physiotherapist Marlene Brand came to move my father's limbs. Close friend Ken Jenkins brought laughter and warm concern into the sickroom. The wider church family expressed the depth of their concern and desire to help by making sure that every day in those last months of my father's life a main meal was provided for all in our house. There were phone calls, letters, flowers, and cards from so many, ranging from government ministers to rural peasant farmers.

* * *

The love story between my mother and father had begun under the yellow acacia trees at the side of a dusty mountain road on a clear winter's day so many years ago. My mother had loved my father in his strength, his drive to forge ahead, his wit and quick thinking, capable and resourceful and handsome as he was.

Now all that was gone. My father was weak and barely able to move. He was no longer vital and energetic; his thinking was slow and his answers unpredictable in content and clarity. His head had been battered by brain surgery and radiotherapy, and his hair had grown back in strange tufts and clumps.

Yet in wonder, we watched that love story continue to unfold even in this hideous, unwanted twist in the journey. My parents' love for each other had not faded or grown stale but rather entered new depths of warmth and closeness, despite the depredations of a cruel and merciless tumour. He needed her, called for her, leant on her, asked for her comfort, and longed for her presence.

My mother responded unstintingly and without reserve. She fed him, read to him, cleaned him, prayed with him, sang with him, laughed and cried with him. Nothing was too much trouble for my mother to do for my father in the final months of his life. No matter how poor the quality of his life became, she did not want to lose him; she wanted to be able to be with him and love him still.

Some of my father's last written words, scrawled to Joy Bath, were a tribute to the wife of his youth: "During my darkest moments of this illness, I longed for the appearance of Christ both vivid and visible, until I realized it was going to come to me through other people. Through Brenda's deep love, care, constant ministering to my needs, and just being there when I most needed her, I have truly felt the presence of Christ."

As the disease gripped him more firmly, while he was still conscious but so aware of death drawing closer, he wanted to change his will. It had been written during the war years when my parents did not know how they might die, but prepared for the worst. Thinking that they were most likely to be caught in the ferocious blast of an anti-tank mine and there might be little to find in the way of mortal remains, my parents had indicated then that they wished to be cremated. But in his final illness, that wish changed. He told us he wanted to be buried alongside his friends who had died in the Vumba. When I heard he wished to be laid alongside those he had served with, I was rocked again at the depth of feeling he had for his friends, and realized again what forgiveness had cost him.

For the last three months of his life my father was paralysed, blind, and incontinent. Barely conscious, he said nothing for days. One morning, not long before the end, Anna was sitting with him. Suddenly, clearly, unexpectedly he said, "I see a city!"

Anna asked gently, "What city do you see, Peter?"

My father replied, "I see the city of God," and then lapsed into silence again.

Those were among the last words he was to speak. In his final days, the sawing rasp of his laboured breathing carried throughout the house. My father was running the last stage of his marathon, persevering in the race marked out for him, looking to his Lord Jesus.

On 12 October 1993 at the age of fifty-six, my father died after eleven months of cruel, heartbreaking illness, his brain eaten away by a vicious cancer. Moments after his death we stood around his body and sang the simple song drawn from Jesus' final words to his disciples:

My peace I give unto you.
It's a peace that the world cannot give.
It's a peace that the world cannot understand.
Peace to know, peace to live.
My peace I give unto you.

A heavily pregnant Anna stood next to me as we sang, squeezing my hand hard. Her contractions had started. My father's longed-for first grandson was on his way into the world the very night his grandfather died.

Early the following morning, I sat alone in my father's room, watching over him, the outline of his body visible under the sheet we had drawn up over his face. Walking back into our room, I heard Anna laugh softly. As she got up that morning after death, there was a liquid patter onto the floor. Her waters had broken.

Anna's labour was long and complex, and ended in an emergency Caesarean section. The anaesthetist was a friend and saw my terror at what might come. She gathered both Anna and me into her arms and prayed for us. I was in the operating theatre when, in a welter of blood and amniotic fluid, our son Joshua Peter David was finally born. On being handed the baby, I looked down and cried out that he was not breathing. Snatching Joshua from me, the anaesthetist rapidly intubated him, and within moments a team arrived to whisk him away.

Head in hands, I sat on a stool in the corner of the operating theatre. My father lay dead on his bed in our family home. My wife lay unconscious on the table before me. My son lay struggling to breathe in an incubator in Intensive Care. In those moments life seemed impossibly, unbearably bleak. Yet to my mind came the words of a man who knew great suffering intimately: "The Lord gave, and the Lord has taken away; blessed be the name of the Lord."[3] Those simple phrases looped endlessly in the darkness of my grief and fear.

* * *

Joshua made a rapid recovery. His arrival eased our mourning. The outburst of his vigorous and healthy new life into a house of death brought us great joy amid our pain.

My father's funeral at Northside Community Church was packed. A friend commented that it was a chance to see a life lived for God in panorama.

The committal took place in Mutare the next day. We gathered by the mass grave of his friends. It was a day of scorching heat, late October in Zimbabwe. The rains had not yet come and the ground was dry and hard and dusty. Behind the painfully vast and arid stretch of the mass interment, a fresh grave had been cut into the blood-red soil.

I stood looking down on my father's coffin, the high, hard walls of earth close on each side. A handful of dust trickled through my fingers, pattering like soft rain on the wood inches above the face I knew so well and loved so much. The burial of my father's body I found so hard. I hated the associations with the utter darkness underground, the place of slow writhing of pale worms, the fine-grained heaviness of dank, inert clay pressing down pitilessly on the remains of someone I loved.

But then I read of Jesus speaking of His own burial, which He described as being in "the heart of the earth".[4] Rather than being pressed down under a blank, inert, merciless mass, Jesus saw Himself as enfolded into something living, beating, warm. I realized Jesus was comparing Himself to Jonah, who had disappeared into the realm of chaos and horror, into the sea and into the maw of a sea monster. It seemed to the witnesses of Jonah's flight into the ocean that he was overwhelmed and lost to the power of those forces.

Yet Jesus calmly stated that even in the extremity of Jonah's situation, God remained supreme over the sea creature and over

Jonah's fate. Jesus saw His burial in terms of being enfolded into the heart of God's earth, a place intimately known by Him, where nothing is hidden from Him, and which God plans to restore to his original rich intent. Impressing me with new force, the words of Jesus brought me comfort.

My father's death plunged my mother into a sea of pain deeper than she had ever endured. She would wake in the mornings for months after he had gone, with tears already running down her cheeks. My mother had prayed fervently for my father to be healed, but he was not. Struggling with this, she mentioned to Bill Sheehan (who had come out to Zimbabwe to help nurse his friend) that she had heard a friend's prayer for my father, asking that he would be given another fifteen years of life. That had sounded so wonderful to my mother. She quoted the example of God granting King Hezekiah fifteen years[5] after he was confronted with a life-threatening illness. Bill thought for a moment and then said, "Brenda, I think that God has already given Peter another fifteen years." It was 1978 that their friends and colleagues were killed, and in 1993 my father died. She realized that God had already given my father fifteen years more.

She remembered that just nine days before the brain tumour struck him down, my father had preached on 1 Thessalonians 4. He had reminded us that the early Christians described death as "falling asleep", and said that this conveyed the idea that the person who had died would wake up, and wake up in the presence of Jesus.

My father had told us that God has given to those who know him a great and wonderful tomorrow – forever with the Lord – and had exhorted us to encourage each other with these words of hope as Paul commanded. He had quoted a hymn which was to become very significant to him during the agony of his illness: "O, that will be glory for me, when by his grace I shall look on his face, that will be glory, be glory for me."

Passionately, my father had declared, "I may die – but if you read my funeral notice in *The Herald* saying that I'm dead, don't you believe it! Don't you believe it! I'll be more alive than ever on that day!"

Five weeks after my father's death, my mother blessed us and sent us to Mozambique. We took our leave of her on a runway, climbing into a light aircraft crammed with our belongings, our newborn son, her precious grandson, cradled in our arms. She stood in the grey November morning, sobbing to watch us go, praying aloud, her arms raised in farewell to us and praise to her Lord. A paraphrase of the words of King David came to my mind: "Shall I give to the Lord that which has cost me nothing?"[6]

* * *

Joy Bath treasured the letters that she and my father had exchanged, the phone calls they had made. She found it comforting to have an old and trusted friend suffering alongside her, wrestling with some of the same thoughts and feelings that she was. His last letter to her told her that he knew he was living through his last few weeks. Although she had fallen sick first, she would outlive him.

A memorial service was held in the Swansea Elim Church that had sent my father out to Rhodesia more than thirty years before and supported him during those years. Joy found the occasion incredibly moving, and cried in my grandmother's arms when it was over. In the car on her trip home, Joy was exhausted, suddenly understanding that the drugs she was taking were fighting a battle that was being lost.

Her attitude to her death changed. No longer a vague acceptance that life might be shorter, she clearly saw that she would die young, still in her mid-forties. She wrote to my mother, "From within me came a firm, almost tangible excitement at the thought of meeting my Lord Jesus face to face."

In the coming months Joy became increasingly breathless,

unable to walk without help, and then blind in one eye. Debbie, her nursing colleague and friend, on leave from Elim Hospital, came to see her. They joked that Joy looked so old she should be nursed on a geriatric ward. Debbie described the precautions that were being taken to protect the staff against HIV in the Elim Hospital operating theatre: "Nowadays we go into the operating theatre dressed for a moon walk!"

Unforeseen feelings of sadness and anger erupted within Joy. If only she had been more careful. Debbie, seeing Joy's reaction, said, "Joy, you mustn't blame yourself."

Joy responded, "Yes, I must. I was in charge – of myself and the rest of you. This is the price I have had to pay for my negligence." Joy began to cry tears of sorrow for the loss of her own life.

Unexpectedly, the Anglican Bishop of Salisbury came to see her, and listened to her with interest and warmth. As a link between them as servants of God he gave her his ring, a simple gold band inscribed with the lettering, *IN TE DOMINE SPERAVI* ("In thee O Lord have I put my trust"). Moved, Joy took the precious gift and wore it for all the days left to her.

Not long afterwards, in early 1995, she went totally blind. And when she was no longer able to eat, Joy became skin and bone, and found even the least movement painful. Her morphine intake was increased, and the daily visits from the district and Macmillan nurses eased her many discomforts. Lying in bed with little to distract her, Joy felt again that God was close day and night. Her family watched over her, doing what they could to bring her comfort.

On Good Friday, Joy's extended family worshipped God around her bed, praying, reading the Bible, and singing. As they sang together, with unexpected strength, Joy flung up her arms and shouted, "Hallelujah!"

Joy died on Easter Saturday, two days before her forty-fifth birthday.

"WE'LL FIND OUT LATER"

God stir the soil,
Run the ploughshare deep,
Cut the furrows round and round,
Overturn the dry hard ground,
Spare no strength nor toil,
Even though I weep.
In the loose, fresh mangled earth
Sow new seed.
Free of withered vine and weed
Bring fair flowers to birth.

Anonymous[1]

Joy's death on Easter Saturday 1995 grieved my mother greatly for many reasons. Joy's passing left her with a profound sense of loneliness. Of the young missionary team that had worked so closely together in the mid-1970s, she was now the only one still alive. While still struggling to come to terms with her many losses, she saw Zimbabwe, her adopted nation, badly damaged by leaders determined to feed their hunger for power at any cost. The investment of her life's work seemed to blow away like sand in a desert wind.

Vulnerable as an older widow living on her own, she was robbed repeatedly. In one frightening incident, thieves brazenly cooked and ate a meal in her kitchen before robbing the house, leaving my mother locked in her bedroom, trembling and crying out to God. Eventually, ten years after my father's death, she fled Zimbabwe and returned to England, leaving behind her family home. She joined a wave of Zimbabweans both black and white scattering across the world. Rampant inflation of the Zimbabwean dollar meant she took very little with her.

Her obedience to the call of the Lord Jesus meant that at the age of sixty-nine she was starting a new life after having lost so much – her husband and her team all dead prematurely, her church community, her home, her money, her life's work, her adopted country. All the work of her hands, the investment of the most productive years of her life appeared lost and gone. Adjusting to life in an England she had left nearly half a century before was a slow process measured in years, and she wrestled with depression.

Far from Zimbabwe at the time, Anna and I were working in Cambodia in education and medical work and alongside the Khmer church with OMF International. I found my mother leaving Zimbabwe in trying circumstances unexpectedly dislocating, a splintering fracture of my sense of rootedness. About that time I was made aware of memoirs that described the events around the Elim massacre, except not as I recalled. The motivation and the actions of the Elim missionaries were questioned, and one of the memoirs described them as naive and foolish, overly involved politically, and implied that they deserved to be killed. Another felt that they had acted ignorantly, unaware of the danger they were exposing themselves to, and that ignorance had ensured their deaths.

Had I remembered events wrongly? Was my recollection of my parents' colleagues unduly coloured by my childhood memories of them? Had I accepted comforting distortions rather than uncomfortable truths?

Beneath the pursuit for the truth of the matter, for an understanding of the geography and mechanics of mass killing, beyond the seeking for what legacy might be left behind ran a quest for a deeper truth. A church leader in Zimbabwe, who had known many of those killed, wrote to me on an anniversary of the massacre, telling me he believed God had absented himself from the scene that night.

The reality of death had lingered so close to us for so long. I asked my father once, pleadingly, if our friends would have felt anything as they died. I hoped for some kind of supernatural body armour, a divine anaesthesia that would have rendered them unable to feel the pain of what was so terribly inflicted. I wanted to know that they were spared, martyrs smiling beatifically in their deaths. If violent death came looking for me, would God enfold me, shield me, cushion me?

I longed for one answer but expected and dreaded another. I asked the question deliberately to lead in one way, "Dad, when they died, God didn't let them feel anything, did He?"

My father looked at me. He paused and his eyes filled with tears. He honoured me with the truth. "No, Steve, I believe they felt everything."

They felt everything. All that was used – axe, bayonet, boot, body, club – to chop, to cut, to stab, to wound, to tear, to batter, to violate the sanctity of the image of God. I knew that God has made the most astonishing claim: "all souls are mine".[2] God claims personal ownership of every human being who has ever lived, who lives, or who will live. Here was God's property being savagely, horribly abused and torn and broken. How could this be? Why would God surrender His rights, wash His hands, turn away, and abandon them to their pain in the dark night? Did God have any kind of purpose to what had happened?

Orphaned Rachel Evans, eight years old, was interviewed by the BBC, broadcast on 29 October 1978. When asked about the death of her parents, she spoke artlessly, with quiet conviction. I found her words arresting: "Well, we'll find out later why God wanted it to happen really. We don't know why God did this but we know it is for a special reason and we'll find out later … maybe. I don't really hate the [killers]. I think they should be ashamed of themselves."[3] Were her words merely the simple rationalization of a child confronted with the unthinkable? Was she simply repeating what others had said to her? Or was there something more?

Provoked to look again, it was a curious sensation to begin to explore the roots of my life, turning over the flotsam and jetsam of what had washed up on the beaches of my memory. An atmosphere of rust and decay, of worthy lives perhaps but lived in dusty, slow-moving corners of what was then a vast world. Those lives, however vibrant at the time, were apparently reduced to black and white photographs; jumpy, scratched silent 8 mm films; old aerogrammes covered in spidery script, and brown-edged curling documents that perhaps no one but me had even looked at for more than thirty years. Was this all they had left behind? Was there any other legacy?

I didn't wish to dwell on the suffering of our friends. But I felt a need to understand what had happened. How did the events of that night unfold? Why was the target of Elim Mission chosen? How does one choose a killing ground? Were the killings planned or did something go wrong with an abduction? Why were the killings so brutal? How was it decided who would kill which missionary? Did the children die before their parents? Why did they separate the missionaries into two groups on the grassy bank? I wanted to try to look at the killings, the massacre in context rather than a "mythological" martyr story ungrounded in time, space, politics, and relationships. I needed also to see the missionaries in their humanity and frailty as well as their courage.

If there was going to be any talk about the purposes of God, I wanted the lens jammed wide open, no matter how much it hurt. My journey to explore the past began in scepticism and doubt.

I was able to track down people willing to tell me about those terrible days more than thirty years ago. The first police officer on the scene on the morning after the killings described to me the scene he found. Retired now, a senior intelligence officer in the Zimbabwean government recounted the confession of two of his men of their involvement in the killings at Elim. A former senior military instructor and political commissar was willing to discuss training in guerrilla camps. A Dominican nun and confidante of Mugabe who was also working for the KGB, the main security agency for the Soviet Union at the time, now living in an Anglican commune in London, told me what she knew.

A Special Branch operative who personally examined the bodies and documentation of the two dead guerrillas involved in the killings at Elim sent me a detailed account of that day. Two Rhodesian Police Anti-Terrorist Unit servicemen who led the team that shot the guerrillas described the firefight. A former British government minister described the patchy and unsatisfactory evidence that he was provided with.

The former head of Rhodesian Special Branch came for lunch. He described the scene in Rhodesian Combined Operations headquarters when news of the massacre came in. Surprisingly open, he told me of his regrets about the war – that if he had his time over again he would have done things differently.

From these contacts, I was able to understand the manner of the deaths. To the question "Why were the Elim missionaries killed?" a number of answers emerged from combatants on both sides in the war.[4] The atrocity had cold political and military logic behind it, strategic (damaging white morale), tactical (removing possible hindrances to infiltration routes), training (ensuring that recruits would be able to kill), as well as personal. The guerrilla commander wanted to punish the missionaries for not responding quickly enough to his letter which ordered them to leave the premises.

The memories that came first to mind and the interviewees who were contactable all seemed to circle around the entirely negative, steel and blood and sorrow. At times I was overwhelmed with a palpable sense of evil. A brooding darkness would menace me even though the warm afternoon sun lit the room. Those moments arrested my writing, bringing the vehicle of memory that was traversing the landscape of the past to a juddering halt. I needed to pause, to seek counsel and prayer.

But as I continued to work, slowly and quietly other memories, other themes, began to emerge. Like the last time I saw "Uncle Phil" Evans, all his hair standing on end, filthy dirty and uproariously cheerful after riding in from Katerere on a motorbike to see Tim and Rachel in the boarding school hostel. Or the warmth of friendship that shone through the personal letters written by Wendy, Cath, Phil, and Joyce to my parents while they were on furlough. Or Mary singing the Statler Brothers' witty lyrics, "Noah Found Grace in the Eyes of the Lord", her eyes laughing along with us as we sat on her living room floor one hot lowveld evening.

I saw again how all our missionary colleagues had loved life. They did not seek martyrdom. They did not intentionally provoke martyrdom. They were walking a tightrope stretched between two infernos. They were the dancing grass avoiding the pounding of the fighting elephants' feet. They had no macabre love of death, no twisted death wish, but rather a fierce love of life and a longing for others to find it too. They were not in love with death but in love with life, with the one who said, "I am the life." They were not intent on heroism or martyrdom, but rather intent on obedience to Christ whom they saw as the highest authority.

All confronted the possibility of violent death in the silence of their minds, in the aching solitude of wakeful nights. Each of the missionaries experienced great fear in the months leading up to their deaths. None was compelled in any way to stay. All contributed to group meetings to discuss the worsening situation. Individually and collectively they decided that they felt God still meant for them to continue, delicately balancing fear and faith.

I puzzled over what Garikai described of the prayers that were cried out that night of 23 June 1978. The missionaries reminded God that they were obedient to His will. They seemed to recognize that it was God who had brought them to this point. They prayed to a God they saw as still in control, despite what they were going through.

At the one and same time they prayed for forgiveness for those who were killing them. They knew that their killers were moral agents, responsible for their violent lawless actions. They believed that God as the righteous judge would hold their killers accountable, and yet they prayed that their killers would repent and find mercy in Jesus Christ.

Plumbing the depths of their dying prayers, I was struck by the fact that they did not see their killers as helpless pawns in the hands of a powerful God who for some capricious reason had decided that they must die. Nor did they see God as someone who was helpless in the face of their pain and anguish and weakness.

They would have known the striking words of the Old Testament figure of Joseph, betrayed and sold by his brothers into slavery in Egypt. Speaking to his brothers when they finally met him again, Joseph said, "You meant evil against me; but God meant it for good, to bring it about that many people should be kept alive."[5]

They knew that Joseph's startling thinking was echoed centuries later in Peter's first public sermon after the death and resurrection of Jesus to a crowd gathered at Pentecost. "[Jesus] was handed over to you *by God's deliberate plan and foreknowledge;* and *you, with the help of wicked men, put him to death* by nailing him to the cross."[6] Peter knew that in the act of executing Jesus, when evil men did their brutal worst, God held them fully responsible for their actions. But in addition, Peter boldly declared that the cross of Jesus was no accident through a moment of inattention by God; it was no Plan B after Plan A had gone wrong; it was not merely passive or allowed by God. Peter stated that in the same terrible event caused by evil men, God was bringing about His good purpose.

But I could not bear this thinking applied to what happened at Elim. How could God purpose the events of that night? Was God evil? Was God a monster? My heart and my mind quailed before this. I ran from it. Yet the idea of the good purpose of God being brought about through the suffering of His people drew me back. The mystery at the core of the Christian faith is the mystery of the cross.

So many reasons had been given for the death of our colleagues: naivety, foolishness, incompetence, as revenge, to derail a peace process, to be taught a lesson, to break white morale, and so on. But what if there was a divine reason underlying it all? What if this was no divine absence, no mistake, no second best, no passive "God allowed it", but rather the entire event lay within the plan and purpose of God that the missionaries should die that night?

I began to grasp that God actively weaves the evil deeds that people do into His sovereign rule over all things, while at the same time never condoning or accepting evil, never depriving men and women of either their freedom or their responsibility for what they do. Sometimes God intervenes to protect His people, but sometimes He places His people in harm's way because that will bring about His good purposes.

If this was the case, I needed to wrestle further with that question, "What might the purpose of God be in the deaths of our colleagues and friends?"

Was the purpose of God for His people to demonstrate a different response to hatred, to break the cycle of violence and revenge? At the time of the attack, my father and the relatives of those killed called for forgiveness for the killers. Given what I saw of the agony of heart and mind endured by those who had lost so much, it was plain that this was not cheap forgiveness, not an easy-going "There, there, it doesn't really matter."

This was forgiveness offered by those who could say, "By your evil actions you have utterly broken my heart. You have taken from me those I love. You have battered those I caressed, violated those I raised in purity, caused anguish to those I loved to comfort. By killing my children you have sought to undo all that I have done in raising them. You have stolen my investment, my life's work of love, sacrifice, prayer, thought, and time. The grief you have caused me shortens my life. My days will be darker, my load heavier, my sadness deeper. A shadow has fallen across the rest of my life that no sunshine will fully erase. I acknowledge all this and yet I choose to forgive you in the name of Christ."

This was a forgiveness from above. As my parents, as the relatives of the slain had been forgiven by God, so they too needed to forgive, leaving the door open to the possibility of re-creating a relationship where, humanly speaking, none could exist. These calls for forgiveness in the storm of recriminations, accusations, calls for further violence, and political one-upmanship were powerfully countercultural.

Was the purpose of God for the missionaries to share in the sufferings of the people of Zimbabwe? The missionary team understood that being a Christian would not always shelter them from suffering. Their lives were shared with the people they felt called to serve: praying, working, eating, educating, and healing. "We were ready to share with you not only the gospel of God but also our own selves."[7]

The missionaries had suffered because they were committed

not only to sharing their lives with others, but also to partaking of the lives of others. Theirs was no separatist Christianity, but rather engaged with and committed to God's beautiful but broken world. They shared the lives of those who lived with injustice and racism and political exploitation, as part of our world which is groaning and longing for its release.

Non-combatants, innocent of the reasons that had precipitated war, they died caught up mercilessly and unjustly in that war. From their own government, there was no demand for justice, no truth-telling after they died. In this, the missionaries joined thousands of civilians killed in circumstances that were never clarified, where responsibility was never taken, where the truth was never told. In this, the missionaries shared the fate of so many who died unjustly in the war in Rhodesia. But all those who died unjustly remain known to God, and their blood cries out from the ground. Jesus promised that one day God will lead justice to victory. God's patience is perfect, but it is not permanent.

Was the purpose of God to bring the hard-of-heart to Himself? One would expect that hardened extremists, practised killers, would be able to kill and kill again, left unmoved by what they had done. The Shona proverb, *chinokanganwa idemo, chitsiga hachikanganwe* ("What forgets is the axe; the wood does not forget"), might have been coined to describe exactly such a group who left a bloody trail of death, who sowed enduring sorrow along their path while remaining hard and unyielding themselves.

Of the group of killers that fateful night, two died in combat several weeks after the killings. But it seems that the prayers of hope and forgiveness that the missionaries prayed as they died were a powerful challenge to the guerrillas that survived – those ruthless, violent young men who killed them.

Of that group who survived the war, two joined the Zimbabwean Central Intelligence Organization. "In a moment of guilt ridden remorse",[8] they admitted their participation in the Elim killings to their senior officer. Both were deeply troubled by recurrent dreams of the attack, and sought refuge in alcohol. Both were killed in road accidents while drunk. Chillingly, their officer wrote, "I suppose, in a way, they were hoping for me to absolve them in some way."[9] But this was something he was not willing or able to offer.

Another survivor was paralysed in a road accident in 1980. Haunted over the years by his involvement in the killings in the Vumba, Chenjerai was overwhelmed by guilt and shame, longing for forgiveness and peace, which he eventually found.

Then there was Garikai and his men. Convicted, suffering shame and guilt, the young men searched for peace, looking for ways of coming to terms with the traumatic, blood-soaked days and nights they had created and endured. They found that peace.

The axe which cut the tree had not been able to forget.

Finding Garikai again, living as he was with a new identity, was a kind of miracle in itself. Trembling, I reworked over and again the wording of the letter I would send him. I was afraid that he would not respond and that nothing would ever come back from him. I was also afraid that his response would be offensive, bitterly angry, or indifferently denying knowledge of me, of my father, of the past. Perhaps Garikai was no longer walking with God, his conversion story was fake, a temporary means to make peace with the past that was no longer needed.

A response came. Holding my breath, I opened it.

> *Steve, oh what joy it has been to receive a surprise note from you. I was wondering what happened to my friend, your dad. He was a very close friend of mine. I am glad he went home where there is no sorrow, grief, or pain. I am filled with bittersweet to learn of what your dad, my cherished friend and brother, went*

*through. But one thing is that he left a great seed of
faith in my life. He made me what I am today. I am so
proud of your dad. A gallant soldier of the cross!*

Married for more than twenty years, Garikai lives quietly,
works in a regular job, cares for his wife, and loves his children.
Committed to a local church, he is an enthusiastic organizer of
evangelistic events in the area, and is also part of a team working
with teenagers at nearby schools. He remains in touch with
members of his former guerrilla section, and told me that they
too continue to live lives of faith in Jesus Christ.

As we corresponded, there were moments of surreality. This was
a man whose actions permanently marked my life and broke my
parents' hearts. Yet we are brothers in the Lord. I called my mother
to let her know the news. She was very glad to hear that Garikai
appeared to be persevering in his faith. Then, in a very human and
entirely understandable way, my mother said, "He did such terrible
things. I'm finding this hard to take in, hard to absorb." Thoughtfully
reflective, my mother wanted to turn again to the cross of Christ,
to the absolute scandal that because of that cross, the murderer can
enter the kingdom of God to stand forgiven and free alongside the
murdered. This is the shattering power of the grace of God.

Sometimes it appears that under the hand of God, the death
of Christians can break through hardened hearts (at a later stage)
in a unique way. This is the depth of the love of God for those
who do not yet know Him. Sometimes God does not spare His
own servants, as He did not spare His own Son, out of love for
those who do not yet know Him.

Was the purpose of God to challenge and inspire a group of
young men and women with the fullness of the claims of the
gospel? Through their deaths, the missionaries demonstrated
to those who had known them that there was something more
precious than life itself, and that was their relationship with God

and their obedience to Him. They did not seek death but wanted to bring life in all its fullness – spiritually through the Word of God, intellectually through education offered in the name of Christ, and physically through the act of healing. They were in that situation because of their obedience to the call of God. Many students drew challenge and inspiration from the lives and untimely deaths of their teachers.

Colin Kuhuni works as a labour lawyer in Zimbabwe. He suffered a savage beating for standing for truth and justice. His Christian faith undergirds his approach to life and work, and he ascribes his willingness to stay in a place of danger for the sake of his principles as a lesson he learned from his missionary teachers years ago.

While doing locum work in the UK, Zimbabwean surgeon Patrick Mandisodza wanted to find out how I was and tell me of his prayers for my family. Covering orthopaedics and accident and emergency, Patrick Mandisodza had been caring for those affected by flooding in the UK. My father's kindness in the name of Jesus to a young boy disabled by both polio and poverty, forty years ago in a remote area of Zimbabwe, had translated into care for those affected by natural disaster in the United Kingdom a generation later.

Willie Shumba, working as the Chief Customs Advisor for the African Union based in Addis Ababa, Ethiopia, and a leader in a Baptist church, wrote to tell me of former Emmanuel students who went on to lead Baptist, Methodist, Assemblies of God, and various Pentecostal churches. He mentioned that each year on 23 June, "I usually take time to thank God for that sacrificial love which made some of us know God, have education and be what we are today… The seed planted has germinated and continues to give living fruits."

Was the purpose of God to bring their lives to a close because their work was complete? In the immediate aftermath of the massacre, there was a meeting of Elim leaders from the United Kingdom with the black leaders entrusted with the work at Penhalonga and Katerere. There was a proposal to close down all Elim work in Rhodesia as the missionaries had been killed.

This idea was very strongly and clearly contested by Pious Munembe, who called for the work that had already been handed over to national leaders to continue. More than that, Pious Munembe drew both inspiration and challenge from the shattering events, recent though they were. "If foreign Christians take their obedience to the Lord so seriously that they are willing to come and live and die in a country that is not theirs," he declared, "how much more should we do for the Lord, we Christians of this country?"

To Pious, it was clear that the season of missionary-led work had ended. Their days had run their course. In fact, never again did Elim International Missions Board have such a large team in the country, even in the years of peace after independence. But that did not mean an end to the work of God! It seemed it was God's time for the national church to fully assume its leadership responsibilities while remaining open to working in partnership with believers from other parts of the world.

Thirty-eight years after his declaration, I met Pious and Evelyn Munembe living in the eastern border town of Mutare. Evelyn still wanted to mother me! Recently retired from nursing, she missed her busy days in the hospital but had found ways to keep busy. I ate her tasty *chibage*, or green mealies. She had baked a plenitude of cakes for my visit. Apparently I was not the size that I should have been, so she pressed on me bananas, sweet potatoes, and groundnuts that she had grown, and her home-made *dovi*, or peanut butter.

Now leading the Elim Pentecostal Church of Zimbabwe, Pious updated me on developments. Elim Mission, Katerere, originally named after the chief, was renamed the Elim

Pentecostal Church Centre Ruwangwe, after the valley in which it is located. The seventy-five-bed Elim Hospital is very busy, with a resident doctor and a new operating theatre block nearing completion. The hospital functions as a referral centre for the network of clinics in the area originally set up by Elim missionaries between 1951 and 1975 but now run by Nyanga Rural District Council.

Emmanuel Secondary School, now called Emmanuel High School, has 660 students, of which 450 come from across the country and board at the school. Two-thirds are girls, a remarkable turnaround given my father's concern in the 1970s when girls made up less than a sixth of the student body. Emmanuel High School is among the top twenty schools in Zimbabwe for O and A Level results. A team of black Zimbabwean teachers maintain the reputation of educational excellence that attracted so many in the past. Faithful Christian witness remains a characteristic of the school.

At the end of the war of independence in 1980, there was only one Elim church still open for public services, in the very north of Zimbabwe's eastern-most province of Manicaland. Now, among the villages of the Ruwangwe Valley alone, there are twenty-four churches. Like jewels on a chain, churches can be found scattered along a 300-kilometre arc, right to the southern tip of Manicaland. Where the Elim work in Zimbabwe first started in the 1940s in the Penhalonga area, there are three churches, primary schools, and a boarding resource unit supporting thirty deaf-mute children as they gain an education.

Manicaland's provincial capital Mutare has five churches, including the centrally located Elim Memorial Church, purchased after the massacre. A plot of land has been purchased nearby to build a Bible College. Close by, the centres of Old Mutare and Marange have churches. The names of beautiful little towns and villages all along the eastern border of Zimbabwe rolled off Pious' tongue, each with its own church: Chimanimani, Mount Selinda,

Chipinge, Tanganda River, as well as a small church hidden in the mountains across the border in Mozambique.

Halfway between Harare and Mutare, Rusape Elim Church has been given a ninety-nine-year lease by Makoni Rural District Council and is building on the fifteen-hectare land a primary school for the surrounding Crofton Community. The land is also used as a campsite and gathering point for Elim churches and conferences, now more central than the Elim Centre Ruwangwe.

Travelling up the escarpment and out of the Ruwangwe Valley heading west, Pastor Ephraim Satuku, supposedly in retirement, has opened a new church at Tanda. At Nyangombe River, where long ago guerrillas blew up the access bridge to the area, there is a church, and Elim have been asked to open a second boarding school there. Nyanga Town has a church, and in Mutoko, from where the Rhodesians sent their airborne troops so long ago, there are four Elim churches. Far to the west, beyond the bounds of Manicaland, there are Elim churches in the central towns of Marondera and Norton as well as eight churches in different suburbs of the capital Harare.

As Pious came to the close of his update, he heaved a great sigh. On asking him why, he told me that that there have been (and remain) many problems and challenges. He was not satisfied with the growth and expansion of the church.

Seeing this as a "holy dissatisfaction", I responded that he had given me an extraordinary overview of the solid growth and development of the work pioneered by the Briens along with Harry Tsengerai and Mateu Marongedza who, in obedience to the call of God, buried themselves in a remote, neglected valley sixty years ago. A missionary team characterized by faithful obedience had taken the vision further, only to meet an abrupt, bloody end. But, challenged and inspired by the witness of their foreign brothers and sisters, Zimbabwean men and women of character and faith had courageously and quietly persevered for nearly four decades.

Together, Pious and I went to visit my father's grave and the mass grave of his friends and colleagues. With the political turmoil and economic meltdown in Zimbabwe, many basic services have been badly neglected. Mutare Cemetery is no exception, and has become a wild, overgrown area of bush. However, the mass grave and my father's grave remain clean and well cared for. Over the decades, every six months Pious has ensured that the graves are tended to keep them that way, doing this as a mark of love and honour for those he once described as his spiritual parents. It remains a very beautiful and peaceful spot, partially shaded by a large jacaranda tree close to the mountains of the Eastern Highlands of Zimbabwe.

We drove up into the Vumba mountains that lie right on the border with Mozambique, finding our way to the plaque that was placed beside the road that overlooks Eagle School. It was sent to my parents by the Evangelical Sisterhood of Mary in Darmstadt, Germany, in 1978. My father had arranged for the plaque to be placed on a plinth close to the road. It reads, "In your distress say to God, 'My father, I do not understand you but I trust you.' Then you will experience his help." A stopping point there and a well-trodden path to the plinth indicated that it has visitors. We stood together there and prayed as a curtain of fine rain swept over us.

What of Eagle School itself? After independence in 1980, Eagle School was strictly out of bounds for decades, used as a training centre for the National Youth Service, a militia more commonly known as the "Green Bombers". Pious suggested that we drive down to the school gate. Nervously, I edged the vehicle down the dirt track.

To my surprise, we were able to enter the school grounds, my first visit in nearly forty years. The grounds remained beautiful, clean and well maintained, although the buildings were in dire need of repair. Emotions ran high as I strolled through the estate

– there was the Evans' home, the McCanns' place, our house. And there too was the place once chosen as a killing ground. The misty rain cleared and the diamond-sharp sunlight lit the grassy mound on the edge of the sports field under the imposing spreading branches of the acacia trees.

Quietly enjoying the anticipation of telling me, Pious chuckled as I asked him how he knew we would be able to get into Eagle School. He had been permitted to hold a retreat there for Elim pastors a few months before. He had found it tremendously moving to see Christian people thronging on to the site, reading from the Bible publicly, scattered in groups across the site to pray and intercede and then join together to fill the air with the evocative high call and deep response of Shona songs of joy and shouts of praise to God – all made more poignant by what everyone there knew lay in the past.

* * *

As I renewed links with old friends, I made contact with Roy and Gwyn Comrie. The Comries were Canadian missionaries who had worked for decades in Zimbabwe. Friends of my parents, they also worked on an Eastern Highlands mission station not far from Eagle School and had been devastated at the time of the killings of the missionaries on 23 June, 1978. Ten years later Roy had met Garikai and heard him speak after he came to faith.

On catching up with Roy's news, I was shocked to hear that his beloved sister Sheila, living alone after her husband had died of cancer, was raped and murdered by an intruder in her home in South Africa in 2007. Eventually a man was arrested whose DNA and fingerprints placed him at the scene. Astonishingly, Roy travelled to South Africa to try to meet with the man. He was told it would be impossible, but eventually he was granted twenty minutes just before the trial began.

In a holding cell with two detectives, the prosecutor, a defence lawyer, and a court clerk, Roy sat on a narrow bench right next to Chris Mnguni, the man about to go on trial for his sister's murder. Roy identified himself. Given limited time, Roy chose to tell the story of the killing of the Elim missionaries, giving an account of Garikai's barbaric crimes, and then told the story of Garikai's transformed life in Christ. Mnguni listened, as did the legal team assembled around the two men.

Roy had been looking down as he told the story, feeling overwhelmed with the situation. He said, "When I looked up, I saw the detective chief inspector's face. He was crying. I knew that God was moving. I felt my weakness very, very deeply at that particular time." Roy Comrie gave Chris Mnguni a Zulu Bible. Chris walked from that meeting into the court room but entered a plea of not guilty to Sheila's murder as his trial began.

Seeing the need, Roy became the catalyst for reviving a defunct chaplaincy programme in the "Murder Plus" prison wing of Westville Prison, in Kwa-Zulu, Natal, one of the biggest prisons in South Africa. Over months, Chris read the Bible in his cell and came to faith. The chaplain wrote to Roy several months later, "Chris keeps growing in Christ and has now confirmed his relationship by following Christ through the waters of baptism. More and more inmates are accepting the gospel of Jesus Christ. That is what we live for."

On a return visit to the prison, Roy was able to join in a meeting of the Christians in the prison, among them Chris Mnguni. Chris got to his feet and asked for an opportunity to speak. Inarticulate at first, choking repeatedly with emotion, Chris told the hushed group of his shame, his deep regret for the night when, high on drugs, he had raped and murdered Sheila. Roy wept on hearing again of his sister's death. Chris spoke of how Roy had met with him, gave him a Bible, and told him of the love of God and His willingness to forgive. As Chris finished his story, Roy walked over and embraced him.

Having decided that as a Christian he needed to tell the truth, Chris asked to change his plea to guilty. Chris was tried and sentenced to sixty years in prison for the rape and murder of Roy's sister, Sheila. Astonishingly, Chris told Roy that his sentence meant that the Lord had called him to spend the rest of his life in prison ministering to other prisoners.

Over these last nine years, more than 130 murderers in the Murder Plus wing have become Christians as a result of the testimony of Chris and others. Roy wrote to me from Cape Town, "We are encouraged by the Lord's growing family in Murder Plus prison wing and the way in which inmates are reaching out to the ones they victimized, seeking forgiveness and reconciliation." He added, "The horror of that long ago massacre and the extension of forgiveness has reaped such an amazing harvest. The power of forgiveness is truly so meaningful, especially when we know that our Saviour is the one who modelled it for us."

* * *

Our pain is real pain, and our loss is grievous and life-long. But in the hands of God, the suffering of His children endured on the path of faithful obedience can bring about unexpected, unlooked-for results. The death of a seed, planted in sorrow and watered with tears, can produce a harvest of righteousness, joy, and gratitude to God.

But more than that. The words that my mother, Anna, and I read to my dying father, words that were pinned to the wall of his sickroom, read, "But this light and momentary affliction is achieving for us a weight of glory."[10] A weight of glory? Can it really be? That the occasion of our deepest sorrows will one day become a fount of our deepest joy?

Like Dostoyevsky, my hosanna has passed through an immense furnace of doubt.[11] My faith has journeyed through the valley of the shadow of death. I only see through a glass darkly, indistinct moving light, vague and fleeting flashes of colour. But I see something, not nothing.

The little I see I am given as promise, a down payment on seeing all, seeing clearly one day. The sorrow is not yet over. The grieving is not yet done. The loss is not yet made good. But God is enough. So much was lost. All will one day be found.

Soli Deo Gloria

THANKS

The clear cold winter's day faded into dusk, the hours fleeting by as retired Elim leaders John and Mary Smyth sat with Anna and I around a table perched above the water's edge, overlooking Plymouth Harbour.[1] John remembered the first time we had met. My brother Paul and I were "driving" our Matchbox cars along a network of roads we had graded in the Katerere dirt outside the kitchen door. My father spoke to us in Shona, the local language. John laughed as he recalled me looking up and answering in Shona, after which I corrected what my father had just said!

Our journey into the past was shadowed as well as sunlit. Thirty-eight years after the massacre, the memory still stung and tore. Several times we sat, lost in our thoughts, tears running freely down our faces. John and Mary were so open, giving freely of their time and memories as I worked on this book. And they were not alone.

Without the generous help of many, this book would never have come to be. I have shared my own memories as well as being privileged to hear the recollections of others – gleaning much from their diaries, letters, documents, and photos. I wanted to tell this story as truthfully as possible, so have avoided embellishment or assumption. Even background detail of a scene is only what I recalled myself, verifiable from the memories of others, or known from documentation. If this has meant a somewhat spare style at times, I felt that to be a small price to pay for only passing on what I had found to be true.

Garikai was willing to read parts of my manuscript, taking

time and trouble to comment and correct, despite there being much he would rather not recall. It was not easy for him even though these are events that have been covered by the grace of God in Jesus. I hope that one day he will be able to tell his own story in his own words.

Grace and mercy came to Garikai through the determined witness of Margaret Lloyd, who told me she was threatened with death more than fifty times due to the sharing of her faith with those caught up in the Zimbabwean war of independence. Finding Margaret after all these years was a minor miracle! She kindly shared with me an unpublished manuscript, *Dear Comrade*.

Former Emmanuel Secondary School students Colin Kuhuni, Willie Shumba, Oliver Manyemba, Patrick Mandisodza, Antony Mandiwanza, and Stembile Mdhluli spent time talking to me or corresponded with me – sometimes at length. I value not only their help but their friendship. David McKenzie read and commented helpfully on early chapters. Richard Whitaker found some rare, out of print sources. Lameck and Rose Zulu and David and Christine Dawanyi told me about Northside Community Church in post-independence Harare.

Journalist Tim Lambon, then a BSAP police officer, recalled the scene at Eagle School on the morning after the massacre. The late Dzinashe "Dzino" Machingura was willing to discuss guerrilla training with me. Fay Chung's book *Re-living the Second Chimurenga* was invaluable – a gripping, disarmingly frank account of her experiences as one of the few Rhodesian-born Asians to join ZANU. She crossed into Zambia and then Mozambique during the war and ended up in the Ministry of Education after Independence where she became my father's boss.

Outstanding work was carried out by Laverne Page of the African & Middle Eastern Division in the US Library of Congress in locating records relating to the official list of ZANLA war dead.

US State Department archivists responded thoroughly to my Freedom of Information Act requests from halfway round the world. Tim Knatchbull, a dear friend and fellow survivor, helped me gain access to film archive otherwise unavailable. Professor Sue Onslow provided valuable insights, as did Professor Paul Moorcroft. I owe Professor David Maxwell a great deal, both as a stimulating and incisive conversationalist as well as a kind friend (even providing a map of the Katerere region from his own research). Jocelyn Mawdsley's warm encouragement was refreshing and her enthusiastic enlistment of Jeremy Harding (who provided some professional advice and told me he thought I could write) kept me going in a dark moment.

Annette McCulloch, Audrey Greenshields (Longley), and Eddie Cross – longstanding family friends who have done so much to build community in Zimbabwe, who knew and loved my parents and our friends who died – gently reminded me of much I had forgotten and told me of things I would not otherwise have known. Friends and siblings in Christ, Pious Munembe and his wife Evelyn make up the background to my life. Pious is now very busy leading the Elim work in Zimbabwe but still gave much time, energy, and prayerful support to me and I am deeply grateful.

Some shared with me at risk to themselves and so have asked to remain anonymous: the first police officer on the scene of the massacre, two members of the small unit that shot dead two ZANLA guerillas involved in the killings, and a very senior officer in Zimbabwe's Central Intelligence Organization who described how two members of his organisation confessed to him that they had been involved. I am grateful for their trust.

Others played different parts: the Tuesday night home group at Al and Claire Reynold's house held this book writing project in their prayers; Neil West scanned and captioned hundreds of photos; Patrick Fung encouraged me to take time to write and Jennie Fung's sensitive words acknowledged my need to understand deeply what had hurt me; Peter and Christine Rowan allowed time and space from the day job to write; Maldwyn Jones provided a warm Welsh welcome and kind support in working in the Elim archives; and Paul Hudson opened the way to access Elim records and provided much encouragement.

Joshua Griffiths searched for research articles at short notice. Aimée Griffiths brought boundless enthusiasm (and marketing expertise!) to this project. My mother, Brenda Griffiths, provided her war diary, reluctant permission to read my father's letters and frequent stern reminders to point always and only to God. Humble and unassuming, she is free of any trace of bitterness and remains full of life, laughter, and practical spirituality.

During the writing of this book I sat at the dinner table with my wife Anna and we talked things through, wrestled with language and ideas, and even wept at times as we "lived with the dead". Anna has patiently loved, served, edited, critiqued, cooked, cleaned, managed business affairs, and organized social events while coping with a husband who was all too often morose and grumpy. Selfless, she leant energy and provided support at a time when she herself was grieving a great loss. While keeping me going, Anna also urged me to stop work to walk, to laugh, to sing, to watch rugby, and to pray. She made a life for us both during the long months of writing. Anna has shaped my writing in a myriad of ways, not least with her scrupulous and courageous editing but also through her thoughtful insights and above all in her private prayer. Anna's name means "grace" and I have truly known grace flowing from her and through her. The Lord has shown me favour and I am thankful.

SELECTED BIBLIOGRAPHY

Referenced

Ngwabi Bhebe and Terence Ranger (eds), *Soldiers in Zimbabwe's Liberation War*, London: James Currey, 1995.

Ngwabi Bhebe and Terence Ranger, *Society in Zimbabwe's Liberation War*, Oxford: James Currey, 1996.

Joaquim Carlos Paiva de Andrada, *Relatório de Uma Viagem Ás Terras do Changamira*, Lisbon: Imprensa Nacional, 1886.

Catholic Commission for Justice and Peace in Rhodesia, *Civil War In Rhodesia*, London: Catholic Institute for International Relations, 1976.

David Caute, *Under the Skin: The Death of White Rhodesia*, Harmondsworth: Penguin, 1983.

Shimmer Chinodya, *Harvest of Thorns*, Harare: Baobab Books, 1989.

Fay Chung, *Reliving the Second Chimurenga*, Stockholm: Nordic Africa Institute, 2006.

Henrik Ellert, *The Rhodesian Front War: Counterinsurgency and Guerrilla Warfare 1962–1980*, Harare: Mambo Press, 1989.

David Freemantle, *A Hole in Our Lives Forever*, Australia: Xlibris, 2011.

Preller Geldenhuys, *Rhodesian Air Force Operations*, New Zealand: Peysoft Publishing, 2014.

Alexander Kanengoni, *Echoing Silences,* Harare: Baobao Books, 1997.

Norma Kriger, *Guerrilla Veterans in Post-War Zimbabwe*, Cambridge: Cambridge University Press, 2003.

David Lan, *Guns and Rain: Guerrillas and Spirit Mediums in Zimbabwe*, London: James Currey, 1985.

Catherine Claire Larson, *As We Forgive*, Grand Rapids: Zondervan, 2008.

Melvyn P. Leffler and Odd Arne Westad, *The Cambridge History of the Cold War, Volume 3, Endings*, Cambridge: Cambridge University Press, 2013.

David Martin and Phyllis Johnson, *The Struggle for Zimbabwe*, Harare: Zimbabwe Publishing House, 1981.

David Maxwell, *Christians and Chiefs in Zimbabwe: A Social History of the Hwesa People c.1870s–1990s*, Edinburgh: Edinburgh University Press, 1999.

David Maxwell, *African Gifts of the Spirit: Pentecostalism and the Rise of a Zimbabwean Transnational Religious Movement,* Oxford: James Currey, 2006.

Wilfred Mhanda, *Dzino Memories of a Freedom Fighter*, Harare: Weaver Press, 2011.

Paul Moorcraft and Peter McLaughlin, *The Rhodesian War: A Military History*, Barnsley: Pen and Sword Books, 2008.

Bruce Moore-King, *White Man, Black War,* Harare: Baobab Books, 1989.

Dick Paget, *Paget's Progress*, Milton Keynes: Authorhouse, 2007.

J. D. Y. Peel and T. O. Ranger, *Past and Present in Zimbabwe*, Manchester: Manchester University Press, 1983.

Heather Powell, *Tsanga Place of Reeds, Place of Healing,* Australia: Bayprint, 2005.

Brian Raftopoulos and Alois Mlambo (eds), *Becoming Zimbabwe*, Harare: Weaver Press, 2009.

Phyllis Thompson, *The Rainbow or the Thunder,* London: Hodder and Stoughton, 1979.

Background

David Blair, *Degrees in Violence*, London: Continuum Books, 2001.

C. J. Chivers, *The Gun,* New York: Simon and Schuster, 2010.

Chris Cocks, *Fireforce*, Johannesburg: 30 Degrees South Publishers, 2008.

R. B. Drummond and K. Coates Palgrave, *Common Trees of the Highveld,* Harare: Longman Zimbabwe, 1987.

Ken Flower, *Serving Secretly,* London: John Murray, 1987.

Alexandra Fuller, *Don't Let's Go to the Dogs Tonight: An African Childhood*, Oxford: Picador, 2002.

Alexandra Fuller, *Scribbling the Cat*, Oxford: Picador, 2004.

Peter Godwin, *When a Crocodile Eats the Sun*, London: Picador, 2007.

Peter Godwin, *The Fear,* London: Picador 2010.

Erik Holm and Elbie de Meillon, *Insects,* Cape Town: Struik Publishers, 1993.

Chenjerai Hove, *Bones*, Harare: Baobab Books, 1988.

Michael Howard, *Recklessly Abandoned*, Kansas City: Out of Africa Books, 1996.

John Knight, *Rain in a Dry Land,* London: Hodder and Stoughton, 1987.

David Lemon, *Never Quite a Soldier*, Stroud: Albida Books, 2000.

Martin Meredith, *Our Votes, Our Guns*, New York: Public Affairs Books, 2002.

Paul Moorcraft, *Mugabe's War Machine*, Barnsley: Pen and Sword Military, 2011.

NOTES

The Dream

1. Shona proverb.

Stream of the Lion Spirit

1. Kopje – literally "little head" but meaning a hilly, rocky outcrop. Afrikaans.

2. J. C. Paiva de Andrada, *Relatório de Uma Viagem Ás Terras Do Changamira*, Lisboa: Imprensa Nacional, 1886, pp. 5-7.

3. The medium was described as being possessed by a "mhondoro" or spirit of a dead chief. When the spirit was not possessing its spirit medium it was thought to enter a lion.

4. I witnessed a similar demonstration seventy years later. Ultimately, the demonstration I saw did not have the same effect on an incipient revolution!

5. National Archives of Zimbabwe, N9/4/18, Monthly Report, Inyanga, April 1904. Quoted by David Maxwell, *Christians and Chiefs in Zimbabwe: A Social History of the Hwesa People c.1870s–1990s*, Edinburgh: Edinburgh University Press, 1999, p. 33.

6. David Maxwell, *Christians and Chiefs in Zimbabwe*, p. 19.

7. Qualifying MPS in 1928.

8. Ian R. Phimister, "The Spanish Influenza Pandemic of 1918 and its Impact on the Southern Rhodesian Mining Industry", in *Central African Journal of Medicine* 19/7, 1973, p. 144.

9. Howard Phillips, "Influenza Pandemic (Africa)", in *International Encyclopedia of the Frist World War*, available at: http://encyclopedia.1914-1918-online.net/article/influenza_pandemic_africa (accessed 13 September 2016).

10. Peter Griffiths, "A great service to Africans: Cecil and Mary Brien of Katerere", *Central African Journal of Medicine*, 20(8), August 1974, pp. 174–75.

11. Ibid.

12. "Dr Cecil Brien: a Tribute", *Elim Evangel*, published following Cecil's death in 1980.

13. Ibid.

14. Jeremiah 45:5.

15. Peter Griffiths (my father) joined the Briens as a junior missionary nine years after they had pioneered the work in the Ruwangwe Valley. It was a source of frustration to him that extracting information from the Briens about their work and those early days could be painfully slow!

16. An inanimate object worshipped for its supposed magical powers or because it is considered to be inhabited by a spirit.

17. The Briens had begun work in the Zambezi Valley with the Evangelical Alliance Mission but had left because of the EAM rejection of Pentecostal practice and what the Briens saw as the agency's refusal to engage with the supernatural world view of the people they were trying to reach. In my view, the long-term impact of a missionary failure to engage in this way is clearly and painfully described in David Lan's book, *Guns and Rain: Guerrillas and Spirit Mediums in Zimbabwe*, which describes the upsurge in traditional religious practice during the war, especially in the Zambezi Valley, and the unpreparedness of cessationist evangelical Christians to understand and respond to such a "revival".

18. David Maxwell points out that in the 1980s, one of the medium's sons also converted, becoming a fervent Pentecostal preacher in Mutare.

19. His great-grandson, Jimmy Thomas, was an outstanding Professor of Medicine at the University of Zimbabwe. I worked as Professor Thomas's Junior House Officer after qualifying from the University of Zimbabwe in 1988.

20. Thomas Morgan Thomas, *Eleven Years in Central South Africa,* Snow, 1873, p. 219.

21. Edward Shizha and Michael T. Kariwo, *Education and Development in Zimbabwe: A Social, Political and Economic Analysis,* Sense Publishers, 2011, pp. 17–18.

22. A scapular consists of two rectangular pieces of cloth, wool, or other fabric that are connected by bands. One rectangle hangs over the chest of the wearer, while the other rests on the back, with the bands running over the shoulders. On the cloth appear images of saints, symbols, or messages.

23. Vatican II, as it is commonly known, took place in Rome between 1962 and 1965.

24. Maureen Sullivan, *101 Questions and Answers on Vatican II,* Paulist Press, 2002.

25. National Archives of Zimbabwe, Native Commissioner Inyanga to Provincial Native Commissioner Umtali, 5 April 1956. Quoted by David Maxwell, *Christians and Chiefs in Zimbabwe* (Edinburgh: Edinburgh University Press), p. 95.

26. Dr and Mrs C. Brien, "Southern Rhodesia: an SOS for Prayer", *Elim Evangel*, 23 June 1953.

Peculiar People and Publicans

1. Corporal B. A. Hurrell RAFVR 1648877 mentioned in dispatches *London Gazette*, 1 January 1946.

2. 1 Peter 2:9 (King James Version, emphasis added).

3. Established by George Jeffreys in 1921, at Leigh on Sea, Essex. http://www.elim.org.uk/Articles/410264/History_Overview.aspx (accessed 13 September 2016).

4. Harvey Cox, *Fire from Heaven: The Rise of Pentecostal Spirituality and the Reshaping of Religion in the Twenty-First Century* Reading, MA: Addison-Wesley, 1994.

5. Yeol-Soo Eim, "The Roots of Korean Pentecostalism" (a paper presented at the eighteenth Pentecostal World Conference, Theological Symposium for Asian Church Leaders, "Asian Issues on Pentecostalism," Yoido Full Gospel Church, Seoul, Korea, 21 September 1998).

6. John 7:17.

7. See Matthew 10:39.

8. The previous Archbishop of Canterbury, Rowan Williams, attended Dynevor.

9. John 8:12.

10. Saul Dubow, "Macmillan, Verwoerd, and the 1960 'wind of change' speech", *Historical Journal*, 54 (4). 2011, pp. 1087–1114.

The River Cuts New Channels

1. Boniface was from Sangoma village. He had come to faith there on Sunday 4 October 1959 through Ronias Mukwewa (the Briens' first convert in the Ruwangwe area) and Brenda.

2. 25 October 1962.

3. The Annexation of Portuguese India (Goa) took place on 18 and 19 December 1961. In a short, sharp military action lasting a day and a half and involving air, sea, and land strikes, the Indian Armed Forces ended 451 years of Portuguese overseas provincial governance in Goa. In India, the annexation was seen as liberation of Indian territory. Portugal saw it as a humiliating defeat, aggression directed against Portuguese national soil and citizens. Reprisals against Indian nationals in Portuguese territories followed.

4. Zechariah 4:6.

5. 10 April 1964.

Among Worlds

1. Harper Lee, *To Kill a Mockingbird,* Warner Books, 1988, p. 224.

2. The photo was taken in March 1968. Alan Renshaw, the shooter, reported the killing of the leopard to the British South Africa Police on 6 March 1968. The reason given for shooting the leopard was "damage to livestock".

3. March 1971. I had a temperature of 103.4, "but an injection soon knocked it down". A course of mepacrin tablets turned me yellow!

4. See Harvey Cox, *Fire from Heaven* for a similar account of the impact of Pentecostal Christianity on violent, exploitative, feral men in the favelas of Brazil.

5. First Communion in December 1972. Prayer Newsletter No. 16, December 1972.

6. Prayer Newsletter No. 16, December 1972.

7. *Kaffir* was a highly pejorative term widely used by white people in Southern Africa to describe black people. The word is rooted in the Arabic term *kfir*, translated "infidel" or "heathen", initially used by Arab slave traders for black non-Muslim slaves.

8. Originally from the Zulu *umuntu*, meaning "person", but now has derogatory overtones.

9. From the Afrikaans *hout*, meaning "wood", and with the implication of being "wooden-headed" or stupid.

10. Probably originally from Portuguese *pequenino*, diminutive of *pequeno*, meaning "small".

11. Used in a derogatory sense of almost any black woman, with the implication that she was a child-carer and nothing more.

12. From the Nguni language meaning "a married woman".

Rushing Wind

1. Prayer Newsletter No. 8, December 1968.

2. Prayer Newsletter No. 10, December 1969.

3. *Sadza* is a stiff maize meal porridge, and *muriwo* is a vegetable relish.

4. The Beits reportedly paid a great deal of attention to the detail of the philanthropic investment of their fortune.

5. On 26 April 1974, a few months before their visit to Katerere, the Beits had been tied up, pistol-whipped, and pushed down stairs by an IRA gang who stole eight million Irish pounds' worth of art from them.

6. Willie Shumba's personal communication.

7. Willie Shumba's personal communication.

8. Mozambique Liberation Front – the main nationalist guerrilla force fighting a conscript Portuguese army in Mozambique, which at the time was an "overseas province" of Portugal.

9. Quoted in Phyllis Thompson, *Rainbow or the Thunder*, Hodder and Stoughton, 1979, p. 20.

The Blind Killer

1. John 14:27; Isaiah 32:18; Psalm 147:14. The last was significant for my mother, who was ill at the time and being X-rayed. She had been forgotten in her cubicle and as she read this psalm she was particularly struck by the words "peace in your borders" – i.e. within the borders of the Mission.

2. D. M. Fremantle, *A Hole in Our Lives Forever*, Australia: XLibris, p. 116.

3. Special Courts came into being as part of the Emergency Powers (Criminal Trials) Regulations, 1976, specifically to deal with offences related to "terrorism in Rhodesia", to provide stiffer sentences and "on-the-spot justice". The jurisdiction of the courts was the same as the High Court. The relatives of those sentenced to death were not told of the day of execution nor were they allowed to take possession of the body. Catholic Commission for Justice and Peace, *Civil War in Rhodesia* (1976), pp. 86–92.

4. *Rhodesia Herald*, 28 May 1976. Sentence of death was passed by Mr Justice Beck and two assessors, Mr H. Nicolle and Mr W. Henning. Mr J. Colegrave prosecuted. The men were defended by Mr A. Bruce-Brand

(who two years later was to attend the inquest of the Elim massacre at the request of the FCO. This trial is also mentioned in *Civil War in Rhodesia*, p. 89.

5. Peter Griffiths, "Emmanuel Secondary School Rhodesia", *Elim Evangel*, 23 January 1971.

6. The Alouette was a French-made helicopter, adapted in various ways to become both the workhorse and the warhorse of the Rhodesian Air Force. Ironically, the meaning of the French word for this helicopter responsible for so much suffering and death is "skylark".

7. Frequently the Soviet TM-46 anti-tank mine was used. Often the mine was "boosted" with extra high explosives packed around the mine. By the end of 1977, across Rhodesia mines were destroying eleven vehicles, and a further six mines were being lifted, every week.

8. This was agreed in missionary conference of 19 June 1976. It was also agreed to put a radio-telephone into my father's office. Plans for emergency evacuation were also worked on.

9. The theory of the time was that the occupants had to sit on hard seats because cushions caused the body to bounce on the accelerating seats, demolishing the spine.

Hammer and Anvil

1. Dietrich Bonhoeffer, *The Cost of Discipleship*, SCM Press, 2015, p. 45.

2. Roy Lynn from Culleybackey Elim Church in County Antrim. History of the church including Roy's story at http://www.cullybackeyelim.com/ (accessed 6 October 2016).

3. In June 1976 the BSAP camp at Ruwangwe was augmented by the deployment of 6 (Independent) Company of the Rhodesia Regiment – a sign of increasing concern at the level of guerrilla incursion in the area.

4. Air gunners were required to be very careful with the ammunition they expended owing to the cost of the rounds and the difficulty of obtaining supplies, with international sanctions in place on the Rhodesian government.

5. Sergeant Technician/Gunner 6149 John "Pat" Graham (aged 25), No. 7 Squadron RhAF, killed in action from a gunshot wound, as a result of ground fire while flying in an Alouette IIIB R5076 in the Inyanga area, Op Thrasher. Source: Roll of Honour, Rhodesian Army.

6. Former ZANLA Commissar Josiah Tungamirai in his paper

"Recruitment to ZANLA: Building up a War Machine" describes this as "press-ganging" and explicitly links it to British Royal Naval practice. Ngwabi Bhebe and Terence Ranger, *Soldiers in Zimbabwe's Liberation War*, Heinemann, 1995, pp. 40–41.

7. "Terrorists kill 12 black men who were building a fence at Musani School in the Mutema TTL, Chipinga area", 5 October 1976. Cited in A Newspaper Chronology of the Rhodesian Bush War December 1972 to April 1980, from notes by John White.

8. Others who had left around 22 September 1976 were James Kaunye, Langton Katerere, Tendai Gwizo, Ernest Chipise, and Brian Mafondokoto. Some of these men were Emmanuel students and others local teenagers.

9. In September 1976, Kissinger was actively involved in negotiations, along with South Africa's prime minister John Vorster, to hasten the transition to black majority rule in Rhodesia. Their proposals were reluctantly accepted by Ian Smith but rejected by the leaders of the two main black nationalist groups, and the war continued.

10. See "6 Independent Company: The Rhodesia Regiment / The Rhodesian African Rifles. A Brief History by G. D. P Morgan (Company Sergeant Major)". Available at http://www.rhodesianforces.org/6IndepCoy.htm for a Rhodesian forces account of the action. Rhodesian Services Association Incorporated, "Contact! Contact!", June 2010, reports the death of Trevor Blythe in April 2010 in Harare. He was rendered quadriplegic by this attack in 1976. Available at http://www.rhodesianservices.org/user/image/publication06-2010.pdf (both articles accessed 19 September 2016).

11. Equivalent to £110 in 2015.

12. Rheims-Cessna F337 "Lynx" fixed-wing aircraft armed with French SNEB unguided air-to-ground rockets and frantan (napalm) bombs.

13. Willas Chinoya, District Assistant, Internal Affairs, killed in action, in an ambush at Kazozo Kraal, Inyanga North, 13 November 1976. Source: Roll of Honour, Rhodesian Army.

14. Galatians 6:10a.

15. Ezra 8:21–23, 31–32.

16. Air strike report 571, Rhodesian Air Force Operations, p. 305, records eighteen aircraft involved but describes it as an "external operation", possibly because ZANLA retreated across the border into Mozambique.

17. Rifleman Frederick Koen (20) of 3 (Independent) Company, Rhodesia Regiment, was killed in a contact in the Tanda TTL, Makoni District on 25 November 1976. Source: Rhodesian Army Roll of Honour.

18. "A kind of bomb that started fires" was what Brenda was told. Probably this was frantan, a 1.8 metres (5 ft 11 in) long Rhodesian-made napalm bomb developed by the Royal Rhodesian Air Force during the 1960s. They were filled with about 73 litres (16 imp gal; 19 US gal) of napalm. During development they were given the name "frangible tanks" to obscure their real purpose. The common abbreviation "frantan" stuck when they entered service.

19. Prayer Newsletter, 6 December 1976.

20. Elim Archives, Reports and Notes South Africa and Rhodesia, J. C. Smyth, *Final Report of Visit to Rhodesia*, July 1977.

21. Former Rhodesian Army serviceman David Freemantle records this allegation in his memoir *A Hole in our Lives Forever*, p. 268.

22. Isaiah 43:2.

23. "Bible women" were mature local Christian women who learned literacy skills and about the Bible after coming to faith. They worked alongside missionary societies to travel through villages, visiting women in their homes and introducing Bible study, singing, and prayer. They often distributed the Scriptures very effectively, being able to go where foreigners could not go. The role of Bible woman was the first independent ministry role available to Christian women in Asia and Africa.

24. Wendy White, Prayer Letter, March/April 1977.

25. I worked here for a brief period as a government doctor, and recall a referral coming in from Ruwangwe, a stinking horrible infected incomplete abortion which left us all retching as we choked our way through a dilation and curettage in the heat of a non-air-conditioned operating theatre.

26. Ngwabi Bhebe and Terence Ranger, *Society in Zimbabwe's Liberation War*, Oxford: James Currey, 1996, p. 67.

27. Ephesians 4:3.

A Greater Danger

1. Tim Keller, *King's Cross,* Hodder & Stoughton, 2013, pp. 101–102.

2. Air Strike Report Number 668 09/04/77 Op Thrasher. Preller Geldenhuys, *Rhodesian Air Force Operations,* Peysoft Publishing, 2014, p. 310.

3. Possibly Warwick, E., Trooper, First Battalion, Rhodesian Light Infantry, killed in action, 9 April 1977. Source; Rhodesian Army Roll of Honour. The other remains unnamed and unrecorded.

4. Broadcast in the UK on 24 February 1977. Covered in the *Elim Evangel*, 12 March 1977.

5. Both that question and response were cut from the final broadcast.

6. Briefly defined in four main strands of thought as: reverence for the Bible and a high regard for biblical authority (biblicism); the necessity of being "born again", that the central message of the gospel is justification by faith in Christ and repentance, or turning away, from sin, with conversion differentiating the Christian from the non-Christian, and that the change in life it leads to is marked by both a rejection of sin and a corresponding personal holiness of life (conversionism); a belief in substitutionary atonement, in which Christ died as a substitute for sinful humanity by taking on himself the guilt and punishment for sin and so can offer humanity forgiveness of sins and new life (crucicentrism); and an active expression and sharing of the gospel in diverse ways that include preaching and social action (activism).

7. The Rhodesian Army were establishing a battle camp in the area with truck movement, were expecting mines to be laid, and had prepared a "reaction stick", and a medic was on standby. A guerrilla had cycled to what seemed to be a good spot to lay an anti-tank mine. As he was in the process of burying it he had heard the Elim Mission lorry coming and had run for it, in his panic leaving the bicycle by the side of the road. The Army unit in the battle camp heard the Mission truck approaching from the east, anticipated the detonation, and dispatched the reaction unit and medical team on hearing the explosion. David Freemantle, *A Hole in Our Lives Forever*, p. 196.

8. Brenda Griffiths' diary entry made on 31 May 1977.

9. 11 June 1977 – Cpl Frank Hamp-Adams, Rhodesia Intelligence Corp (RIC), killed in action in a landmine explosion near Ruwangwe, St Swithin's TTL, Inyanga district, Op Thrasher.

10. John Smyth, "Final Report of a Visit to Rhodesia", July 1977.

11. Pious Munembe – personal communication.

12. ZANLA recorded the landmine incident in its field reports: "Date and Time of Operation: 21/7/77, 8:38 am Place of Operation: Inyanga – Ruangwa to Inyanga Road Type of Operation: The mine was detonated by a vehicle belonging to LN (sic) Mission. This surprised the comrades

because these people had been told not to use the road. No one was killed but there were three white teachers in the truck." ZANU Archives, File: Chitepo Sector 2: Chitepo Operational Report, 21 July 1977, by B. Chakamuka. Quoted by Janice McLaughlin in *On the Frontline: Catholic Missions in Zimbabwe's Liberation War,* Baobab Books, 1996. However, the dates in the operational report and in my mother's diary differ by a day.

13. Isaiah 55:12.

14. Mr Chikoore was travelling home on his bike when he came across the pathetic straggle of children who said they would walk to Inyanga. Knowing this was not possible, Chikoore went to phone the police (which is how my mother and father came to know about this) and arranged for them to stay at St Mary's and Marist Brothers Missions.

15. One of the students was on both the first and third buses. On travelling home from Umtali, they were on a local bus which also hit a landmine, meaning they were blown up three times in three days.

16. Acts 20:22 onwards.

Eagle School

1. George MacDonald, *Sir Gibbie,* Hurst and Blackett, 1879.

2. Haggai 2:9.

3. It is unlikely this had much to do with the subsequent attack as the African staff were left completely uninvolved and unharmed. However, it did have a deleterious effect on morale.

4. Brian Raftopoulos and Alois Mlambo (eds), *Becoming Zimbabwe,* Harare: Weaver Press, 2009, p. 155. Norma Kriger, *Guerrilla Veterans in Post-War Zimbabwe,* Cambridge: Cambridge University Press, 2003, p. 6.

5. 1 John 4:18.

6. Interviewed in Harare, 3 June 2016.

7. Evidence given at the inquest by Elias Chikoshana.

The Devil's Kick

1. Guerrillas were called *magandanga* by the Rhodesian Ministry of Information. In Shona, a *gandanga* means a person who lives in the forest, randomly cutting the throats of passers-by: a most vicious and terrible person. The word was sometimes taken and subverted by the guerrillas themselves.

2. It was a waning gibbous moon just three days after full. The moon rose at around 8.30 p.m. that night in that latitude/longitude.

3. Levi Kombi's testimony to the inquest gave the last known location of the missionaries while still alive.

4. 1 Peter 5:6–11.

5. The inquest was told that the entire period between 7.00 p.m. and 8.25 p.m. had been quiet. No sounds of struggle or screaming had been heard – the relevance being that the missionaries were still alive at that point.

6. Information given at the inquest by Andrew Tinonesana, teacher.

7. Information about the speaker and his weapon given at the inquest by Elias Chikoshana, vice principal.

8. A newspaper reported an interview with a black teacher who stated the speech was about six minutes long.

9. Information about the guerilla speaker given at the inquest by Elias Charamba, student. He also said, "I don't know what it is called but they told us that whenever they come across sell-outs, that sell-out is told to swallow that thing which is attached to the firearm."

10. From personal correspondence between Peter Griffiths and Phyllis Thompson. Thomas Muripira had become a Christian following the landmine incident in which his Christian friend Leonard Bhunu had been killed.

11. Years later, writing about the school, Colin said, "I could not imagine going to a school with a better environment for mental, spiritual, and emotional growth."

12. When interviewed, this former British South Africa Police (BSAP) Ground Cover Section Officer requested that his real name not be used.

13. Odzi was the western boundary of Umtali Rural, Cashel was the southern boundary, the international border with Mozambique was the eastern, and Dangamvura was northern boundary. Umtali Rural covered the Tribal Trust Lands around, including Zimunya TTL.

14. This former BSAP Cadet requested that his real name not be used.

15. African traditional axe.

16. The axe belonged to school clerk Levi Kombi and had been taken from the woodpile next to his house. Evidence given to the inquest. A post-mortem showed that Phil Evans was killed with the axe that was found

still buried in Cath Picken's body so these must have been sequential and could not have taken place at the same time. Phil and Cath died within a few paces of each other. Source: post-mortem examination by Dr Antony David Owen.

17. Officer Poole's testimony about bodies, positions, relative distances were all confirmed independently by Detective McDade's map and measurements submitted to the inquest.

18. Philippians 1:20–21.

19. Jeff Lucas, *Lucas on Life,* Authentic Lifestyle, 2001, pp. 216–17.

20. Personal correspondence from BSAP Section Officer Tim Lambon.

21. Unedited satellite uplink footage provided to the author from BBC archives.

22. Grand Reef Forward Air Field.

23. "As far as I am aware, the BSAP were the only people who followed up on this massacre and I was very much in the picture as far as the follow-ups which took place, resulting in the contact which ensured after resulting in the kills and captures (as you are well aware of)." BSAP Ground Cover Section Officer interviewee.

24. *Everyman* programme interview with Florence Evans broadcast on 29 October 1978.

25. Daughter of David White and grand-daughter of Sir Thomas White, Chair of the Joint Tunnel Committee of the Mersey Tunnel opened in 1934 by King George.

26. *Yorkshire Post*, 26 June 1978.

27. Romans 8:31–32, 35–39.

28. Acts 7:59–60.

29. *Daily Mail*, 30 June 1978.

30. Hebrews 11:32 – 12:3.

31. Personal communication from John Smyth.

32. *Elim Evangel*, July 1978.

33. Referring to the words of John 12:24-25: "Unless a grain of wheat falls into the earth and dies, it remains alone; but if it dies, it bears much fruit. Whoever loves his life loses it, and whoever hates his life in this world will keep it for eternal life."

In High Places

1. "Letter to Three Students" (October 1967) as translated in "The Struggle Intensifies", in Leopold Labedz (ed.), *Solzhenitsyn: A Documentary Record,* Harper and Row, 1970.

2. Source: Public Records Office, minutes of British Cabinet Meetings, Thursday 29 June 1978.

3. Record of Debate on Rhodesia (British Missionaries) – in the British House of Commons at 12.00 p.m. on 26 June 1978.

4. Further work in reviewing secret documentation now released from FCO files in the UK reveal that the FCO had a contact called Gaylard who was Secretary to the Cabinet in Rhodesia, who remained in contact with Combined Operations during the pursuit. Gaylard was providing information to FCO rep Mr Graham.

5. Secret FCO report "Rhodesia: Military Aspects", 19 June 1978, obtained from the UK Public Records Office.

6. "Southern Africa: Front-Line States Back U.K.-U.S. Plan", 1 October 1977. Available at: http://web.stanford.edu/group/tomzgroup/pmwiki/uploads/3127-1977-10-01-FF-b-LIA.pdf (accessed 20 September 2016).

7. Source: copies of cables obtained from the UK Public Records Office.

8. Cable dated 27 June 1978, obtained from the UK Public Records Office.

9. *The New York Times*, Editorial 27 June 1978, p. 14.

10. Either the traffic was removed from the files or a decision was taken not to pursue the facts further.

11. Sources: 1. FCO files: press statement by R. G. Mugabe, President of ZANU on 25 June 1978. 2. FCO files: Interview with Robert Mugabe and *Tempo* magazine on 25 June 1978, published in Maputo on 2 July 1978. 3. David Caute, *Under the Skin: The Death of White Rhodesia,* Penguin, 1983, pp. 253–58.

12. FCO files: Meeting Maputo 28 June 1978 Evetts (First Secretary of the British Embassy) and Zvogbo, ZANU Secretary for Information and Publicity.

13. Report: "Call on the Secretary of State by the International Missions Director of the Elim Pentecostal Church", 27 June 1978, referring to a meeting on 26 June 1978. Copy of report obtained from the UK Public Records Office.

14. Source: Former BSAP Section Officer Tim Lambon, personal communication.

15. Source: CID officer McDade testifying at inquest. Elim archive, accessed 15 February 2016.

16. In addition, CID officer McDade testified at inquest that the diary "contained small details that only the perpetrators would have known of". Elim archive, accessed 15 February 2016. Police Officer Tim Lambon took a copy of the diary, which remains buried in Harare. Personal communication.

17. David Caute, *Under the Skin: the Death of White Rhodesia*, p. 256.

18. Reported in the official organ of the Zimbabwe African National Union the *Zimbabwe News*, Vol. 10, No. 4 p. 27, covering the period July–August 1978: "At 9.50 p.m. on August the 1st, an enemy base situated along the Vhumba road four kilometres from Umtali in Zimunya was attacked by a heavily armed ZANLA detachment. Thirty (30) enemy troops were killed and many others were seriously injured. Seven military trucks, five 7-ton trucks of the racist road department and a D.C.7 caterpillar were set ablaze. The camp administration offices were razed to the ground. This camp was being used to defend road department personnel who were carrying out repairs on this mine disrupted road."

19. Published by the Prime Minister's Office, 1983. Printed by Jongwe Printing and Publishing Co. (Pvt) Ltd, Harare, p. 126.

20. Philippians 1:21 – the same text that my father spoke on at the EBC graduation.

21. Buried in the footnotes of Terence Ranger and Ngwabi Bhebe's second book, *Society in Zimbabwe's Liberation War*, is a reference to an interview that British historian Professor David Maxwell conducted with my father on 9 July 1991 regarding this meeting with Laver.

22. It would seem that either Laver shared a source with the US State Department or that the US had decided to pass on the INR report to the Foreign Office. The record of this second meeting in November 1978, together with any note or record of such a communication between Mugabe and the FCO, is no longer available or held in the FCO records.

23. Lord Owen personal communication: Lord Owen's careful response to me many years later did not reflect what his subordinate Laver reported as fact to my father. He refers to the fact that I might have come across some National Archive material "giving advice to Ministers as to who we thought was responsible at the time. But I doubt there would be certainty."

Burning On, Burning Bright

1. J. R. R. Tolkien's character Sam Gamgee has these thoughts in *The Lord of the Rings book III Return of the King,* UK: Harper Collins, 1994.

2. Revelation 6:11.

3. Letter from David Ayling to Peter Griffiths, 1 December.

4. Letter from Brenda Griffiths to David Ayling, 17 February 1979.

5. 2 Corinthians 4:17–18.

6. Letter from Peter Griffiths to David Ayling, 18 August 1979.

7. Peter Griffiths to David Ayling quoting Acts 15:25–26, 20 September 1979.

8. Letter to David Ayling from Peter Griffiths, 5 January 1980.

9. Peter Griffiths to David Ayling, 11 October 1980.

10. Originally £20,000 – equivalent to more than £91,000 in 2015.

11. Elim Evangel Mission News, May 1985, p. 2.

Whispers and Rumours

1. Alexander Kanengoni, *Echoing Silences,* Heinemann Educational Publishers, 1997, p. 91.

2. Letter from Brian Edwards to Peter Griffiths, 20 April 1983.

3. Letter from Brian Edwards to Peter Griffiths, 23 May 1983.

4. Published a few days before on Friday, 28 November 1980.

5. Letter from Devil Hondo (Garikai) to Margaret Lloyd from an unpublished manuscript entitled "Dear Comrade" written by Margaret Lloyd. Used with permission from both Margaret Lloyd and Garikai.

6. According to multiple former combatants in their memoirs and in newspaper interviews.

7. Fay Chung, *Reliving the Second Chimurenga,* Stockholm: Nordic Africa Institute, 2006, p. 88.

8. Analysis of "Fallen Heroes of Zimbabwe", the official list of ZANLA war dead, confirmed from ZANLA's own records that in 1978 around 30 per cent of guerrilla deaths were disease-related rather than combat-related.

9. Fay Chung, *Reliving the Second Chimurenga*, p. 198.

10. Patricia Choguguza, *Gender and War: Zimbabwean Women and the Liberation Struggle* (online). Available at: https://www.brunel.ac.uk/__

data/assets/pdf_file/0009/185922/ET62ChogugudzaED.pdf (accessed 7 October 2016), p. 18.

11. Ngwabi Bhebe and Terence Ranger (eds), *Soldiers in Zimbabwe's Liberation War*, pp. 47, 179.

12. Zimbabwe Air Force Air Chief Marshall General Josiah Tungamirai in Ranger and Bhebe (eds), *Soldiers in Zimbabwe's Liberation War*, p. 44.

13. Former head of Zimbabwe People's Revolutionary Army (ZIPRA) intelligence Dumiso Dabengwa, in Ranger and Bhebe (eds), *Soldiers in Zimbabwe's Liberation War*, p. 34.

14. This uprising eventually led to the overthrow of Ndabaningi Sithole, previously head of ZANU, and his replacement by Robert Mugabe.

15. Wilfred Mhanda, *Dzino: Memories of a Freedom Fighter*, Harare: Weaver Press, 2011, pp. 50–1.

16. Fay Chung, *Reliving the Second Chimurenga*, p. 131. Chung outlines on page 133 how Tongogara's veterans were resurrected in the war veterans revolt of 1997 and how they were used in the "land resettlement programme".

17. A child soldier is any person under the age of eighteen who is a member of or attached to government armed forces or any other regular or irregular armed force or armed political group, whether or not an armed conflict exists. Child soldiers perform a range of tasks including participation in combat, laying mines and explosives; scouting, spying, acting as decoys, couriers or guards; training, drill or other preparations; logistics and support functions, portering, cooking and domestic labour; and sexual slavery or other recruitment for sexual purposes. Quoted by E. Martz (ed.), *Trauma Rehabilitation After War and Conflict*, p. 315.

18. Fay Chung, *Reliving the Second Chimurenga*, p. 66.

19. Garikai made this statement as part of an astonishing and dreadful two-page confession in tiny writing which he sent to Margaret Lloyd after his conversion, contained in an unpublished manuscript entitled "Dear Comrade" written by Margaret Lloyd. Used with permission from both Margaret Lloyd and Garikai.

20. Ngwabi Bhebe and Terence Ranger (eds), *Soldiers in Zimbabwe's Liberation War*, pp. 160–61.

21. Interview between Garikai and Peter Griffiths, Friday 10 June 1984. These reasons were also stated to me in a recent interview by the BSAP Ground Cover Section Officer Poole.

22. Personal communication with BSAP S/O Poole, BSAP S/O Lambon, and notes in the diary recovered from ZANLA guerrilla Luke Mazvimbo.

23. Correspondence between Phyllis Thompson and Peter Griffiths in 1979 revealed that a guarded report was passed on to my father months after the killings, providing just a glimpse into the final moments of his colleagues and friends. Someone had been in a position to witness the killings and reported this single episode of the interaction between Phil and Wendy.

24. Matthew 10:28.

25. As his men completed their gruesome task of torturing a man to death, and Jesus breathed his last, so the execution detail commander said, "Certainly, this man was innocent!" (Luke 23:47).

26. Heather Powell, *Tsanga Place of Reeds, Place of Healing,* Australia: Bayprint, 2005, p. 177.

27. Personal correspondence with Isobel Staunton.

28. Captain Richard Paget, *Paget's Progress,* Milton Keynes: Authorhouse, 2007, p. 242–3.

29. Letter from Peter Griffiths to Brian Edwards, 30 May 1983. Elim Archive, accessed 15 February 2016.

30. Captain Richard Paget, *Paget's Progress,* p. 244.

31. Letter from Peter Griffiths to Brian Edwards, 11 July 1983.

32. Letter from Garikai to Peter Griffiths, 6 February 1986.

33. Letter from Peter Griffiths to Brian Edwards, 4 September 1988.

34. Personal communication in 2012 with David McKenzie, former Treasurer, Northside Community Church, Harare.

35. 2 Corinthians 5:17.

36. Sermon preached by David McKenzie on 10 June 2012 at All Saints and St Margaret's Church, Lowestoft, UK.

37. Correspondence with Northside Community Church leader Lameck Zulu, March 2016.

38. Norma Kriger, *Guerilla Veterans in Post-War Zimbabwe* (Cambridge: Cambridge University Press, 2003), p. 188.

More Alive Than Ever

1. Letter Peter Griffiths to Joy Bath, November 1992.

2. Letter Peter Griffiths to Brian Edwards, 6 October 1989.

3. Job 1:21.

4. Matthew 12:40.

5. 2 Kings 20:6.

6. 1 Chronicles 21:24.

"We'll Find Out Later"

1. Anonymous, *The Lion Christian Poetry Collection,* Oxford and Grand Rapids: Lion Publishing, 1995, p. 227.

2. Through the prophet Ezekiel 18:4.

3. *Everyman* programme broadcast on 29 October 1978.

4. ZANLA guerrilla Garikai, British South African Police Section Officer Poole, British South African Police Section Officer Lambon, among others.

5. Genesis 50:20.

6. Acts 2:23 (NIV UK, emphasis mine).

7. 1 Thessalonians 2:8.

8. Personal communication with a former high ranking Special Branch Officer who became the Director of Internal Operations (DIN) of the Central Intelligence Organisation for the Zimbabwean government, after Independence.

9. Ibid.

10. 2 Corinthians 4:17.

11. Fyodor Dostoyevsky, *Last Notebook (1880–1881),* Literary Heritage Литературное наследство, 83: 696.

Thanks

1. 28 October 2015.